THE PEACEMAKERS

Manu Bhagavan is a historian and has also authored or (co-) edited five books. He teaches at Hunter College and the Graduate Center, the City University of New York, where he is Professor of History and Chair of the Human Rights Program at the Roosevelt House Public Policy Institute. Manu has been a fellow of the American Council of Learned Societies and president of the Society for Advancing the History of South Asia. He has appeared on CNBC, National Public Radio (NPR), CNN-IBN, BBC World Radio, Press TV, World Citizen Radio, INI9, HuffPost Live and Al Jazeera English. Manu lives in New York City with his wife and daughter.

PRAISE FOR *The Peacemakers*

'Priceless book on India's visionary role in global affairs.'—*Afternoon Despatch & Courier*

'Bhagavan's archival research is extensive and commendable. The language is lucid . . . It is almost like a short novel, which maintains the interest of the reader right up to the last page . . . the book is a must read.'—*Strategic Affairs*

ADVANCE PRAISE FOR *The Peacemakers*

'This riveting story recovers one of the most important moments in India's relationship to the world at large. It captures the extraordinary passion with which a remarkable group of men and women dared to dream of "One World" founded on justice. It vividly describes how this high idealism was matched by an equally adroit political rhetoric that catapulted India to moral leadership. The book combines dramatic flair with rigorous and path-breaking scholarship. It is a must read for anyone interested in India's role in global affairs.'—Pratap Bhanu Mehta, President and Chief Executive, Centre for Policy Research, New Delhi

'*The Peacemakers* is a welcome and compelling challenge to sterile consensus about the kind of ideas that guide India's world view. Bhagavan excavates the record of India's formative years to reveal the extraordinary internationalism that guided the republic's founding figures. Universalism and not narrowly constructed Third Worldism, Bhagavan demonstrates in this ground-breaking work, inspired India's early international engagement. For Gandhi and Nehru, Bhagavan argues, the pursuit of one world and respect for human rights were integral to the construction of democratic India's concept of sovereignty.'—C. Raja Mohan, Contributing Editor, *The Indian Express*

'Manu Bhagavan has written an important book which documents the central place of human rights as India achieved independence. Written with grace and verve, *The Peacemakers* is the inspiring story of how principles that gave birth to the Indian state animated its constructive role, setting the agenda for the United Nations. That One World vision has yet to be realized but India's leadership could once again move humanity toward a more just and peaceful condition. This is a book that should be required reading for all who care about the potential of India to advance human rights and international justice.'—Jonathan Fanton, President, American Academy of Arts & Sciences

The Peacemakers

India and the Quest for One World

MANU BHAGAVAN

HarperCollins *Publishers* India

First published in hardback in India in 2012 by
HarperCollins *Publishers* India

Building 10, Tower A, 4th Floor, DLF Cyber City, Phase II,
Gurugram Haryana – 122002, India
www.harpercollins.co.in

P-ISBN: 978-93-5177-178-4
E-ISBN: 978-93-5029-469-7

2 4 6 8 10 9 7 5 3 1

Typeset in 11/14 Goudy Old Style at
SURYA

Printed and bound at
MicroPrints India, New Delhi

For Sree and Priyanka

Contents

Preface

This book originally began as an exploration of the ideas and ideologies that informed discussions related to the drafting of India's new Constitution, written from 1946 to 1950. Over the course of my research, I became fascinated by a discernible strand of internationalist thought that appeared in the archival records, a line of thinking that had never been the subject of any serious academic inquiry. Part of this had to do with disciplinary boundaries. Most historians of South Asia ended their investigation of the past at 1947, the moment of independence for India and Pakistan. The reason was rather straightforward. Most records after this moment were sealed and so historians ceded this ground to scholars in other disciplines. Anthropologists, sociologists, economists and, of course, political scientists have all since used their rich research methods to uncover many fascinating aspects of the post-colonial subcontinent.

Still, the methods and tools of the historian can help to shed new light on well-worn territory. Over the last decade or so, a number of historical scholars have begun to breach the 1947 barrier, prominent among them being Ayesha Jalal, Yasmin

Saikia, Dipesh Chakrabarty, Joya Chatterji, Sarah Ansari and Ramachandra Guha. I count myself among those working in this relatively new field.[1]

The problem, of course, is that many official post-Independence records, at least in India, remain closed. But the few records that I was able to access there piqued my interest. To compensate for the lack of available material in India, I consulted material, both published and unpublished, in twenty archives outside the country. The result, this book, is an innovative account of Indian international relations in the years leading up to its independence and more than a decade after. In particular, *The Peacemakers* makes three distinct historical claims.

First, this book highlights the ways in which Gandhi and Nehru worked together in the years after the Quit India movement to create a coherent vision for the new Indian state. The two are often seen as distant in this respect, with Gandhi favouring local, village rule and Nehru relying on a powerful central state with an industrial base.[2] I argue that while both remained committed in some ways to these varying ideals, the two agreed that an external, democratic authority, world government, was needed to check the power of the state. Both felt that the nation state–the dominant form of world organization since the seventeenth-century Peace of Westphalia ended the Thirty Years' War and established modern notions of state sovereignty in Europe–was pernicious and oppressive, and they jointly imagined a future, One World, that would move past this old violence-prone arrangement.

One World was to be built on an entirely new framework that was emerging at the same time that Gandhi and Nehru were evolving their new vision: human rights. *The Peacemakers* dramatically alters our understanding of the process by which 'human rights' developed into a fundamental plank of contemporary international law. Human rights today are largely built on the foundation laid by three major United Nations instruments: the Universal Declaration of Human Rights, the International Covenant on Civil and Political Rights, and the International Covenant on Economic, Social, and Cultural Rights. All three of these are seen as the product of Cold War history, and especially of an overly influential American presence. The splitting of civil and political rights from economic and social rights in particular is seen as a move by the West to push economic and social rights, preferred by the non-West, into second-class status.[3] This book challenges these claims by revealing India's central role, led by several prominent women, in the production of all three documents. It was India that steered the effort to create two separate covenants of rights, using its own new Constitution as justification and foundation. This is a fact that significantly alters the relationship of universalism and difference underlying modern debate on the origins and repercussions of human rights law.

To get past the divisions of the Cold War, Nehru formulated a doctrine of foreign policy known as Non-alignment. This principle has famously come to be seen as an incoherent practice of neutralism that frequently leaned towards the Soviet Union.[4] But *The Peacemakers* conclusively shows that Nehru's Non-alignment, in fact, was but one element of his larger goal, which was One World. Non-alignment was certainly not about 'neutrality' in the vein of Switzerland. It was instead a proactive, Gandhian means of equal engagement with two, opposed warring factions.[5] Its purpose was to bring the two sides together in an atmosphere of respect and trust. Then, at the global negotiating table, differing systems could be brought into harmonious relationship, recognizing and affirming the strengths of the other while simultaneously improving on the weaknesses of each. The result would be a more just world for all.

This book, then, intertwines the histories of Indian foreign relations, domestic constitutionalism, international human rights and activism in the United Nations, and recasts the towering intellectual and political figures of mid-twentieth-century India. *The Peacemakers*, in short, is one of the first, truly international histories of the post-colonial subcontinent.

The Cast

LEADING ROLES

Mohandas K. Gandhi	The Mahatma ('Great Soul')–'apostle of non-violence'
Jawaharlal Nehru	First prime minister of India
Madame Vijaya Lakshmi Pandit	India's lead representative to the UN; sister of Nehru
Hansa Mehta	India's representative to the UN Commission on Human Rights, 1947–52

SUPPORTING ROLES

Asaf Ali	Indian ambassador to Washington DC in 1948
Robert Boothby	Ally of Winston Churchill
Pearl S. Buck	Famed novelist
Nikolai Bulganin	Premier of the Soviet Union
Winston Churchill	Prime minister of Great Britain
Albert Einstein	Legendary scientist

Madame Chiang Kai-shek	First lady of China
Nikita Khrushchev	First secretary and premier of the Soviet Union
Franklin Delano Roosevelt	President of the United States
Eleanor Roosevelt	Chair of the UN Commission on Human Rights
Walter White	Secretary of the NAACP
Wendell Willkie	Republican presidential candidate, 1940
Jan Smuts	Prime minister of South Africa
Hamidullah	Nawab of Bhopal and leader of the Chamber of Princes

SELECT CAMEOS

W.E.B. DuBois	Distinguished leader of the NAACP
Adolf Hitler	Leader of Nazi Germany
Generalissimo Chiang Kai-shek	President of the Republic of China
Fiorello LaGuardia	Legendary mayor of New York City
Clare Booth Luce	Republican member of the US House of Representatives
Henry Luce	Publisher of *Time* and *Life* magazines
Muhammad Ali Jinnah	Leader of the Muslim League
V.K. Krishna Menon	Foreign policy advisor/official and friend of Nehru
Vallabhbhai Patel	The Iron Man of India
Tej Bahadur Sapru	Eminent Indian constitutional lawyer

J.J. Singh	President of the India League of America
Joseph Stalin	Premier of the Soviet Union
Earl Warren	Governor of California and future chief justice of the US Supreme Court

ORGANS OF THE UNITED NATIONS IN 1951

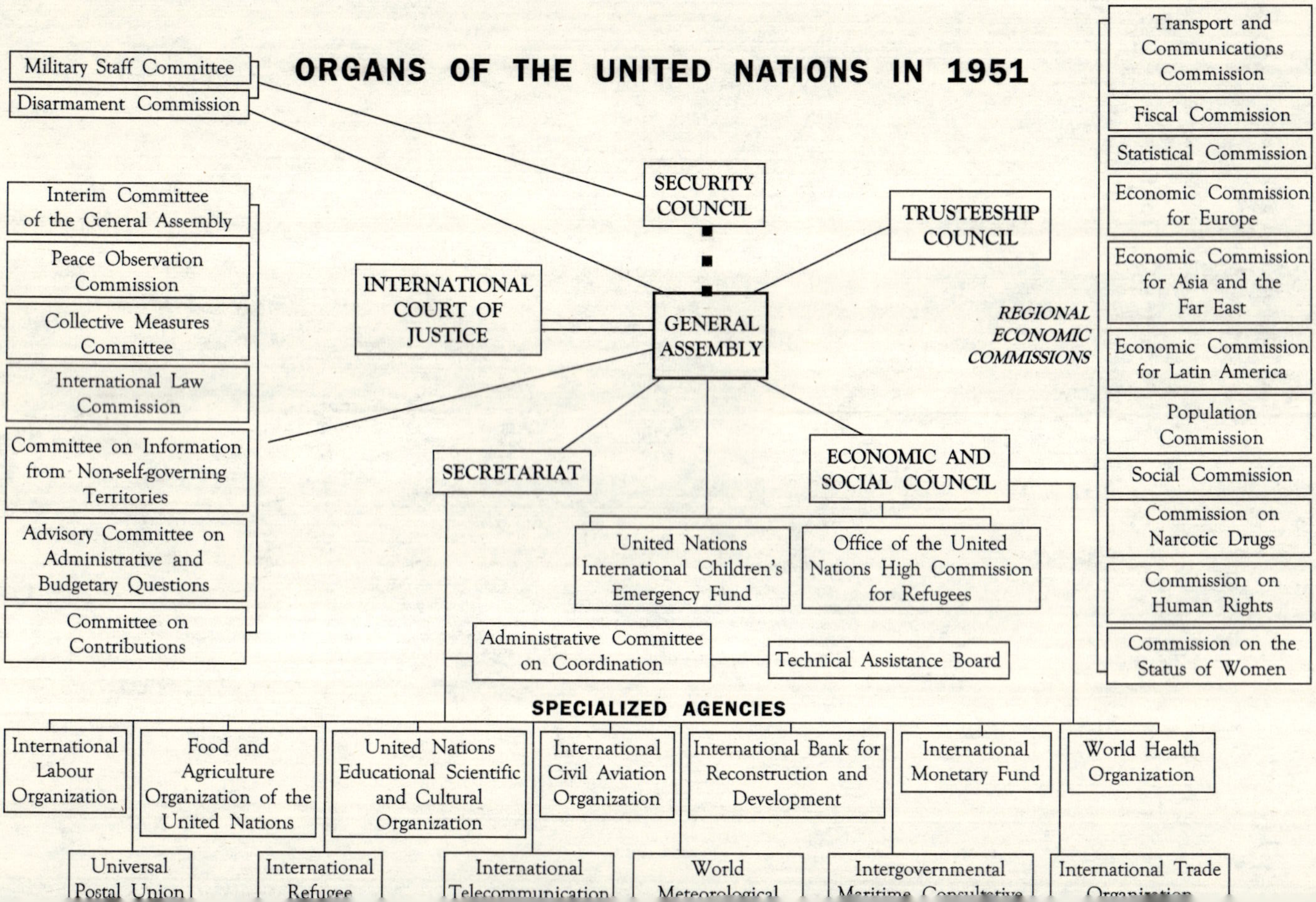

PROLOGUE

This is the story of India's efforts in the years leading up to its independence from Great Britain, and for more than a decade after, to forge a common destiny for all humankind. Seeking to bridge the ideological differences that divided East from West, capitalist from communist, India sought to construct a new global infrastructure around an innovative, and equally new, concept: human rights.

The world in the first half of the 1940s was a scary place. The forces of Hitler and Mussolini were on the move in Europe, and Japanese imperialists were equally aggressive in the Pacific. There was real fear that the Axis Powers might actually succeed in taking over. And there was also sorrow and disgust that the globe had been consumed by such conflict once again. Not many years had passed since the Peace at Versailles put an end to what was then known as the 'war to end all wars'.

Against the shadow cast by the Nazis, the light of India's 'apostle of non-violence', Mahatma Gandhi, seemed to shine all the more bright. As the war ground on, many people throughout the world looked to Gandhi for deliverance, a way out of the morass in which they found themselves.

It took Gandhi some time to figure out how to respond. The problem was the continued colonial stranglehold Britain had over India. Gandhi and all other Indian nationalists found this completely unacceptable. And yet the threat posed by Hitler and his minions was obvious. For Gandhi, there was only one answer. The principle of non-violence had to go global. Only the music of non-violence could counter the harsh drumbeat of war. It was a soothing thought, but the question was how. Non-violence was a way of life for Gandhi, but it was a difficult concept to practise, even for Gandhi's most ardent followers.

This was where Jawaharlal Nehru stepped in. Nehru was Gandhi's protégé, one of his closest friends, and his chosen successor. A gifted orator and a charismatic personality, Nehru was by nature given to blending the ideal with the practical.

Nehru and Gandhi laid out a vision that would make the world safer and more just. Premised on the end of imperialism and domination in all its forms, they proposed creating a world federation in which all peoples would be equally represented and to which they would contribute fairly for purposes of defence and finance.

This vision coincided nicely with an idea emanating from the Allied Powers to create a new world security organization, what would come to be known as the United Nations. The Big Three—the United States, Great Britain and the Soviet Union—conceived of this new institution as a means to promote international dialogue and prevent the outbreak of another major war.

The idea caught on like wildfire. People across the planet were desperate for another way, and they found very appealing the notion that they could participate in a new institutional framework to create peace. The fact that US President Franklin Roosevelt frequently discussed the promise of extending freedom to all people contributed to universal hopes for the new world body.

Yet for all the euphoria, there remained the real possibility that the new United Nations would simply retain old imperial systems and race-based politics, especially since both Britain and the United States helped maintain such policies in spheres under their control. Gandhi was especially critical and called for fundamental change. Imperialism and domination of all kinds had to go and the world remade. The first step was the independence of India.

Nehru's sister, Madame Vijaya Lakshmi Pandit, was the most powerful advocate of this new vision. She had travelled to the United States to convince Americans of the justness of India's cause and had won many friends, among them some of the United States' most prominent citizens: Nobel laureate Pearl S. Buck, New York City mayor Fiorello LaGuardia, and publishing magnate Henry Luce. Her appeal allowed her to lead an anti-imperial and anti-racist coalition at the San Francisco summit to create the United Nations. As her ally W.E.B. DuBois put it, they were there 'to help save the world'. She led the charge against the most tenacious defender of the old order: Winston Churchill.

Just as World War II was coming to an end, the United Nations came into existence. War-weary Britain simultaneously began the process of freeing India, with Nehru taking over an interim government. Excitement bubbled over everywhere. It became a true, global utopian moment, when anything seemed possible. The UN symbolized this great hope.

The Nuremberg trials, which prosecuted Nazis for villainy they had committed under Hitler's regime, helped reveal the level of atrocities committed during the war, and also what might be done to hold criminals accountable. Revulsion at Nazi actions convinced people everywhere that a new global standard had to be created, a norm accepted that made such behaviour absolutely unacceptable. The trials popularized the new concept of human rights. What this term meant, or encompassed, was still under development, but there was virtually unanimous global consensus that an architecture of such human rights had to be created.

But even as discussions got underway, the world once more began to fracture into hostile camps. The Cold War was taking hold.

Nehru and Gandhi were more convinced than ever that there were only two possible roads that humanity could travel. One, on which they currently found themselves, led to destruction. The other, salvation.

Why did the world keep succumbing to war? How could the planet be made more just, more safe and more equal for all people?

The problem, as they saw it, was the order of nation states that had dominated since the seventeenth century's Treaty of Westphalia. This system concentrated power in the hands of the few. Injustice was allowed to thrive within the borders of any sovereign state, with no mechanism for redress. And no institution could challenge a state should it behave in a threatening manner.

As Nehru became prime minister, he realized that India, at the forefront of decolonization, was itself a potent symbol for reimagining a better future. What he would do at home would impact what he wished to accomplish on a global scale at the UN.

It was in Nehru's hands, and those of his compatriots, to define the contours of the new post-colonial state. In constitutionally designing India, he hoped to set a new standard for what was possible, to use India's unique geographic position and history to blend elements from divergent doctrines of human rights, and to help integrate the world politically.

Of course, Nehru faced several major hurdles on the vast and varied home front, chief among them challenges from the hundreds of monarchies that ruled throughout the region, as well as religious and ethnic violence set against the backdrop of the demand for Pakistan. His answer to these problems was wrapped up in his grander plan.

Nehru called his solution One World, after a famous book by the American Wendell Willkie. Willkie had been an early and vocal advocate for Indian independence, and through that, for a more moral and just world free of political and economic imperialism and race-based power. One World had caught the attention of many across the political spectrum and thus had captured precisely the type of future Nehru wanted.

In One World, state power would be checked, the freedom of individuals and groups expanded. Questions of minorities, migrant peoples and endemic poverty would all be addressed, and Gandhi's legacy would go global. Madame Pandit, one of the most admired women in the world, led the fight in and through the United Nations to make all this a reality. All that stood between the Indians and success was their own fallibility, diplomatic intrigue, and the blinding haze of mistrust and overwhelming fear caused by the Cold War.

1 The World at War

Staring into the Abyss

In the summer of 1941, the world trembled in fear. The Axis Powers of Germany, Italy and Japan had unleashed devastating force in campaign after successful campaign. Adolf Hitler had launched his blitzkrieg on Europe two years back, taking Poland, France and the Netherlands, and had now begun a major assault on the Soviet Union, in contravention of the Hitler–Stalin Pact. German and Italian forces were spread throughout Northern Africa. And Japan, already deep inside China, was pushing into Southeast Asia.[1] How had it come to this?

The First World War (also known as the Great War), which had come to an end with the Armistice of 1918 and the Peace at Versailles in 1919 between the Allied Powers (which included Great Britain, France and the United States) and Germany, was supposed to have been the war to end all wars. Most Europeans were exhausted from the fighting, worn down by the grinding attrition of trench warfare. They longed for peace and wanted to stay out of conflict at any cost.

Versailles had captured the mood of many, and the imagination of millions. The American president, Woodrow Wilson, had put forward his Fourteen Points, a set of principles and plans through which Wilson sought to establish lasting peace in Europe. Among the most innovative of Wilson's proposals was a suggestion to establish a new international organization dedicated to partnership and an enduring alliance of all states. It was to be a League of Nations.

But Wilson failed to sell his plan to his own people, and the United States ultimately rejected membership in the new institution. Without the United States, the League could not hold universal sway. Powers squabbled among themselves and the organization proved incapable of carrying out its mission to head off conflicts and diplomatically solve international crises.

The League led a short and troubled life, its decline mirroring the deteriorating emotional health of Europe and the larger world in the face of a new, looming threat. There was real euphoria at the end of the Great War, but the Treaty of Versailles (and several related agreements such as the Treaties of St German and Sevres) created an imperfect peace from the start. The United States, which had entered the conflict only at the last moment, remained reluctant to involve itself politically in the affairs and squabbles of Europe, though economically and culturally it embraced numerous ties.[2] Britain and France were utterly depleted by the war, and developed a revulsion to further conflict. Both countries were deeply in debt to the United States, which refused to forgive their loans. Since they equally desired to exact punitive revenge on the Germans, the victorious powers devised an elaborate system to resolve the matter. Germans would have to pay heavy reparations to the

British, the French and the Belgians, who in turn would pay the United States back with the money. But first the Germans would receive the money to pay for reparations in loans from the United States.[3]

The arrangement left the Germans feeling humiliated and resentful, a perfect environment for Hitler to breed his hate. Hitler spelled out his racialized view of the world in his *Mein Kampf*, published in two volumes in 1925 and 1926. As the book came to be circulated widely in Germany and Europe, Hitler used his warped charisma to rise to power. He lashed out at perceived enemies, especially Jews and Marxists.[4]

When the American stock market crashed in 1929, the loans–reparations–repayments triangle collapsed as American banks tried to pull their money back in. Governments cancelled both reparations and loans to contain the crisis but simply did not act fast enough, and the Depression soon spread globally.[5]

In the US, the Depression led to the election of Franklin Delano Roosevelt (FDR) in late 1932. In his 'First Hundred Days', Roosevelt moved quickly to combat the Depression, his policies coalescing into his New Deal. His warm, ebullient personality also helped fight the utter despair of the times, forging a new bond between the American people and the government.[6]

Inversely, the weak republican government of Germany did not address the situation effectively, and the resulting turmoil gave Hitler and his Nazis greatly increased support, reflected in rising parliamentary strength. Hitler was appointed Chancellor of Germany in 1933, and weeks later used a mysteriously set fire at the Reichstag building (home of the German parliament) to increase his authoritarian powers and crush his opposition.[7] Within a year and a half, he had absolute control over the German state.

Hitler was determined to create a new German empire. He wanted a purified space for Germans to live and operate, free of the other peoples of the world he deemed inferior. To help accomplish his goals, Hitler entered into an uneasy alliance with Italy and Japan, both of which had sided with the Allies in the First World War, but were unhappy with their spoils of victory. Both Italy and Japan wanted to increase their spheres of control, the former into Africa, the latter into China and the rest of Asia.

Each of the three had begun expanding in the late thirties, notching up several major victories. The Western powers were unable to effectively meet these challenges. The Soviet Union was jolted by Japanese attacks in 1938 and 1939. In China, Generalissimo Chiang Kai-shek and his Kuomintang withdrew inward in the face of Japanese aggression.[8]

Germany's invasion of Poland in 1939 finally led France and Great Britain, with their empires in tow, to declare war. The United States, although neutral, would, in time, begin to aid the Western powers. In January 1941, Roosevelt used his annual speech on the State of the Union to rally the American people with a new call to support the Four Freedoms essential to liberty: Freedom of Speech, Freedom of Religion, Freedom from Want and Freedom from Fear.[9] All four, Roosevelt argued, were at risk because of the Axis.

Over the year, FDR increased American support for the war effort. He reached out to the Soviet Union after they had been surprise attacked by the Germans in Operation Barbarossa in the summer of 1941, despite the Hitler–Stalin Pact's mutual agreement of non-aggression. Shortly thereafter, the United States and Great Britain laid out the principles of what would become known as the Atlantic Charter, a vision for the post-war world essentially founded on the Four Freedoms.

The United States officially entered the war after the Japanese surprise attack on the US naval base at Pearl Harbor in Hawaii on 7 December. Weeks later, those who stood against the Axis signed the Declaration of United Nations in support of the Atlantic Charter. A new global alliance was born, and with it, the prospect of a new post-war world.

The Crisis of Imperialism

As the war raged, nationalists in India struggled to find the right response. Throughout the thirties, they had been in discussions with the British government on the nature of some kind of post-colonial settlement. The British government in India had passed an Act in 1935 that served as a new constitution. The Act authorized national elections and enfranchised most of the indigenous population. Hope for full freedom from the colonial yoke had grown steadily over these years. But after the German Anschluss with (the annexation of) Austria and as the Nazis marched across the Sudetenland expanding their control into Czechoslovakia, Britain and the other European powers had to focus their eyes closer to home.

As the British focused their attention on Hitler, Indians turned their gaze towards Gandhi. By the late thirties, Mohandas K. Gandhi had emerged as the unquestioned leader of the Indian nationalist movement. There were, of course, nationalists of many different stripes, with varying ideologies and agendas, and a host of organizations, from the Communist Party of India to the religious nationalist Hindu Mahasabha, vied for legitimacy and authority. But Gandhi's Indian National Congress was the most important organization for much of the early twentieth century, and by far the most dominant power, further strengthened by the elections that followed the 1935 Act, when they emerged the victor in virtually every contest.

For Gandhi and his colleagues, the underlying cause of the new world war, as much as the previous, was imperialism. Expansionist policies, racist views and the will to dominate inevitably led to conflict and grief. Imperialism simply found its most egregious expression in Hitler.

This was a troublesome conclusion, for it clouded the way forward. In the wars that Gandhi had lived through previously, especially the Great War, he had sided with the British. Though an ardent champion of non-violence, he had argued that the British, on the wrong side of many issues related to India, were nonetheless friends and good people. It was India's obligation to come to their aid as best they could. Gandhi organized an ambulance corps, and later even urged his compatriots to join the war effort. While non-violence was his paramount concern, he had to balance his belief in this principle with his sense of obligation to his colonial brethren. British promises to reward India for her support no doubt figured in the equation.

But the British did not follow through on these pledges. So when it appeared in the late thirties that Britain would again have to forego its commitments to India to face down another war, Indians generally, and Gandhi in particular, were hesitant. Britain could not simply take Indian support for granted. Imperialism was an evil that had to be removed, as much for Britain's soul as India's mortal condition.

So in 1938, the Congress passed a resolution at its meeting in Haripura adopting an anti-war stance. They specifically charged Great Britain with fighting to defend their imperial interests, rather than the cause of liberty as they claimed.

Gandhi also wrote if not favourably of Hitler, at least of him as an opponent who needed to be confronted the same as any other. He counselled negotiation and reason and saw no reason why Hitler, as the British themselves with regard to India, could not eventually be made into a friend.[10]

But as the forties dawned, so too did the realization that Hitler was someone categorically different from almost any other person Gandhi had encountered. Gandhi had trouble coming to terms with this. His entire philosophy and way of life was premised on the ideal that anyone—everyone—could feel the kinship of humanity. By resisting opponents in a certain way—one that treated them with respect and dignity while simultaneously shedding none of one's own—a certain empathic bond would be created between the clashing parties. It was Gandhi's universal principle, and it meant that all people, in a sense, were one. All were capable of realizing the error of their ways, and thus all were potentially good.

Hitler confounded this view. Gandhi struggled with reconciling his deeply held beliefs with Hitler's existence. Gradually, he came to see Hitler as the exception to the rule. Hitler was the opposite of everything that Gandhi stood for, the Moriarty to Gandhi's Holmes. He was Gandhi's negative and had to be stopped. But for Gandhi, there was only one way to achieve this. He counselled: 'Hitlerism will never be defeated by counter-Hitlerism . . . If my argument has gone home, is it not time for us to declare our changeless faith in non-violence?'[11]

Gandhi saw Hitler as the ultimate expression of violence, and thus only non-violence could effectively combat this kind of threat. If Hitler was beyond reach, this was not so for the millions of Germans who followed him. *They* could be touched, and empathic bonds built, he concluded.

But few understood these details of Gandhi's thinking. To many people, even his closest friends and admirers, Gandhi seemed erratic. Many feared that the old man was in decline. To an extent, Gandhi realized his own marginalization and therefore named Jawaharlal Nehru his successor in January 1942.

Nehru was Gandhi's dashing lieutenant. He came from a

family of great privilege—Kashmiri Brahmins who had moved to Delhi in the service of the Mughal empire. Nehru's father, Motilal, was an acclaimed and wealthy lawyer and a prominent member of the Indian National Congress in his day.[12]

Growing up, Nehru wore his aristocratic pedigree on his sleeve. He was schooled at Harrow in Britain, and completed his higher education at Trinity College at Cambridge University.

But Nehru was one of the first to fully realize Gandhi's significance and soon became the Mahatma's closest friend and associate. The two shared a deep bond, even if they did not always see eye to eye on matters.

In 1942, with Nehru's future as leader now official, the Congress high command had to confront an unhappy membership. Nearly three years had passed since the war had begun and Britain's attention remained far from India. Everyone realized what the UK and its Allies were up against, but they also felt the needs of India's millions could no longer be pushed aside. As early as 1939, the Congress had broached the idea of supporting Britain's war effort in return for independence, though these efforts gained no traction.

In March 1942, finally, Winston Churchill, named British prime minister in 1940, sent Sir Stafford Cripps to India to discuss a possible deal. Many in India held out high hopes for the Cripps Mission. This made the disappointment they felt sting all the more once they concluded that Cripps simply could not deliver the goods. Cripps seemed to have good intentions, but publicly was non-committal and vague. The Indians wondered if he actually had any authority. The dialogue went nowhere.

QUIT INDIA

The British, though, were in an increasingly precarious place. The Battle of Britain and the ongoing Battle of the Atlantic, during which the Germans unleashed their air and sea power against the Allies, and the attack on the American base at Pearl Harbor had brought into vivid relief what an existential threat the Axis Powers posed. Now, the Japanese were at India's eastern doorstep. Churchill did not want to be distracted by India's concerns but desperately needed its support. This did not mean that he was ready to concede to the nationalists' demands. Bringing India into the Allied fold had been the primary motivation for sending Cripps to the subcontinent.

Gandhi and the Congress high command were aware of this when the Mission failed, so in short order they proposed India's full support in return for immediate governmental power. The British, however, did not take them up on the offer.

After huddling in consultation, the Congress demanded the immediate independence of India in July. This was Gandhi's call. Nehru, the actual head of the organization, disagreed with the decision but deferred to his mentor, trusting his wisdom, instincts and judgement.[13]

A few weeks later, on 8 August 1942, the All-India Congress Committee passed the Quit India Resolution at its meeting in Bombay. Gandhi had originally introduced the Resolution in late April, but it was rejected in favour of a version drafted by Nehru.

Gandhi's document asked for the immediate withdrawal of Britain from India. In the face of an Axis attack led by Japan, India would allow Britain to fight them and would assist by offering non-violent resistance to the aggressors.[14]

Nehru saw the main Resolution as an opportunity to lay out a vision for a new India. He felt the burden of leadership that

Gandhi had bestowed upon him. The world, not just the Alliance, was in grave peril. The moment called for a mix of idealism and sober assessment. He had to make clear why the independence of India was fundamentally important to the Allied war effort as well as to any peace that might follow. This had to be a statement addressing the problems of the present while simultaneously painting a better future.

Nehru took the Resolution very seriously and poured his heart and soul into it. While he maintained Gandhi's original political intent, this was also Nehru's moment to step out of the Mahatma's shadow. He began by stating that 'the immediate ending of British rule in India is an urgent necessity, both for the sake of India and for the success and cause of the United Nations'.

'India, the classic land of modern Imperialism, has become the crux of the question,' he declared, 'for by the freedom of India will Britain and the United Nations be judged, and the peoples of Asia and Africa be filled with hope and enthusiasm.' The war was being fought for freedom and democracy. 'A free India will assure this success by throwing all her great resources in the struggle for freedom and against the aggression of Nazism, Fascism and Imperialism. This will not only affect materially the fortunes of the war, but will bring all subject and oppressed humanity on the side of the United Nations and give these nations, whose ally India would be[,] the moral and spiritual leadership of the world.'

Nehru then spelled out what he thought a newly independent India had to do. 'On the declaration of India's independence, a provincial Government will be formed and free India will become an ally of the United Nations . . . [The Government's] primary functions must be to defend India and resist aggression with all the armed as well as the non-violent forces at its command, together with its Allied Powers, and to promote the well-being and progress of the workers in the fields and factories and elsewhere to whom essentially all power and authority must belong.'

With a broad case made for the relationship between an independent India and the war effort, and a clear willingness to use force against the Axis—a definitive break with Gandhi's position—Nehru then turned to outlining the nature of a new Indian state and what place it would have in a post-war order. This vision statement would guide Indian policy for the next several decades.

'The provincial Government will evolve a scheme for a constituent assembly which will prepare a constitution for the Government of India acceptable to all sections of people. This constitution according to the Congress view, should be a federal one. With the largest measure of autonomy for the federating units, and with the residuary powers vesting in these units.'

'[T]he Committee is of opinion that the future peace, security, and ordered progress of the world demand a world federation of free nations, and on no other basis can the problems of the world be solved. Such a world federation would ensure the freedom of its constituent nations, the prevention of aggression and exploitation of one nation over another[,] the protection of national minorities, the advancement of all backward areas and peoples, and the pooling of the world's resources for the common good of all. On the establishment of such a world federation, disarmament would be practicable in all countries, national armies, navies and air forces would no longer be necessary, and a world federal defense force would keep the world peace and prevent aggression.'

If this was the future, and the key to a just and lasting peace, Nehru knew that there remained a long road to travel. 'The

Committee regretfully realizes, however, despite the tragic and overwhelming lessons of the war and the perils that overhang the world, the Governments of few countries are yet prepared to take this inevitable step towards world federation.'[15]

The Resolution was Nehru to the core: idealistic but realistic, visionary but grounded in the immediate concerns of the present. It was at once a declaration of independence and a policy blueprint for a new post-colonial Indian state.

But for the British, the Resolution meant only one thing: seditious activity in a time of war. It simply could not stand. The entire nationalist leadership was immediately arrested and put in prison, location undisclosed. There most would remain until the war's end, in 1945.

2 India in New York

Enter Madame Pandit

Among those who were jailed as a result of the Quit India Resolution was Vijaya Lakshmi Pandit, Nehru's younger sister, the middle one of three siblings. This was not her first confinement. A committed, if less famous, nationalist fighter and Gandhian, Nan, as she was affectionately known, had spent several terms in prison for her political activism. After the 1935 Act that created a new constitutional framework, she had stood for election and won, becoming the first woman cabinet minister in India, holding portfolios on local self-government and medical and public health in the Government of the United Provinces (present-day Uttar Pradesh). She was talented and respected, and unbelievably courageous,[1] but few knew in the 1930s just what a force she would become.

In the summer of 1938, having just led an effort to contain a cholera outbreak in her state, and having lost her mother and her aunt,[2] Mrs Pandit was near physical and mental exhaustion, and needed a brief respite abroad to tend to her own health. She and her husband, Ranjit Pandit, also a committed Gandhian nationalist, planned a trip to Europe. But just as the date for travel neared. Ranjit was elected to an important leadership post within the Congress and was unable to travel.

As it turned out, Jawaharlal Nehru was departing for Europe to attend a peace conference in Paris, so Mrs Pandit decided to join him. The trip took her to Czechoslovakia to discuss her work in the United Provinces with the Czech Minister of Health, and she was there as the Sudeten crisis unfolded. Nehru in the 1930s was vocally and unwaveringly anti-fascist, and he and his sister both expressed repeated concerns about the threat the new right-wing governments of Europe represented. By the time British Prime Minister Neville Chamberlain signed the Munich Pact with Hitler in September 1938, famously appeasing the Nazis by tolerating their actions in Czechoslovakia in a naive attempt to ward off armed hostilities, Mrs Pandit and her brother were in England. She was startled to see packed churches, with people thanking God that war had been averted. She was near tears, wishing they were right, but filled with foreboding of evil tidings to come. While on this trip, Mussolini reached out twice to Nehru, inviting him to Italy as Il Duce's guest. Nehru declined.

By the time the Nehrus got back to India, the situation in Europe had turned from grim to deadly. War had begun.

Britain brought India into the war without consulting the region's newly elected representatives. In short order, Indian troops were sent into battle in various foreign theatres. The elected legislators were incensed and resigned en masse in protest in 1939. The Congress explained that it was willing to support the Allied war effort in exchange for independence but was rebuffed. The British government in India then abrogated the 1935 Act, eliminating elected governments and empowering regional governors with greater control. Gandhi instructed select individuals to provide civil resistance. The government swiftly arrested anyone they thought implicated. Both Mrs Pandit and her husband were incarcerated in this sweep.

But as the war progressed, and Japan advanced towards British India's eastern borders, Churchill (who had succeeded Chamberlain as the prime minister in 1940) grew more agitated about the chances of success. He desperately wanted India's support. The Indian leadership was released in order to negotiate with Cripps in March 1942.

While discussions with Sir Stafford were underway, Nehru's daughter Indira returned to India from her studies at Oxford University. She was engaged to her long-time friend Feroze Gandhi, and the wedding was held in March.

Coinciding with the wedding, the Chinese leader Generalissimo Chiang Kai-shek and his wife visited India. They bore an unofficial message from President Roosevelt. The three of them wished to convey the severity of the world situation and their sincere hope that the Indian leadership would hold off any further disobedience campaigns. In return, the Chinese and the Americans would apply pressure on Churchill to free India.

While this message did not resonate, the Chinese leaders were a huge personal success in India. At this point, Mrs Pandit was the president of the All-India Women's Conference. Madame Chiang was a potent symbol for many, a strong and charismatic Asian woman striving to defend her people from Japanese imperial aggression. The two women shared good chemistry when they met several times in Delhi. During one of these visits, Madame Chiang suggested that Mrs Pandit send her daughters abroad for their education. The war had made things dangerous, and opportunities in India were few. Madame Chiang encouraged Mrs Pandit to think about Wellesley College in the United States, her alma mater, and offered to look into the possibility during her forthcoming American tour. She did, but by then Mrs Pandit was in prison again as a result of the Quit India declaration.

Gandhi had written warmly to the Chiangs in June 1942, thanking them for their visit, wishing them well, and explaining to them why he felt demanding immediate independence for India was necessary.[3] Chiang Kai-shek replied by reiterating his concerns and urging restraint.[4] In his speech in Bombay on 8 August, Gandhi was much more fiery, insinuating that the Chiangs and the Americans might be colluding with the British to keep India in bondage, though he hoped that this was not true.[5]

The Chiangs did not seem to take the criticism personally. When Mrs Pandit was briefly released on parole after seven months in prison to look after her health, she quickly cabled Wellesley to see if her two eldest daughters, Chandralekha and Nayantara, might get admission to the prestigious institution. Nayantara was very young but had already acquired enough credits to qualify. To her surprise and delight, Wellesley cabled back almost immediately to accept. Chandralehka would attend on a scholarship provided by Madame Chiang.

On the night she was released from jail, Mrs Pandit was astonished upon returning to her home in Allahabad to find teams of police officers ransacking her house. She demanded to know what they were doing and was told that they were searching for a copy of a letter that Nehru had written to President Roosevelt in April, just after the failure of the Cripps mission.

She assured them that the letter was not in the house and that they had to leave after restoring things to order. They obeyed. Most importantly, she had boldly protected Nehru's letter, which she indeed had. The letter implored President Roosevelt to support the cause of Indian freedom as a means of bolstering the Allied war effort. Nehru promised to organize a strong and forceful resistance to the Axis.[6]

Mrs Pandit had to return to prison once her health leave expired, but she continued to fare poorly and was formally released in July 1943. She soon learned that her daughters had reached the eastern United States safely, no small thing in the midst of a world at war. They had travelled with troops by ship across the Pacific to California, stopping in Australia, and then had journeyed across the vast landscape of the continental US. Mrs Pandit was overwhelmed by the news of her girls' safe journey, and she felt that service was the best way to express the gratitude she felt. So she travelled in haste to Bengal, where one of the worst famines of the twentieth century was underway. She immediately perceived that this was a manmade issue, caused by poor governmental policy, but she could hardly know that Churchill was actively preventing resources from reaching the desperately needy people.[7] She was horrified by the gruesome scenes she witnessed, even as she led efforts to redress them.

The work in Bengal was staggeringly difficult but Mrs Pandit kept at it. She returned home in late 1943 for a much-needed break. She had not seen her husband Ranjit in quite some time. He had been imprisoned for the Quit India campaign. Mrs Pandit had been allowed a few visits, but had not had such opportunity since her travel to Bengal. She finally managed to see him during this break and was shocked to find that he was at death's door. Although it was against his wishes, as he did not want any uncommon treatment of any kind, she got special permission to have him transferred to a hospital. It was too late. He died in mid-January 1944.

Ranjit Pandit's death took the floor out from under his wife's feet. While she had always been a confident and capable person, the next few months rattled her thoroughly. She had had a most loving relationship, so it came as a devastating shock to her when she learned that her husband's relatives were claiming Hindu customary law to exclude her from all of her family's assets. She suddenly found herself with very few resources. She moved to cut back her expenses and was warmed to receive an outpouring of support from all corners, as business associates waived fees and promoted familial affinity above profit.

But Mrs Pandit was furious at the turn of events, and that women generally could be treated this way. The fact that she was the president of the All-India Women's Conference made the situation all the more ironic, and biting. Gandhi offered her comfort, which she found helpful. Then she steeled herself and worked with her old family friend, Sir Tej Bahadur Sapru, to file a lawsuit against her husband's family. It was an unwinnable case, since customary law was quite clear on the matter. So her stand was in many ways unthinkable. But Sapru was one of the most eminent constitutional thinkers and lawyers in all of southern Asia, widely respected, and his presence assured the suit would draw considerable attention. Her husband's family did not like the glare of the spotlight cast on them, and they conceded to pay Mrs Pandit a certain sum, though it was nowhere near her due. Gandhi and her brother, but not Sapru, counselled her to accept the offer and, further, to make peace with her husband's family. She was bitter and found this a very difficult road to travel but ultimately concluded that the counsel was wise and formally agreed to the terms.

Gandhi had been released from prison and was in Bombay.

His life-long partner, wife Kasturba, had passed away in prison in February, just after Ranjit, and he was heartbroken. He was freed in May due to poor health. Nehru remained in prison and, though he got the news, the channels of communication were too slow for him to stay involved in most matters.

Mrs Pandit stayed with Gandhi for two weeks once she had brought her case to a close and she found the Mahatma to be of great comfort. From there, she went back to Bengal and redoubled her efforts to aid those stricken by the famine. She created a chapter of Save the Children, an international organization dedicated to bettering the lives of young people around the world, and in mere weeks raised considerable resources. Among the most notable contributors were Madame Chiang, first lady of the United States, Eleanor Roosevelt, and Pearl Buck. Buck was the Pulitzer- and Nobel Prize-winning author of the celebrated book, *The Good Earth*. She was a lifelong admirer and friend of China, and Asia more generally. In 1944, she was also the honorary president of the India League of America, a prominent pro-Indian independence organization founded in 1937 'to interpret India and America to each other'.[8] Together, these three women contributed $25,000, the equivalent of approximately $320,000 in 2010 purchasing power terms.[9]

Mrs Pandit's success brought her significant attention and renown. Gandhi suggested that she might consider making a trip to the United States to advocate for the independence of India. The trip abroad would also help her to move past the troubles of the previous months. She found this to be an interesting challenge, and a potentially welcome escape. The Allies had scheduled a meeting of the Pacific Relations Conference to take place in Hot Springs, Virginia, to discuss the future of Asia in a post-war world. Mrs Pandit would attend the Conference as an observer, along with a small delegation.

The only problem was that her passport had been impounded by the British.[10] Their search of her house for Nehru's letter to Roosevelt was only a small part of a much larger concern. The British, led by Churchill, were dramatically opposed to the very idea of Indian independence at this stage. American anti-imperialism, eloquently championed by FDR, was well known and was getting on Churchill's nerves. The last thing the British wanted was someone of Mrs Pandit's calibre speaking in the United States and holding personal meetings with American power brokers.

A Global Gulliver and the Introduction of One World

The British had good reason to worry about America's stand. Aside from Roosevelt's direct admonitions, the message had also been conveyed to Churchill through other channels. Most prominently, and most irksome to Churchill, was the public rebuke he received from Wendell Willkie, Roosevelt's special envoy. Willkie had been FDR's Republican challenger in 1940, running a quixotic campaign against the wildly popular Democrat. Willkie was very concerned about international affairs, and was quite popular in his own right, so Roosevelt, sensing political opportunity, asked his former opponent to join his administration.

By 1942, India was an issue of great interest to many in the United States. There was real fear that the subcontinent might fall to the Japanese and affect the outcome of the war. Among US progressives, there was also a great sense of solidarity with the Indian quest for independence. The National Association for the Advancement of Colored People (NAACP), in particular, equated India's struggles with the larger fight for racial justice throughout the world. Walter White, the distinguished secretary of the NAACP, met Lord Halifax, the former British viceroy to India and then ambassador to Washington DC, in late April at the behest of Willkie to discuss the conditions of people of colour in the US and their outlook in light of the war. The discussion quickly intertwined affairs in India with matters of race, and culminated in a grand proposal. White suggested that President Roosevelt should send a delegation to India led by Willkie, and consisting of a prominent legal mind as well as a notable person of colour knowledgeable about race matters. This delegation would guarantee any promises of independence made by Great Britain, and by transparently confronting the US' own shortcomings, help to convince Indians of American good faith.[11] Halifax approved of the idea and White raced to make things happen. He immediately contacted Eleanor Roosevelt, Pearl Buck and a number of other allies to try to mobilize opinion and resources in support of Willkie's trip. FDR thought highly of the plan and directed White to contact Sumner Welles of the US State Department to get the process rolling.[12]

The plan hit its first roadblock in June when Roosevelt indicated that the delegation should not go forward at that time because Gandhi had recently been making statements accusing the United States of upholding British imperialism. FDR claimed that he feared that any US delegation might only further cement such views.[13] This irked Buck, who commented to Walter White: 'I am sorry the President does not want to do anything in India until the situation changes. I don't think the situation ever will change until America takes some stand that will convince Mr. Gandhi that the interest of the United States is not to preserve and perpetuate British imperialism in the Orient.'[14] White was so impressed with Buck's call-to-arms that he publicly made the same demand a few days later in a speech at Madison Square Garden.[15]

Buck's comment was in response to a letter that White had written her informing her of the president's hesitancy. He had simultaneously written to Clare Booth Luce, a stalwart Republican in the US House of Representatives, one of the first women in Congress and wife of publishing magnate Henry Luce, who ran *Time* and *Life* magazines. Mrs Luce had recently returned from a trip to India and was one of the few prominent Americans with first-hand knowledge of what was happening in the subcontinent. She thought that the United States had to act and crafted a proposal with suggestions on how best to proceed. She and White requested an audience with FDR to discuss these ideas, but were told that the president was too busy. White wrote to the president's secretary protesting and indicating that the fight was not over.[16]

On a broad level, Roosevelt agreed with the principle behind White's suggestion–that an American team with official sanction should travel abroad to get a first-hand account of the global situation, and to convey a sense of American good intentions. In late July, Reuters reported that Willkie intended to go to India, setting off a flurry of British diplomatic activity. But when Willkie's itinerary was published shortly thereafter, India was not on the list. Behind the scenes, though, India remained a possible destination–it had been the point of the entire trip as originally conceived by White. The press continued to report that Willkie might visit India.[17]

In late August 1942, soon after the Quit India movement was launched, Willkie embarked on what would be a fifty-day tour of more than a dozen countries. He travelled in a plane dubbed 'Gulliver', after the famous eighteenth-century Jonathan Swift adventurer.[18] As he was departing, Clare Booth Luce wrote to

Willkie about his pending trip. 'Wendell, it seems to me that your whole trip will acquire enormous meaning for the war effort and for America and for the lives of millions of people if you manage to bring off a meeting with Nehru, and Gandhi.' She warned him not to be seduced by 'mellifluous 19th century' British charms, and provided him with a letter of introduction to Nehru.[19] India, obviously, was still the point.

Churchill claimed that he was not personally worried about Willkie visiting India, for the Republican was a well-known Anglophile, and Churchill believed that he had completely won him over in personal meetings the two had earlier. But the government in India, especially Viceroy Linlithgow, was adamant that he should not be allowed to visit, fearing that he might meet Gandhi or Nehru.[20] Whether to placate Linlithgow, or for other reasons, it was Churchill who would personally veto Willkie's travel to India.[21]

The machinations were all for naught, as Willkie had harboured serious doubts about imperialism from the start, and was a staunch believer in the Atlantic Charter. He was determined to meet as wide an array of people as possible on his trip, talking to everyone from Turkish Prime Minister Sukru Saracoglu to Josef Stalin. In China, he met the Chiangs, and it was he who convinced Madame Chiang to make her trip to the United States in 1943. The Chiangs in turn reinforced the importance of India to him.[22]

Willkie was disturbed by the delusions of many Britons, who acted as if nothing would ever change about their world. He found the Chiangs utterly convincing. So when he returned to the United States following his tour, he decided on a dramatic course of action. He took to the airwaves and made a passionate plea against imperialism. Front and centre in his address was the case of India. He said: 'Besides giving our allies in Asia and

Eastern Europe something to fight with, we have got to give them assurance of what we are fighting for . . . They are not so sure of us. Many of them have read the Atlantic Charter . . . They ask: What about a Pacific Charter? What about a World Charter . . .? "Is freedom supposed to be priceless for the white man or for the Western world but of no account to us in the East?"'

He boiled his message down: 'Many of [the people I met on my trip] also asked me the question which has become almost a symbol all through Asia: What about India . . .? From Cairo on, it confronted me at every turn.'

Picking up on the concerns expressed by Pearl Buck and Walter White back in June, he added: 'People of the East . . . cannot ascertain from our government's wishy-washy attitude toward the problem of India what we are likely to feel at the end of the war about all the other hundreds of millions of Eastern peoples . . . In Africa, in the Middle East, throughout the Arab world, as well as in China and the whole Far East, freedom means the orderly but scheduled abolition of the colonial system.'

He concluded: 'As Americans we must also recognize that we share . . . the responsibility of making the whole world a commonwealth of free nations . . . India is our problem . . . We must win the peace . . . [Hundreds of millions of people in Eastern Europe and Asia] are no longer willing to be Eastern slaves for Western profits. They are beginning to know that men's welfare throughout the world is interdependent. They are resolved, as we must be, that there is no more place for imperialism within their society than in the society of nations. [The people of the East] want us to join them in creating a new society, global in scope, free alike of the economic injustices of the West and the political malpractices of the East.'[23]

Willkie's speech hit a nerve and was on everyone's lips the

next day. Clare Booth Luce sent Willkie a telegram declaring him a 'global Abraham Lincoln'.[24] Letters poured into the president's administration. With few exceptions, most praised Willkie and FDR for the trip, the speech, and for lending support to India.[25] Roosevelt used the opportunity to affirm that the Atlantic Charter held true for everyone.[26]

Willkie's speech had gotten under Churchill's skin, not least because it had proven the prime minister's understanding of the Republican to be wrong. Roosevelt's statement sent him over the edge. It was to this that he famously quipped: 'I have not become the King's First Minister in order to preside over the liquidation of the British Empire.'[27]

Willkie was undeterred, and the following year, in 1943, he penned an account of his world tour, titling the book *One World*.[28] He incorporated many of the statements from his speech, and expanded on them. The book was candidly anti-imperial and anti-racist, condemning the United States for Jim Crow in terms equal to his harsh critique of colonialism. Willkie envisioned a grand world alliance as the way forward to a permanent and lasting, just peace.

The book was a hit. It took some months, but it eventually found its way to India, and into Nehru's prison cell. He read it in late 1943 and was greatly impressed.[29] The idea of One World caught his imagination and he instantly saw that it strongly resonated with many features of his Quit India Resolution. He mulled over the possibilities.

While Nehru was making use of his prison days to better intellectually formulate his own plan for the future, Vijaya Lakshmi Pandit had gone back to Bengal to continue her famine work. A trip to the United States, while of interest, did not seem possible because of her passport status. The British government was also looking into further steps to prevent her from making the trip, but she remained unaware of this fact.[30] But there were other forces at work, aside from the will of the British. Mrs Pandit received a mysterious invitation from the Chinese consulate to a dinner party in Calcutta. She declined but the hosts insisted. She found herself at an event for American Air Force personnel, who were focused on Burma. She had a pleasant conversation at dinner, in which she casually spoke of her interest in the United States, the fact that her daughters attended Wellesley, and that she did not really know that much about the country, though she was interested to visit. She did not know that her dinner-mate at the table was General Stratemeyer, the head of the Allied Air Command in the East. Stratemeyer, with the direct aid of the Roosevelts, arranged for Mrs Pandit to make her trip, and within weeks, in mid-December 1944, she found herself in a military plane headed for New York City.[31]

INDIA IN NEW YORK

Mrs Pandit arrived in the United States' biggest city in the early hours of the morning and was taken to the Waldorf-Astoria hotel. All her needs would be taken care of for a month, she was told. Still dazed from the long travel, she managed to place calls to her daughters and to Pearl Buck. Nayantara and Chandralekha were shocked and delighted to learn that their mother was in the country with them. Buck took Mrs Pandit shopping soon thereafter, and Mrs Pandit was startled by the glitz and glamour of America's financial capital: she was taken to Saks Fifth Avenue, and to others of the finest shops in the city. It was Christmas time and New York was glittering. And the Waldorf, of course, was not half bad either.

But Mrs Pandit was not wowed by all the opulence. Instead, it made images of 'abandoned, diseased babies . . . [and] piled-up corpses of men and women' burn all the brighter in her mind.[32] The famine and the desperate poverty of people throughout the Indian subcontinent was all she could think about, and she felt out of place amidst this American splendour. She quickly moved to a different, more down-to-earth hotel and tried to get her bearings. But she soon realized that there was no escape from the Ritz (or the Waldorf) of New York City.

For more than a month, her schedule was filled with galas, as New York's powerful business, literary and political celebrities put together events with people eager to meet Mrs Pandit and learn about conditions in India. Gandhi's fame, and her brother's, as well as Willkie's speech, had stoked a fire of interest in the subcontinent. Almost no one had heard of Mrs Pandit herself, but that was soon to change.

The first major affair was organized by the Chinese consulate, which threw a grand party. New York's glitterati turned out in full force, and Mrs Pandit was the talk of the town.[33]

Mrs Pandit realized she was among friends, if misinformed ones. She was going to have to do more than attend the Conference at Hot Springs. It was her job, she realized, to bring the reality of her part of the world into the living rooms of the American people.

To figure out how best to go about this, she held long conversations with her closest allies in the States: Roger Baldwin, one of the creators and the first executive director of the American Civil Liberties Union (ACLU); the journalist and Gandhi enthusiast Louis Fischer; Council on African Affairs' president Paul Robeson; and Walter White. She had to reach all corners of the country, and talk to people from all walks of life. This was the only way to ensure that her message got through, and that she also came to fully understand the nature of life in the United States. She would have to go on tour to lecture far and wide.[34]

Pearl Buck put her in touch with the Clark H. Getts, Inc., a lecture bureau with a prominent list of clients that included the pianist Ignacy (Jan) Paderewski, the writer Theodore Dreiser, and the filmmakers Martin and Osa Johnson.[35] Getts had formerly worked for the National Broadcasting Company (NBC) and was well connected. He had been a journalist in China—hence his connection to Buck—and was very interested in issues related to Asia and injustice. Clark and Osa had married in 1941, several years after Martin had died from injuries sustained in a plane crash. Clark and Osa were a power couple, she being one of America's most well-known figures.[36]

His background notwithstanding, Getts represented the utter ignorance about the Indian region that Mrs Pandit faced in the US in the 1940s. There were very few people of South Asian descent anywhere in the continental states. The largest community was a small population of Punjabis in the western state of California. Getts summed up the situation when he told Mrs Pandit that Americans would expect her to 'look exotic' and wear jewels.[37]

Mrs Pandit laughed this aside. The man clearly knew nothing of the situation prevailing in India. It was obvious that she had her work cut out for her. She confidently assured Getts that she had the presence and the speaking skills to command any stage. Simple saris would do fine, and anything else was an unnecessary 'prop'. She made only one demand. Her short time in the States had brought home the vivid injustices of racial segregation throughout the region. She had seethed with anger at the colour bar she saw everywhere and had made clear that all of her speeches had to be open and freely accessible to all people. Getts was in agreement, and so a year-long, coast-to-coast tour was arranged. Over the course of January and February, she had several engagements lined up in New England, and one in Washington. Her audiences ranged from the most intimate to auditoriums with a thousand people.[38]

Before Mrs Pandit embarked on her tour, and just prior to approaching Clark Getts, she had had to fulfill the obligation that had officially brought her there. She attended the Virginia Conference on the post-war future of Asia. After meeting her daughters in a joyous reunion for the Christmas holidays, she travelled down the East Coast to serve as leader of the Indian delegation to the proceedings from the sixth through the seventeenth of January 1945. In her opening statement, she riffed from the Quit India Resolution, declaring, 'we cannot think in terms of national issues; that has been disastrous in the past. In the future we need a wider vision, and international rather than national perspectives . . . I appeal to you to consider matters from a wider view, thinking of the world as one family where each nation can contribute to the welfare and strength of the other.' She praised the Atlantic Charter, slammed Churchill for declaring that it would only be selectively applied, and urged the group to help build unanimous consensus on the Charter's universal application.[39] This was an oblique reference to India's independence, which she cast in relation to building a new kind of international framework for the world.

Mrs Pandit stayed fairly quiet after her opening statement. This was her first exposure to formal diplomatic affairs, and she felt it best to observe and learn. She did not at all care for what she heard. Imperialist ideas were rampant, as the western Europeans spoke of the need to look after the 'weaker peoples' of the world. The language was all the more horrifying, since everyone spoke in high-minded terms, disguising their true intent. To the other diplomats, the meaning was of course clear, but the ordinary person might be bamboozled by the eloquent turn of phrase. The only Western exception at the Conference, Mrs Pandit thought, were the Americans, who were unsophisticated enough to actually say what they thought. This would change quickly, of course. In the context, she found the Americans utterly charming. The whole event was a most informative experience, as she learned what went on in the backrooms of the Men Who Ruled the World.

The weeks after Hot Springs were lined up with a number of speeches and meetings from Boston to Washington DC. On 18 January, Mrs Pandit was received at New York City Hall by the legendary mayor Fiorello LaGuardia.[40] They were mutual admirers. LaGuardia had read and enjoyed Nehru's autobiography. But he considered Gandhi a saint, and therefore someone who did not belong in politics. 'You come here and ask the Americans for their moral support. How far will anybody's *moral* support take you toward your freedom? Now if you had asked for *arms* I could have understood . . . Of course you have my sympathy but it's of little value.' Mrs Pandit found these comments amusing, though she, and later Gandhi and Nehru as well, were very appreciative of the mayor's support. In any event, LaGuardia's observation struck a chord with her.[41] While arms were out of the question for a follower of Gandhi, what was it she wanted from the Americans?

Aside from the welcome that New York's mayor gave her, other associates put together three important receptions. One was a dinner held in her honour by Ambassador William Phillips, Roosevelt's personal representative to India and the former head of the London branch of the Office of Strategic Services, the precursor to the Central Intelligence Agency (CIA).[42] Phillips had been a strong supporter of Indian independence.[43]

On 26 January, Pearl Buck organized a massive celebration with a thousand guests to mark 'Indian Independence Day'.[44] Buck worked in her capacity as the honorary president of the India League, sharing credit with the organization's tireless official president, J.J. Singh. With Mrs Pandit as the guest of honour, dinner was served at the luxurious Hotel Commodore. The programme underscored India's anti-fascist stance, quoting from Congress Resolutions from 1939 through 1942 condemning the Munich Pact and promoting democracy, in order to demonstrate that India's call for independence was in no way meant to obstruct the Allied cause, as some imperial propaganda had been suggesting. It linked India's stand on independence and democracy with the ideals of the United States Declaration of Independence. It also highlighted the Quit India Resolution's talk of a world federation and proclaimed that a democratic world order was the ultimate objective.[45] While the speakers spoke of a rising Indian anger, 'born out of agony' as Buck memorably phrased it, Sirdar J.J. Singh, the president of the India League, warned that 'no peace can exist nor any Dumbarton Oaks proposals be successful as long as imperialism exists'.[46]

The US, Britain, China and the Soviets had met in late 1944 in Dumbarton Oaks outside of Washington DC. There they discussed possibilities for a post-war world, outlining general proposals for a new international organization to maintain the peace. Their proposals were the outline of what would come to be known as the United Nations, carrying forward the official title of the wartime Allies. This, though, was a matter that needed further discussion, and even as J.J. Singh spoke, planning was underway for Stalin, Churchill and FDR to meet again in Yalta to follow up.

The day after the Commodore reception, Mrs Pandit lunched

with Eleanor Roosevelt, and then on the twenty-eighth went on CBS radio to present a speech on India and World Order. She spoke with fire and castigated the US for not being more supportive of the Indian cause.[47] Her comments quickly caught the attention of US authorities, who felt compelled to defend themselves. On 29 January, Undersecretary of State Joseph Grew noted that the United States was a friend to both the British government and the Indian people and that it stood ready to help 'in any appropriate manner' to find a solution for India. While hardly a resounding rejection of colonialism, this public statement nonetheless was widely interpreted as proof of Mrs Pandit's impact.[48]

The next day, Mrs Pandit spoke at the annual meeting of Save the Children in NYC. There, and at other stops during her trip, she spoke of the famine in India and raised funds towards relief.[49]

Her final gala for the time being was scheduled for 3 February. This time the hosts were Henry and Clare Booth Luce. The Luces were great admirers of India. Henry was on the board of the India League, along with Albert Einstein and other luminaries. He had been working in 1943 with Pearl Buck and others to alleviate the famine in India.[50] Clare Luce had been an early and ardent supporter of India. While travelling there in 1942, she had initiated a correspondence with Nehru, whom she deemed the 'greatest and truest friend that the cause of Democracy and the cause of the United Nations [the war-time Allies] has in all of Asia'.[51] Nehru had received one of her letters on 8 August 1942, just before he was arrested, and he kept it with him while he was in prison.[52]

The Luces hosted Mrs Pandit over a fabulous dinner at the Waldorf. It was the hottest ticket in town, and the guests at the party read like a veritable who's who of the rich and famous: Mr and Mrs John D. Rockefeller; *The New York Times* publishers Mr and Mrs Sulzberger; the governors of New York, New Jersey and Connecticut; the founder of Pan Am, Juan Trippe; Pulitzer-prize-winning journalist Herbert Swope; and many more. [53] The Luces delivered the cream of American publishing, journalism, business and politics (especially from their Republican circle). Mrs Pandit, with characteristic wit, thanked everyone for coming on behalf of India's imprisoned leaders.

The irony was wicked, but it was delivered in a benevolent fashion. Mrs Pandit contrasted the grandeur and lavishness of America's riches, and its well-meaning citizens, with the grim state of affairs in India.

But all of these experiences—the hobnobbing, the electric speeches, the friendly push-back, the constant anti-imperial crusade—were just the warm-up act. On 1 March, Mrs Pandit was booked to appear on America's Town Meeting of the Air, a wildly popular radio programme broadcast from New York City's Town Hall to seven or eight million people across the country. From 1944 to 1945, it was sponsored by *Reader's Digest*, then the most widely read magazine in the United States, which helped publish the transcripts to ensure an even wider audience. The Town Meeting's format was live debate. A speaker would have several minutes to make their best case, and they would have an ally of sorts in one other speaker, though there was no assurance that the two would agree on much. They would face-off against two opponents who held to the same pattern. Then, all of them would open themselves up to live questioning from the audience. It was nerve-wracking for even seasoned radio veterans, often resulting in a 'verbal bloodbath'.[54]

Mrs Pandit was scheduled to challenge Robert Boothby on the question of whether colonial empires were a threat to world peace. Boothby, an Englishman, was a polished speaker, and highly regarded. He had met Adolf Hitler in the early 1930s and quickly sized him up as a 'terrifying' threat.[55] Boothby was a British Member of Parliament and the former parliamentary secretary to Churchill. Owen Lattimore, an advisor to Chiang Kai-shek and former editor of *Pacific Affairs*, spoke in the affirmative along with Mrs Pandit, while the radio personality John W. Vandercook was allied with Boothby. The vast audience, the heckler-friendly give-and-take format and the eminence of the speakers made this a high-stakes affair. If Mrs Pandit stumbled, she could effectively harm India's chance at independence as well as the larger cause of anti-colonialism.

Mrs Pandit was the first speaker. She came out swinging: 'Is it not absurd that in the sixth year of World War II we should debate a subject like the one chosen for this evening?' It was a jaw-dropping way to begin.

To a hushed hall, she cited her brother's Quit India Resolution, and called for European powers to release all of their colonial possessions. She ended: 'The post-war world cannot be built on old and rotten foundations. There must be a new concept in which all people can share. Military standards of security will not be guarantees of lasting peace. Political thought must change. Asia will be the testing ground of the promises of the United Nations and the continuation of colonial empires will be a danger to world peace and to the progress of humanity.' The audience applauded politely. But now it was Boothby's turn.

Boothby defended empires as keepers of the peace. He noted that he hoped India would in short order have 'complete dominion status', but that empires were the best formation in which to consider grand alliances. His speech was interrupted several times by applause. He had been charming and gracious, a velvet hammer.

But Lattimore was ready to spar and to applause; he opened

by saying 'how emphatically I support Mrs Pandit'. His speech too was broken several times by applause, as was Vandercook's in the final opening statement. By the end of the first round, purely on debate points, it seemed a fairly even match.

The second round consisted of crossfire among the speakers, each allowed to directly question one another. Mrs Pandit led off by asking Boothby, who had defended Britain's benevolent rule in India, how he might account for the famine that had been ongoing for the past two years. Boothby sought to brush this off, but Mrs Pandit came back with statistics on annual per capita health spending by the British government in India. Boothby found himself on the defensive, and he would never recover. While Lattimore and Vandercook both got in a few punches each, it was clear that the night belonged to Mrs Pandit. She repeatedly received applause from the audience, the only one of the speakers so recognized in this round.

Boothby tried to turn things around. He tried to point out that Britain did not need to finance India since it was 'self-supporting'. Mrs Pandit cut in: 'India supports herself and England, that is the whole trouble.' Annoyed, Boothby continued that this then meant that the whole issue of British health care spending in India was irrelevant. He was again cut off mid-sentence: 'It is because Mr Boothby doesn't realize the money is ours and the control is his,' Pandit chortled, clearly delighting now in the battle, and pleased at the turn of the tide.

As the debate moved to round three, questions from the audience, Mrs Pandit was in her element. She fended off one particularly persistent questioner, and remained an audience favourite. Vandercook tried to move away from the topic of India but was shouted down by the audience. Boothby continued to jab, but it was pointless. Mrs Pandit ended the evening to applause. It was a star-making turn, and in the process she acquired the sobriquet by which she would forever be known in the international arena: Madame Pandit.[56]

One person who attended the forum in person, Helen Cantor, wrote a letter that eventually found its way to the British Foreign Office. She told them that 'T.N.T.' was 'tossed around' by the participants. Then she demanded to know: 'Who and why is Robert Boothby? I am afraid that he is not serving too well as goodwill ambassador . . . and he is doing harm.' The Foreign Office noted dryly in an internal memo that the next 'General Election will presumably at least have the advantage of returning Mr. Boothby to home pastures.'[57]

Madame Pandit's performance garnered her attention far and wide. But an even greater challenge lay on the horizon. At the behest of the Big Three (the US, England and the Soviets), representatives from around the world were soon to gather in San Francisco to discuss the creation of a new world organization to maintain peace and security. Anti-imperial forces were coalescing to take a stand at the meeting, having agreed that Madame Pandit was the one person who could best champion their cause, to ensure that *justice* was included in the institution's conception.

3 SHOWDOWN IN SAN FRANCISCO

THE GREAT POWERS AT YALTA

As Vijaya Lakshmi Pandit was landing in New York, President Roosevelt was consumed by preparations for meetings between the Big Three that would take place in Yalta, in the Crimea. The Yalta Conference was meant to follow up on an earlier 1943 conclave in Tehran, where the overall camaraderie between Roosevelt, Stalin and Churchill had produced fruitful dialogue. In Tehran, the three had tentatively agreed that some kind of post-war world organization was necessary to maintain the peace.[1] The Allies needed to meet again to discuss this matter in greater detail, in the context of the latest developments in the war.

On 6 June 1944, the Allies launched Operations Overlord and Neptune, landing troops in France and beginning an eastward march. The Soviets, in the meantime, had launched an offensive of their own and the Red Army was moving swiftly west. The pincer attack was meant to crush the German forces in-between.

As the military advanced, the imperative for post-war planning dramatically increased. Administration officials from the Big Three and China met in Dumbarton Oaks and agreed on a tentative framework for creating a new international organization to help maintain peace and security. The primary purpose of the new body would be to use collective arrangements to ensure the prevention of aggression. Fostering 'friendly relations' between countries and peoples and working together to solve major economic and social challenges were seen as essential to fulfilling this central mission.[2] Ironically, for a meeting meant to lay the foundation for international camaraderie, the Soviet and Chinese delegations needed to meet separately with the Americans and the British since the two non-Western giants did not get along.

Dumbarton Oaks nonetheless established the basic parameters of the post-war framework for peace. But several major issues remained unresolved, including a timetable for implementation, and details of representation and voting procedures. The Soviets were especially concerned about the latter two issues. The heads of state would have to meet in person to resolve the matter.

The meeting was scheduled for early February 1945. Roosevelt was already on the ground by the time Churchill arrived, and the two joined in procession, Roosevelt by open car, as part of the welcome ceremony. By this point, FDR was a very sick man. He would be dead within two months. At Yalta, he appeared thin, his skin 'transparent', and his eyes somewhat glazed. As he rode in the procession, his mouth hung open and his mind seemed in a distant place. People immediately began to gossip. Despite the great strain, Roosevelt nonetheless pulled it together long enough to participate fully in all the discussions that followed.[3]

Stalin, Churchill and FDR met over the course of several days, from the third through the eleventh. The question of a world organization came up four times over the course of the meetings, which also focused on the futures of Germany and Poland, and touched on a wide range of other issues, including Japan, Yugoslavia and Greece. There were really only two broad areas of discussion regarding the international institution: details related to the Security Council, and the date to hold a conference to officially establish the new organization. On vivid display was Churchill's benevolent paternalism, a hallmark of his worldview that also justified his continued belief in imperialism. At their meeting of 6 February, Churchill declared that 'smaller nations of the world' had to have a right to bring grievances against anyone they so chose in the world forum. The Great Powers, meaning the Big Three in this case, had to make clear that their intent was to serve, not rule, the world. Thus, he concluded, he supported Roosevelt's proposal that any state party to a conflict must be able to present its point of view, though it would have no vote on the matter. To illustrate his point, Churchill declared that China should be allowed to ask for the return of Hong Kong. China could present any case it wished, as could Great Britain in response, and the matter would be left to the Security Council to decide, with Great Britain having no vote, or veto, in the matter. It was Churchill at his most magnanimous. The only caveat was that 'there was no question of [Great Britain] being compelled by the Security Council to give Hong Kong back to China if [Great Britain] did not think this was the right step . . . to take'.[4] It was, again, Churchill at his characteristic best. He gave away nothing while fostering the illusion of full democratic dialogue and dissent.

A few days later, on 9 February, after agreement had been reached on the basic structure of the Security Council and on the world organization's initial voting membership, Churchill voiced concern about issues related to 'territorial trusteeship and dependent areas'. The three powers had agreed that this was to be a matter of continued consultation between them and would also have to be publicly discussed at the soon-to-be-held international conference for establishing the organization. Churchill, though, made one thing clear. He 'could not agree . . . to any British territory being made the subject of a system under which it would be open to other Powers to make criticisms of the work which [Britain] had done in our Colonies, and which called upon [Britain] to justify [its] standard of administration.' Churchill would only agree to allow planning to move forward if it was 'made clear' that the trusteeship proposals would not affect 'the integrity' of the British Empire 'in any way'.[5]

Churchill's determined defence of the British colonial enterprise was clearly at odds with FDR's stand on the issue, but the president was simply far too weak to effectively counter his Atlantic neighbour. Churchill's concerns were acknowledged and discussions proceeded to other matters.

A few days earlier, Roosevelt had suggested that the Big Three agree to an international meeting to launch the new global institution as early as the following month of March. Churchill resisted the date, fearing that it was simply too soon. Administration officials were left to hash out the details and they came back with a proposal to hold a meeting a month later. Churchill, Stalin and Roosevelt all agreed, and the date was set. On 25 April, countries from all over the world, including those who were part of the Alliance, some Soviet satellites and members of the British Commonwealth and Empire, would be invited to send delegations to what was to be called the United Nations Conference.[6] It was to take place in San Francisco. There, the future of the world was to be decided.

SHOWDOWN IN SAN FRANCISCO

J.J. Singh and other friends of the India League first broached the subject of Madame Pandit leading a counter-delegation to the San Francisco Conference a few days before the Indian Independence Day celebration Pearl Buck had hosted on 26 February. The British were going to handpick representatives from India, and many felt that this move was meant to shield the goings-on in the British Empire from the prying eyes of the world.

On the twenty-second, Pandit telegrammed Gandhi to inform him of the request and asking for his endorsement of her participation. Gandhi wrote back that he was not going to interfere in this matter.[7] Madame Pandit then confirmed her participation and the stage was set for dramatic confrontation in San Francisco, her fiery anti-colonial message brought up against Churchill's adamant defence of imperialism. What happens when an unstoppable force meets an immovable object?

As preparations got underway, Gandhi released a statement to the press regarding the upcoming Conference, which outlined a vision for what he wished to see accomplished at the meeting. Gandhi made clear that he did not know the details of what was about to transpire, since he was an 'outsider'. But he lambasted the 'world security' framework as one built on 'mistrust and fear'. He described war as something built on deception and fraud, and urged the Allies to give up faith in war's 'efficacy'. For good measure, he added that places such as India should be free to name their own representatives or they should have none at all, giving some wind to Madame Pandit's back as she led the charge.

Gandhi stated that four steps had to be taken to help ensure a lasting and just peace. First, India had to be made independent. This, in turn, had to herald freedom from exploitation for all peoples of the earth. The goodwill washing as waves over the world had also to reach the shores of Germany and Japan. Old opponents had to be made friends, so that the basis of further discord would be removed. The Axis should not be subjected to humiliating, punitive measures, he claimed, distantly echoing conclusions reached at Yalta.[8] And finally, Gandhi called for international disarmament and the establishment of a world police force. This police was 'a concession to human weakness' and not an instrument of peace in itself. Together, these steps would lay the foundation for a new world.

What did this new world look like? Gandhi quoted in detail Nehru's Quit India Resolution, calling for a world federation, with a unified world federal defence force and pooled resources. 'Thus the demand for India's independence is in no way selfish. Its nationalism spells internationalism,' he declared.[9]

Soon after he released this statement, Gandhi was interviewed by Ralph Coniston, a writer for *Collier's Weekly*, a magazine with a distinguished history in the United States. Their work had led to better labour and food safety laws, and *Collier's* was generally seen as one of the leading sunshine publications, one that shed bright light on matters and helped to create more responsive, effective government.

Coniston tried to pin Gandhi down a bit more. When asked what he would like to see accomplished in San Francisco, Gandhi replied: 'Parity among all nations.' He called for an end to domination and for stronger nations to be 'servants of the weak', an idea that interjected notions of ethics into international relations.[10]

Coniston wondered if Gandhi was being too idealistic. Gandhi agreed that he very well could be, but that status quo politics that defended the authority of the Great Powers would only lead to another catastrophic war.

This led Coniston to zero in on the possible product of the meeting in San Francisco. Gandhi called for a world organization 'based predominantly on truth and non-violence'. Gandhi went further, and laid out a distinct new vision. 'Yes [I would have a world government.] I claim to be a practical idealist. I believe in compromise so long as it does not involve the sacrifice of principles. I may not get a world government that I want just now but if it is a government that would just touch my ideal, I would accept it as a compromise. Therefore, although I am not enamored of a world federation, I shall be prepared to accept it if it is built on an essentially non-violent basis.' He concluded by referring again to the Quit India Resolution, noting that India's independence was a necessary precondition to further participation in evolving world government.[11]

In many ways, this was an opaque statement. What was the distinction between 'world government' and 'world federation'? What exactly was the 'world government' that Gandhi wanted? A clue lay in his reference to the Quit India Resolution that called for the elimination of national armed forces and for the pooling of resources, which seemed to indicate a form of integration greater than the one implied by federation. Then again, the same resolution called for a 'world federation'.

If the nuances had not been thought through, a broad direction in which to move had been charted out. The first step, though, required the independence of India, for only in rejecting the overt exploitation and power politics of colonialism could a true foundation be laid for equity and harmony between peoples. The voice of all people had to be heard for 'world government' or 'world federation' to make sense and be effective, and this simply could not be accomplished if some continued under heel.[12] It would be up to Madame Pandit to make this case to the world.

The British were particularly wary of her presence. Sir Frederick Puckle, the agent general for India in the United States, remarked in his report of 31 March 1945 that Madame Pandit's speeches had 'obtained a fairly wide coverage'. He added that her 'charm and oratory have had their effect'. Puckle's job was to get the British message across, which primarily was one of British beneficence and the greatness of her policies in the colonies and elsewhere. Madame Pandit's talks were in stark contrast to this mission. The trick was how to deal with her, for direct assault might amplify her message. So Puckle downplayed her importance, concluding that her effect had 'been less than might have been expected'.[13]

The Americans were sensitive to the feelings of their wartime ally. On 4 April, Eleanor Roosevelt wrote to Secretary of State Edward Stettinius, Jr suggesting that it might be unwise at this point in time to 'stir up feeling against Great Britain', something that was relatively easy to do since the American people were 'on the whole . . . in sympathy with the nationalist movement in India'. She noted that women 'from all sides' were bringing the Indian issue to her attention, highlighting the efficacy of Madame Pandit's advocacy. But with the war still unfinished, the future of the world to be decided in mere weeks, and her own thinking clouded by her husband's collapsing health, Mrs Roosevelt uncharacteristically wondered if the US government should take steps to stop Pandit and her colleagues. Stettinius responded a few days later that the British embassy had recently conveyed the view to the U.S. State Department that Madame Pandit 'may be doing [her cause] more harm than good', a cunning claim since all evidence, and the UK's own assessment, indicated the contrary. The Americans had relayed the British view to Madame Pandit via diplomatic channels.

Stettinius added that no action should be taken against Madame Pandit, first because of the American tradition of free speech, and second because they did not want to give the impression of 'conspiring with the British' to stifle India's 'aspirations for self-government'. He concluded by pointing to the vast reach of the information services of the Indian Agency General, a representative of the British government in India in the United States affiliated with the British embassy. Madame Pandit was up against a propaganda juggernaut. If she really were such a threat, Stettinius said, the British could always just revoke her passport.[14]

But this was exactly the reason for Mrs Roosevelt's sensitivity to British sentiment. Madame Pandit had no passport, and was travelling in the United States by courtesy of FDR himself.[15] The waves she was making would reflect on Anglo-American relations, which had to remain rock solid overall in light of the war.

As letters between Mrs Roosevelt and her Secretary of State went back and forth, Madame Pandit travelled to Baltimore, where she spoke to an inter-racial and international audience, pleading for the 'Four Freedoms for Asia', referencing President Roosevelt's famous 1941 speech. At a reception the previous evening, she had outlined her expectations for San Francisco. 'I am not at all optimistic about the conferences between the great nations [since] . . . they are building the future on old foundations, which must be destroyed before the vision of Dumbarton Oaks becomes fruitful.' Nonetheless, 'we, the common people, really can control the destiny of the world'. If the United Nations Conference itself was a setup by the Great Powers, the hope lay in the activities of regular people. She was assuming this great burden and would speak in San Francisco as a representative of the common people, to give voice to their concerns, and challenge the power and authority of the mightiest men in the world.[16]

Highlighting the real threat that they perceived, and belying their public devil-may-care attitude, British Intelligence Service staff secretly attended her presentation the next day. During her talk, she declared to ovation: 'India sympathizes with all races fighting for freedom and equality and the Indian people is in entire sympathy with the colored people of America. India stands for full equality of all races and creeds.'[17] As usual, the room was mesmerized.

Over the next few weeks, members of the India League, its ally the National Committee for India's Freedom and a variety of other organizations all began their westward march. Each country was allowed to have non-governmental representatives serve as consultants to the official delegation, but the United States was the only country that took advantage of this opportunity. The NAACP served in this capacity, and brought its considerable resources to bear.[18] In them, Madame Pandit had a fiercely loyal ally. The organization's Walter White had advocated India's cause for years, and had created the plan for Wendell Willkie to travel to the subcontinent. White and a number of other race activists had spoken frequently with Madame Pandit since her arrival, and she, in turn, had reinforced the message of universal racial justice.

Indeed, coinciding with her appearance in Baltimore, the NAACP convened a conference of black Americans and colonized people in New York City, with representatives from India present, to discuss matters of racial injustice and imperial control. They condemned colonialism, and took issue with the system of trusteeship. They readied such remarks for presentation in San Francisco, the banner carried forward by Walter White himself and the legendary W.E.B. DuBois. DuBois was one of the founding figures of the NAACP, and the first African American to receive a Ph.D from Harvard. The magnitude of what was to unfold in California was lost on no one. DuBois commented that he was travelling to San Francisco 'to help save the world'.[19]

Madame Pandit arrived at the Conference and immediately threw herself into a whirlwind of activity. On the twenty-sixth, she delivered a fiery speech denouncing 'British stooges'. The American press drooled. The *Chicago Tribune* was perhaps the most hagiographic (and sexist), praising her 'dazzling white robe . . . alluring curves . . . Oxonian accents and scrapping American slang.' They noted that she 'pulled no punches on Prime Minister Churchill' and that she 'began twisting the British lion's tail'.

In her speech, made in the very hotel in which the British foreign secretary, Anthony Eden, was staying, she zeroed in on Churchill's declaration that he had not become the king's first minister to watch over the dissolution of the empire, which he had made in response to Wendell Willkie's 'One World' radio address. Madame Pandit compared this statement to Churchill's more recent democratic protestations, laying bare the prime minister's two-facedness.

The British again did their best to undermine her credibility, hatching a plan to place plants in Pandit's audience to throw her off her game. Instead, she turned the tables when interrupted and mercilessly mocked her inquisitors, eventually driving them out of the room with audience support.[20]

The next day, Madame Pandit changed tactics, directing her attention more towards her American audience. She spoke 'with force that recalls the chill fury with which Madame Chiang Kai-shek once brought the American congress to tears'.

'It should not be I, coming to you Americans who fought for your independence to tell you India wants her freedom,' she thundered. 'You should be standing on your street corners, demanding freedom for us. If you acquiesce in denying freedom to others, you end freedom for yourselves.'

Widening her fire to all the Conference attendees, she demanded more than mere platitudes. 'Every speech at this conference echoes things we believe, but words are not enough.' She called on delegates to stay true to the mission of the Conference, and bring the principles of the Atlantic Charter to all people.[21]

Her words made an impact, and many were dazzled. As one admirer, a Colorado woman named Frances Eagan, wrote: 'I love you [for your fine stand for your country]. I <u>know</u> your [sic] right in your stand–don't let them bluff you out. I hope that you win every point-+some you have not brought out yet.'[22]

Amidst her efforts, she continued to denounce the three Indian delegates at the Conference. She demanded that they stand aside since they did not represent the true voice of Indians in any capacity. Her withering criticism soon led one of those delegates, Sir Feroze Khan Noon, to declare his support for Nehru. Noon asked Gandhi to retire and allow Nehru to 'come to the forefront'. Noon had been serving on the viceroy's executive council in the area of defence since 1943.[23] His comments were immediately picked up. Rumours began to swirl that Churchill was ready to make a deal in the face of the continued embarrassment he faced over the Indian question, successfully made a priority issue by Madame Pandit.[24]

But no offer ever came. After waiting a few days once the news of Churchill's possible move broke, Madame Pandit released a memo to all UN delegates demanding freedom for India. She had intended to release such a memo from the outset, but held her fire briefly when an agreement seemed possible.[25] The document bore all the hallmarks of her eloquent, but acid, tongue: 'The continuance of such a situation [as colonialism] affecting the honor, liberty, peace and progress of one-fifth of mankind is irreconcilable, alike with the concepts that have inspired the United Nations Conference and with the new world order which, it is hoped, will be ushered in . . .'

'I speak here for my country . . . but I also speak for those countries which, like India, are under the heels of alien militarists and cannot speak for themselves . . . The voice of some 600,000,000 of the enslaved peoples of Asia may not be officially heard at the Conference, and those who have usurped their birthright of freedom may cynically claim to speak for them; but there will be no real peace on this earth so long as they are denied justice.'

She soared in her conclusion: 'The recognition of India's independence now will be a proclamation and an assurance to the whole world that the statesmen of the United Nations, assembled in this solemn conclave in San Francisco, have in truth and in honor heralded the dawn of a new and a better day for an all but crucified humanity.'[26]

On the heels of the release of this statement, Gandhi made another statement to the press, attacking Noon's claims, and revealing just how closely he was paying attention to events unfolding half a world away. He mocked Noon's comments, noting that Nehru was Gandhi's 'brother', that he was already named 'successor', and that he was already out in front. Gandhi demanded that Noon request the British government in India to release Nehru from prison immediately and threaten to resign if his wish was not carried out.[27]

Back in the United States, Madame Pandit received a letter from the secretary general of the Conference, Alger Hiss, stating that the issues raised in her memo were not 'germane' to the agenda of the meeting. The delegates were not trying to craft a peace agreement between countries but rather trying to create a new international organization.[28]

Despite the clear signal that she was fighting a losing battle, that she would not be able to accomplish much of substance at the Conference, and that the will of the Great Powers would carry the day, Madame Pandit doubled down in her efforts. When Secretary Eden defended the Cripps mission, saying that he didn't stand there 'in a white sheet' (meaning regret or admission of an error), and placed the onus for its failure squarely on the Indians, Pandit gamely turned the British-ism on its head, acerbically recasting it in American terms and cloaking Eden in the garb of a Klansman. 'I will pass up the point whether Mr. Eden should or should not be wrapped in a white sheet if only as a contrast to the black shroud with which his Government has surrounded India.'[29]

She was getting quite under the British skin, so much so that they changed their tactics. While before, as Stettinius had told Mrs Roosevelt, they expressed diplomatic nonchalance towards Madame Pandit's activities, they now tried to silence her. Madame Pandit was scheduled to address the California legislature on 14 May, but the British exerted pressure on the governor of California, Earl Warren, to rescind the invitation. Lord Halifax, then the British ambassador to Washington, had spoken to the same audience days earlier and assured them of the wondrous progress being made at the United Nations Conference. Madame Pandit was sure to show him up and Halifax personally appealed to Warren.[30]

The invitation remained but Warren, in one of a few blemishes on his illustrious career, chose not to attend, as did the speaker and several other members of the assembly. The majority, though, stood their ground and attended the session. Madame Pandit reminded them that they could not 'rejoice over the end of fascism in Europe when imperialism, its twin brother, is permitted to function in the colonies'.[31]

Her talk and the actions of Warren and Halifax did not escape the attention of the residents of California. One Long Beach resident, after inviting Pandit to speak in her area, wrote a scathing letter to the governor, which inveighed against the officials who had missed the speech, giving in to British pressure. 'It is either that the spirit of Justice is dead in the breasts of many of our representatives or they are positively ignorant of the conditions as they have been and are in India today.'[32]

British efforts and propaganda to the contrary, Madame Pandit was winning hearts and minds. The support she received continuously recharged her. She had up until this point taken only glancing shots at the issue dearest to Churchill's heart: trusteeship. A few days after her speech to the legislature, she released a detailed statement on the subject: 'The issue of eventual "independence" for now dependent peoples under the proposed international trusteeship system is probably the most crucial question that has so far come up before the . . . Conference.'

She focused on the key issue, the type of language that would go into the United Nations Charter: 'Great Britain, France and the Netherlands, all colonial powers, have proposed "self-government" as a substitute for "independence". What is the difference? The word independence means what it says and is clean-cut. The British formula of "self-government"—an ancient weasel word—was deliberately designed and has long been used in India and elsewhere to offer the shadow but never the substance of independence to subject peoples.' The former minister for local self-government spoke from experience.

She went on to cite the case of Burma as illustrative of the true intent behind the deployment of the term 'self-government'—the 'negation of true independence'. '[The British] will do anything but get off the necks of those whom they bestride,' she bitingly concluded.

Madame Pandit knew that any chance at that point of countering Britain's power lay in American influence. The United States, from ordinary people to many in authority, was by and large convinced of India's case, she had come to believe. In her statement, she flattered her hosts, hoping 'that saner and juster conceptions of the future of the world will prevail . . . and particularly that the United States . . . will not permit its traditional position and vast prestige to be tarnished by concession to palpable maneuvers on the part of Britain . . . to secure a new lease of life for their . . . colonialism and . . . imperialism'.[33] China and the Soviet Union supported the use of the term 'independence', and the NAACP contacted Stettinius to inform him of the necessity of a similar stand, to remain in line with all previous US statements.[34]

Churchill, of course, had long been annoyed by American pressure on the issue of colonies. His temper had flared when Willkie and Roosevelt pressed their case publicly, and he was not about to give in now. FDR had died a few days before the San Francisco meeting had gotten underway, and President Harry Truman held nowhere near the kind of sway with Churchill that his predecessor did.[35] The British convinced the Americans that 'self-government' was a reasonable goal, pressed their case, and the US went along. Chapters XI and XII of the new UN Charter structured the trusteeship system according to British will. Chapter XI, in particular, read: 'Members of the

United Nations . . . recognize the principle that the interests [of non-self-governing people] . . . are paramount, and accept a sacred trust . . . to develop self-government, to take due account of the political aspirations of the peoples, and to assist them in the progressive development of their free political institutions, according to the particular circumstances of each territory and its peoples and their varying stages of advancement.'[36] The United Kingdom's Foreign Office gloated that the language 'prescribes the principles of Colonial Administration . . . it does not empower the United Nations organization to intervene in the application of these principles by the Powers concerned.'[37]

It was over. Churchill had won.

BACK TO THE FUTURE

Before leaving San Francisco, Madame Pandit spoke at the Scottish Rite Auditorium at a meeting sponsored by the National Committee for India's Freedom. Dr Syud Hossain, the chair of the committee, delivered remarks that highlighted India's overall stand, and some of Madame Pandit's sharper criticisms in particular.[38] The committee also devoted the May issue of its newsletter, the *Voice of India*, to discussion of Indian independence and the United Nations Conference. Madame Pandit and Roger Baldwin were among the contributors, and they tenaciously continued to make their case.[39]

But the setback was apparent to all. In early June, Madame Pandit travelled to Chicago, where she spoke to a gathering organized by the Chicago Civil Liberties committee, a group closely associated with the American Civil Liberties Union. She confessed: 'I am bitterly disappointed in the San Francisco conference. These Asiatic millions demand at least big steps toward independence. It does not appear that they will get much, if anything.'

Seething about Churchill's underhanded manipulation of the Charter language, she vented: 'I don't know why this couldn't have been an honest, above board meeting of the nations . . . It seems thru [sic] our leaders, our powerful politicians throughout the world, we always give lip service to certain fundamental truths, but that we can never seem to translate this lip service into action.'

She astutely observed that the 'effort seems to be entirely to allocate the power among the Big Five rather than to share power'. And then she warned darkly that 'unless the future being planned for the world includes equality, freedom and justice for all people, the planning is futile, there can be no international security'.[40] A few days later, the San Francisco meetings drew to a close.

At just about the same moment, Jawaharlal Nehru was finally released from prison. Madame Pandit had been exchanging letters with her brother since she had begun her travels, and shared with him all the interesting highlights, from her radio takedown of Robert Boothby to her concerns about the meeting at Hot Springs. To one of these letters, Nehru had responded: 'We are all, or nearly all, internationalists today, but for each one of us internationalism has its own particular significance.'

'We in India, circumstanced as we are, cannot help being rather narrow in outlook in world affairs . . . And yet I do think that basically India is more suited to internationalism than many other countries . . . Once the present distemper is past we ought to be able to adjust ourselves, without too great difficulty, to a new scheme of things'.[41] In his letters, he told her to keep at it, and offered words of encouragement. Upon his release, he sent her a letter while trekking in the Kashmiri Himalayas, recuperating and recharging from his years behind bars.

He wrote: 'You know that your work in the States has been very greatly appreciated here by all kinds of people. You have done a splendid job, as perhaps no one else could have done in the circumstances. The immediate consequences of what you have done may not be obvious but I am sure that the remoter consequences will be considerable.'[42] It was one of Nehru's more prescient predictions.

Nehru's support helped convince Madame Pandit to refocus. Her energies had been directed at accomplishing something in San Francisco. For now, the goalpost again had to be moved and she had to think about what change might come at some subsequent date.

In late October, she was invited to meet Harry Truman in the White House. She was blunt. India looked on America as a friend, she told him, and appreciated the moral support that the country extended to their struggle. But she could not understand how the United States could provide arms that were used to suppress freedom struggles throughout Asia. Her trip to the United States had come full circle, as she found herself repackaging the very words of advice Mayor LaGuardia had given her at the outset of her trip.[43]

Truman was straightforward in his response. He said that he had raised the very same concern with Clement Attlee, the newly elected British prime minister, at the just completed Potsdam Conference, complaining that American aid more broadly was being misused. Attlee simply said that aid, and arms, once given, could not be controlled.[44] The exchange highlighted the complexities of international relations, and one of the reasons why diplomacy was often perceived as insincere, as everyone was mired in a web of conflicting national interests and strategies.

A few weeks later, in a speech in Detroit, Madame Pandit

made her grievances public: 'Colonial peoples deeply resent the use of American war materials to crush the Indonesians. Without the aid of American capital and materials, none of the imperialistic powers are [sic] in a position to restore the status quo. Therefore America is morally responsible for what is happening today in southeast Asia.'[45] She was clearly still stinging from her loss in San Francisco, and the betrayal of the United States. It was one of the few times she so directly turned on her hosts.

She reframed her comments in a speech days later in Chicago. America and India shared ideals and aspirations, she reminded her audience. 'You have an [sic] unique opportunity,' she told them.

'You are at the top of the world. You won the war . . . You are the only one who has the money . . . You, therefore, can make a pattern for good living throughout the world.'

At the end of her tour, she tried to boil her message down to its simplest terms. 'My job is to ask Americans whether freedom is indivisible, or do they think it is a monopoly of certain groups . . . ? We have got to give to our neighbors the things we have in the world today.'[46]

With that, Madame Pandit wrapped up her stay in the United States and left for India by plane. Her brother hurried to Karachi to meet her.[47]

She was greeted in January 1946 with a hero's welcome. Ten thousand people crammed into a space for 3,000 to congratulate Pandit on her successful tour and to welcome her home. As she arrived, the crowd surged. It was adulation befitting a rock star, though, of course, there were as yet none of those around.

Addressing the throngs, she said: 'I come back with happy memories of my visit and I am convinced that the American people will stand by us in our fight for freedom.'

To great excitement, she added: 'I have tried to emphasize the urgent necessity of Independence for India not only because of her own rights but freedom of India is a pivot of world peace structure . . . An India functioning as free and equal partner with other nations will be a tremendous force in the building up of a new world order.'

Then, looking out to the horizon, she steeled her gaze. 'We have firm foundation of the past and we will build up the future.'[48]

She could not, at that point, know how fast events would move. Within months, with Nehru assuming transitionary leadership of India, Madame Pandit would be headed back to New York to make her new world a reality.

4 THE NEW HOPE

A DREAM RENEWED

In 1946, Britain's vice-like grip over its colonies began to loosen. Thoroughly exhausted by the war, which by the end of the conflict had consumed over half the country's Gross National Product (GNP), the United Kingdom was a ravaged land, if not one as thoroughly devastated as its continental neighbours. Unlike during the First World War, this time around Great Britain had been forced to cannibalize its own resources and thus had a weak hand with which to rebuild, a troubling scenario when faced with the reality of the loss of 30 per cent of its total housing, 3.5 million homes in London alone.[1] Combined with ceaseless pressure from the Americans to give up its overseas possessions, Britain no longer possessed the will nor the means to maintain its empire.

Under these conditions, Jawaharlal Nehru took over the

leadership of a new interim government in India in September. Within days, he summoned his sister from her home in Lucknow to Delhi and, in one of his first acts after taking power, requested her to lead India's delegation to the new United Nations. Nehru, Gandhi and Lord Wavell, the British viceroy, all unanimously agreed that Madame Pandit was the most appropriate person for this posting. When she protested, Sir Girja Bajpai, a career civil servant who had been Britain's agent general in Washington during the latter part of her just-completed trip to the US, responded: 'You managed pretty well on your unofficial tour–I personally witnessed that!'[2]

Madame Pandit's actions in San Francisco had awakened Nehru to the possibilities that the new world body represented. For him, this was an opportunity to make good on a long-held dream. For as early as 1919, when President Woodrow Wilson had redefined international relations with his radical plan to remake the global order, Nehru had come to believe in the value of international organizations. He found Wilson's promise of a League of Nations to guide world affairs on the basis of peace and justice to be alluring and profound. So when the League failed to gain traction, and further failed to address the needs of colonized people or to even meaningfully incorporate their voices, Nehru found himself bitterly disappointed. 'President Wilson's brave words have remained but words, and the "fourteen points", where are they . . . ? The great moment has passed and for ourselves it is again the distant hope that must inspire us, not the immediate breathless looking for deliverance.'[3]

When World War II broke out, Nehru imagined what the world could be like after the conflict. This was manifested in two material ways, the first the 1942 Quit India Resolution (see Chapter 1), and the second his famous *Discovery of India*, written from 1942 to 1945 and published in 1946. Nehru began work immediately upon his arrest for Quit India and released the book once he was freed. The *Discovery* is a voyage into India's past, but is as much about the future, as Nehru marshals history to make his case for what he thinks India and the world should be like in the days to come. What was the cause of conflict, and how to create a just peace? While imperialism was a driving factor, there was a more elementary condition that contributed to antagonisms and bellicosity. Although he was careful in his choice of words, Nehru was hardly cryptic in his formula for a better tomorrow: 'We shall have to put an end to the national state and devise a collectivism which neither degrades nor enslaves.'[4]

He is even clearer elsewhere in the *Discovery*:

> Sometimes we are told that our nationalism is a sign of our backwardness . . . Those who tell us so seem to imagine that true internationalism would triumph if we agreed to remain as junior partners in the British Empire or Commonwealth . . . They do not appear to realize that this particular type of so-called internationalism is only an extension of a narrow British nationalism . . . Nevertheless India, for all her intense nationalistic fervor, has gone further than many nations in her acceptance of real internationalism and the co-ordination, and even to some extent the subordination, of the independent nation state in and to a world organization.[5]

With San Francisco, Nehru concluded that the moment was at hand at last to see his vision, which had been germinating since the Fourteen Points, made into a reality. If the League was the dream that died, the United Nations was the new hope, the great second chance to refashion the world in a more just and non-violent way.[6] Unlike the last time, India could now play a direct and active role in shaping the new organization. Nehru felt the burden of history and was wary of repeating the mistakes of the so-called Wilsonian moment.

Just a few days after he assumed office, Nehru broadcast from New Delhi: 'The world, in spite of its rivalries and hatreds and inner conflicts, moves inevitably towards closer cooperation and the building up of a world commonwealth. It is for this One World that free India will work, a world in which there is the free cooperation of free peoples, and no class or group exploits another.'[7]

A year back, while Madame Pandit was still touring the United States, Albert Einstein, who had grown increasingly worried about the development of atomic weaponry, published a press interview in *The New York Times* arguing that there was 'no other salvation for civilization and even for the human race than the creation of a world government . . . As long as there are sovereign states with their separate armaments and armament secrets, new world wars cannot be avoided.'[8] In 1946, a few months before Nehru spoke, the Federation of American Scientists published a pamphlet on the 'full meaning of the atomic bomb'. It was entitled *One World or None*. In it, Einstein wrote: 'It is necessary that conditions be established that guarantee the individual state the right to solve its conflicts with other states on a legal basis and under international jurisdiction. It is necessary that the individual state be prevented from making war by a supranational organization supported by a military power that is exclusively under its control.'[9]

The pamphlet made the notion of One World, circulating since Willkie's bestseller, even more popular. It also helped to expand the concept to include ideas of global government.

One World had captured Nehru's imagination since he first encountered Willkie's book in prison in 1943. Willkie's plan was imbued with an anti-imperial sensibility and a ringing call for global justice, both ideals that Nehru held dear to his heart.

Coincidentally, Einstein's conceptualization of One World resembled the structure Nehru had envisioned in the Quit India Resolution. It also used Gandhi's language from his Coniston interview on world government, while it resonated with Nehru's concerns about the nation state.

For Nehru, One World had the benefit of widespread appeal. Just when Einstein was writing, Churchill, out of power, was observing the Iron Curtain falling on Europe. The Cold War was beginning. If Nehru was going to make any headway in fulfilling his dream in such chilly conditions, he was going to have to find common ground on which otherwise divided people and statespersons–capitalist and communist–could warmly stand.

When he briefed Pandit and her delegation about their new duties, Nehru focused on three principles meant to guide their every action. First, he exhorted them to hold true to high ethics and morality, even as they faced the difficult challenge of facing the demands and corruption of 'practical problems'. Second, he instructed them to steer clear of 'rival power blocs' and to work to help bridge differences and divides created by such blocs. Finally, he reminded the delegation 'of India's total acceptance of the UN Charter and her determination to work with other member nations to make it a reality'. He particularly pointed out that the Charter's preamble was almost precisely India's own promise to the world: 'to promote social progress and better standards of life in larger freedom.'[10]

This was an idealistic pitch, broadly demanding that the delegates take the high ground in all of their dealings with the UN. But how could India 'totally accept' the UN Charter, when its language was the very point of contention in San

Francisco? Madame Pandit had vociferously opposed the proposed language of the Charter, which she contrasted unfavourably with that of its predecessor, the Atlantic Charter. And she had lost. The UN Charter contained the terminology and phrasing preferred by the Great Powers (see Chapter 3). The specific bone of contention lay in chapters XI and XII, which were dedicated to the colonies and trustee lands. The Atlantic Charter had declared simply that the US, Great Britain and its allies agree to 'respect the right of all peoples to form the government under which they will live; and [that] they wish to see sovereign rights and self government restored to those who have been forcibly deprived of them'.[11] Churchill had immediately rejected any notion that the Atlantic Charter implied that the UK had to give up its colonies.[12] His government fought to change the wording as they drafted the UN Charter in 1945, and thus chapter XI read: 'Members of the United Nations . . . recognize the principle that the interests [of non-self-governing people] . . . are paramount, and accept a sacred trust . . . to develop self-government, to take due account of the political aspirations of the peoples, and to assist them in the progressive development of their free political institutions, according to the particular circumstances of each territory and its peoples and their varying stages of advancement'.[13] This wording made all the right gestures without giving away a thing, and it was enough to appease the Americans who had become almost dogmatic in their opposition to the continuation of the pre-war colonial enterprise.[14]

The anti-colonial alliance had been blistering in its criticism of the ideas of 'sacred trust' and 'self-government', which the Indians correctly discerned as euphemisms for the legitimacy of colonialism. Their failure at San Francisco to redact the passages, many had assumed, actually meant that colonialism would be more secure and stable in the post-war order, sanctioned, apparently, by the UN Charter.

But India rejected this proposition in its entirety. At a UN plenary meeting some time later, Madame Pandit made plain that '[the] Indian delegation, believing in the freedom of all peoples, wished to see the early termination of [the] colonial system, and the speedy attainment of self-government by all peoples inhabiting colonial or Trust Territories. It insisted on the strict observance of chapters XI and XII [of the UN Charter], both in spirit and letter. In particular, it urged the colonial Powers to realize that the two hundred million people inhabiting the Non-Self-Governing Territories read into the provisions of the Charter relating to such territories far more than the colonial Powers were inclined to do so.'[15]

When Nehru spoke to his new UN delegation, he conceived of India as 'about-to-be independent'.[16] By the time Pandit made her remarks at the UN, India was. So India specifically, and all colonized people generally, acquiesced to the power of the UN by reading the Charter in their own terms, in 'spirit and letter'. It was India's very participation in the United Nations, as a full, equal, free and highly involved member, that ensured that the Charter could and should be read in this way. As a post-colonial country, the first in the non-Western world, they now represented the physical manifestation of chapters XI and XII and their very presence imbued both the document and the organization it constituted with the anti-imperial ambitions of the Atlantic Charter.[17]

The British were undone by their own shrewd wordplay. Madame Pandit had proved a cunning chess player. Seeing San Francisco as a setback rather than a defeat, she continued to wage the campaign she began on America's western coast until she saw victory. This tenaciousness and persistence would be the key to India's long-term strategy in international affairs.

Nehru's declaration that his country totally accepted the UN Charter was a forward-looking statement of policy rather than a banal platitude for those about to work for the new organization. So too were the other principles: the foundation of Non-alignment was laid when Nehru admonished his team to steer clear of power blocs and assuage problems that may stem from them; and morality was meant for more than suasion, it was meant to guide actions and interactions in the vein of Gandhi's method of satyagraha (literally 'truth force').

But if these three tenets comprised the tools needed to steer India's ship of state through the sea of global affairs, it was the line from the preamble to the UN Charter that provided the overall map charting course and destination. Put another way, India accepted the UN Charter in toto *to what end*? India had to stay non-aligned *to what end*? India was meant to use moral force *to what end*? Nehru's answer: to promote social progress and better standards of life in larger freedom. If India, believing in 'the freedom of all peoples', hoped to see colonized people attain self-government, what did it wish to achieve in the name of 'larger freedom?'

THE SOUTH AFRICA QUESTION

Whatever Nehru's lofty vision, Gandhi was more immediately driven by practical matters. He, and Wavell, wanted Madame Pandit to take up the cause of Indians in South Africa. The South African parliament, under the leadership of Prime Minster Jan Smuts, had just recently passed the Asiatic Land Tenure and Indian Representation Act, commonly known as the Ghetto Act. The law in effect segregated the Indian community in South Africa and denied them a variety of basic rights and privileges. The community there was outraged and rose up against the Act.[18] In addition to this, the South African state moved to annex South West Africa (today's Namibia), a former colony of Germany that had been acquired by South Africa under the mandate system following the Peace at Versailles in 1919.[19]

Gandhi felt the Ghetto Act was a terrible affront to human dignity and wanted to see its repeal. And the notion of annexation stung for the old anti-imperialist. But Gandhi was also concerned, as he always was, by the process by which change could be effected. Smuts was Gandhi's old sparring partner from his earliest campaigns: Gandhi had begun his career in civil resistance as a lawyer in South Africa, and had experimented with many of the techniques that he would later refine in his Indian campaigns. For Gandhi, Smuts was wily and wrong-headed. He was also a friend.[20]

Gandhi counselled Pandit that the United Nations was not going to be a 'debating society', but rather a place to forge international amity.[21] His advice resonated with Nehru's more formal directions. But Gandhi also more specifically implied that he wanted Smuts to be treated with dignity and respect. The means were just as important as the ends, and Pandit was warned not to aim either for showmanship or victory at any cost.

Madame Pandit took the advice from Gandhi and Nehru to heart. She accepted her portfolio and travelled back to New York where she joined her team and took up her new assignment. She immediately began to look into the situation in South Africa, and had at her disposal a report that had been prepared and submitted to the UN in August by the Indian delegation. The assessment was grim, with nearly thirty pages devoted to detailing forms of discrimination against people of Indian origin that included disenfranchisement of all women and many men, restrictions on the acquisition and occupation of land, the refusal of trading licences, segregation, prohibition of interracial marriages (with whites), and a variety of other offences.[22]

Indian government officials began considering the South Africa question in earnest in September and October, producing a variety of confidential memos discussing various angles of the issue and the problems that the delegation may have to face as a result. Nehru was keenly involved from the outset, asking detailed questions about laws and debating tactics, and ensuring that everyone in the delegation, while free to provide dissenting opinions privately, moved in lock-step in public.

Among the things that most concerned Nehru was the way India was going to respond to South Africa, which had already made a preliminary defence to the UN secretary general that the matter was basically a domestic one. The General Assembly, and the United Nations more generally, were prohibited from interfering in the internal affairs of member states under Article 2(7) of the UN Charter, the so-called 'domestic jurisdiction' clause.[23]

As the Indian team looked into the case closely, they concluded that Nehru had put his finger on the crux of the matter: the nature of, and limits to, Article 2(7). They speculated, correctly, that Smuts and his advisors would argue that Indians settled in South Africa were South African nationals, and hence were subject to the laws of that land, whatever they might be. And so the Indian course of action had to be a direct assault on the very principle of domestic jurisdiction. For though the laws passed by the South African parliament might be considered legitimate within the state, 'yet those laws affect the fundamental human rights of Indian subjects there'.[24] Human rights were advocated in the UN Charter, if in the preamble, and were thus the means by which the Indians could argue that the actions taking place in South Africa stood in violation of the principles and vision upon which the United Nations was founded. The legal advisors pointed out that any violation of the Charter contravened Article 14, which allowed the General Assembly to act no matter the origin of the problem. Further, they laid a strong case regarding why the preamble held significant juridical weight, meaning that all member states to the Charter were *bound* by its conventions as if by a constitution. All member states' sovereignty was subject to the provisions and restrictions of the UN Charter, ipso facto 'domestic jurisdiction' simply did not apply.

The Indians were wary of how dull all of this sounded. 'Dry, arid, and technical questions of law' do not good political theatre make.[25] The team concluded that their appeal had to be one of broad strokes, focused on the specific facts at hand in South Africa and laid out in moral tones. In short, the case was one of the violation of fundamental human rights which formed the basis of all international civilization, and no state could hide behind domestic jurisdiction to cover it up.

It was up to Madame Pandit to strike the right balance. She was the public face of India, and it was she who had to convince the world's representatives. If she spoke in overly general terms, the Indians would likely fail to puncture the domestic jurisdiction defence. If she steeped her comments in legalese, she would lose her audience.

Her opening remarks, delivered to the entire Assembly on 25 October 1946, a year and a day after the United Nations officially came into existence, proved that she was more than up to the challenge. She was pitch-perfect in her delivery.

She first spelled out India's specific vision for the United Nations. She talked about her country's resolve to follow the Charter 'in spirit and letter', and added that they stood 'for the independence of all colonial and dependent peoples and their full right to self-determination'.

She continued: 'We believe that peace and freedom are indivisible and the denial of freedom anywhere must lead to conflict and war . . . We seek no dominion over others–we claim no privileged position over other peoples, but we do claim equal and honorable treatment for our people wherever they may go and we cannot accept discrimination against them.'

Madame Pandit went on to say that the UN Assembly represented millions throughout the world and served as the court of world opinion. South Africa stood in violation of the Charter, she charged, and therefore was of concern to all the world's people. Brilliantly, she wove together a narrative of tragedy that was sure to strike a chord with peoples from all communities: those embittered by racism, those subject to imperialism, and those devastated by Nazism and fascism. The assault on the dignity of one group was an assault on all groups. It was the logic of human rights, linked to the horrific recent past.

She ended with a stirring plea: 'We move, in spite of difficulties, toward a closer cooperation and the building of a world commonwealth. Let us do this with more deliberation and speed . . . Let us recognize that human emotions and the needs of the world will not wait for an indefinite period. To this end let us direct our energies and remind ourselves that in our unity of purpose and action lies the hope of the world.'[26]

Pandit was emotionally electric. The audience–those in the room with her and those hearing about it through news media–was dazzled, many feeling a genuine connection with her words. *The New York Times* raved that she was 'eloquent', 'speaking with much of the fire and intensity as her brother'. Her speech, the *Times* noted, was interrupted by bursts of applause.[27]

If the South Africans were worried, they did not show it. And there was good reason for their confidence. General Smuts had at the outset concluded that the real path to victory lay in simply convincing the Great Powers to support South Africa. Thanks to the American policies of segregation and racial discrimination collectively known as Jim Crow, Smuts 'compromised and shamed' the United States. He then 'bull[ied] and blackmailed' the British as well.[28] With them in the bag, he believed triumph was at hand, for this was the way the game had always been played.

In order for the Indian petition to be brought before the General Assembly, it had to be first considered by the General (Steering) Committee, which had the power to determine which internal committee branches should take up the matter. It was a potential procedural loophole that, if properly utilized, could kill a proposal. And General Smuts sat on the Steering Committee, along with representatives from the United States and Britain. There were fourteen members in total, but South Africa felt secure.

A short while after Pandit's speech, General Smuts raised an objection to India's petition on the grounds that it violated Article 2(7) of the UN Charter. Smuts had acted just as the Indian team had predicted. After some haggling, in which India received loud support from the Soviet delegation, Britain moved that the matter be turned over to the Legal (Sixth) Committee, where they felt the issue would be bogged down in technicalities and lost in limbo. But the United States disagreed, arguing instead that the matter should be taken up by the Political (First) Committee, terrain that in fact was much more favourable to India. To prevent being outmanoeuvred, the British urged that the matter be taken up by both committees, a proposal that received majority support and carried the day. Though Smuts was taken aback by all of this, given that it was not the outcome he had expected, he was persuaded by the British to go along and to accept, with India, that the matter should be discussed in joint sessions of the two committees. This was an idea that came from the Soviets, and the British wanted to prevent a Cold War humiliation by acting as if the suggestion was their own.[29]

Pandit was pleased with all of this, and cabled back to Delhi that they had taken the first round.[30] Both Nehru and Gandhi responded enthusiastically. Nehru noted that 'all India' was 'watching with anxious interest'.[31]

South Africa suddenly realized that it had a real fight on its hands. They immediately released their own memo taking aim at the details of the Indian complaint, blasting the assertion that Indians were even mistreated in South Africa, and claiming instead that Indians benefited more than any other community in the country. Ultimately, they rested their case on a simple question: 'Are [Indians in South Africa] South African Nationals, as they are recognized to be by the law which is objected to . . . ? The choice must be made. The Union of South Africa is a Sovereign State and cannot acquiesce in any interference in its domestic concerns . . .'[32]

Great Britain too had realized that India might actually succeed, and it had turned its attention to analysing the case. Their internal review quickly concluded that India was likely to receive 'substantial' support at the UN. Moreover, British legal analysis showed that South Africa's claim to domestic jurisdiction was unconvincing. The British were terrified. 'It was felt to be most important,' Secretary of State for India Lord Pethick-Lawrence argued, 'to avoid setting a precedent for intervention by the United Nations in matters like this, which had hitherto been regarded as being within the domestic jurisdiction of sovereign states. Once such intervention began, it would be difficult to set limits to it and all nations might be faced with investigations into their internal policy . . .'[33] Madame Pandit and her delegation had to be stopped.

But the Indians were not without allies of their own. Where Smuts saw the world solely as a theatre in which sovereign states were the actors, the Indians saw a space where peoples as well as states could play major roles, and where new solidarities could be built. The actions of governments did not necessarily implicate their people. This was Gandhi's ethic, and the proto-Indian state led by his protégé Nehru tried to practise this as a matter of policy. And thus the Indians reached out to, and received support from, people throughout the United States and South Africa.

Madame Pandit had an impressive rolodex to call upon. Her tour of the US, and her performances in New York and San Francisco, had won her many admirers, both in and out of government circles. And serendipitously, if unsurprisingly, many of them shared the same concerns. Most prominently, Walter White, the executive secretary of the NAACP, and Paul Robeson, the chair of the Council on African Affairs, were horrified by what was going on in South Africa. As early as in 1945, White's antennae had begun to buzz, and he warned of the dangers of the proposed annexation of South West Africa. By late October 1946, following Pandit's opening speech, the NAACP had begun to communicate with associates in South Africa, who pleaded with the organization to intervene on their behalf and to counter the snake oil that Smuts and his team were trying to sell.[34]

With the NAACP and related groups running public relations interference, the Indians turned their attention to the coming encounter. The first meeting of the Joint Committee was held on 21 November. With Smuts present, Madame Pandit methodically stated the overall case. Then, in a dramatic flourish, she concluded by quoting from two speeches made in the 1920s that she claimed resonated strongly with the discussion at hand:

'We, a handful of Whites, are ring-facing ourselves first with an inner-ring of Black hatred, and, beyond that, with a ring of hatred of the whole of Asia; for while a only a few Asiatics are directly affected by the bill, the inclusion of their name will win us the hatred of hundreds of millions of Asiatics from the north of Asia to the south . . . In these circumstances, the Colour-Bar Bill . . . is a fire-brand flung into a hay-stack.' Madame Pandit paused for effect, then, ended: 'Mr. Chairman, the author of these two quotations is the distinguished Prime Minister of South Africa—Field Marshal Smuts.'[35]

It was sheer brilliance. Pandit came across as both reasonable and humane, holding no personal grudges. Smuts was outmatched, and added to his handicap by following her speech with one that had been written much earlier and pre-circulated. He had no precise rebuttal, and India again won the crowd.[36]

Hopelessly cornered, South Africa decided to change tactics. If Smuts' charm and polite sparring were not sufficient, then they would go on the attack with G. Heaton Nicholls as their lead speaker. At the next meeting a few days later, Nicholls could not conceal his utter contempt for the Indian case, and dissolved into a number of crude insults about Indians generally. He ridiculed social and religious customs by charging rampant polygamy, mocking Indian languages, and talking about the need to defend superior Christian civilization. Madame Pandit went to town. Laden with sarcasm and dismissive, she ripped apart his condescending, racist rant with lightning speed, calling him 'deliberately . . . frivolous and offensive'. 'In fact, we have had a long sermon on Christianity . . . I wonder, Mr. Chairman, if the paradox of Mr. Heaton Nichols' speech on this point is realized? He refers to the Christianising mission of the white man but, according to the Immigration Act of 1913, Jesus Christ himself, if he were in our midst today, would be a prohibited immigrant.' She then unleashed an avalanche of facts and figures to buttress the Indian case.[37] Her response was met by warm, supportive laughter and loud applause.[38] Nicholls came across to fellow delegates looking like a smug idiot.

Pandit, however, was far from pleased. She had allowed herself to be swept up by the moment, and had clearly taken pleasure in eviscerating and humiliating Nicholls. Gandhi's words echoed in her ear. Her goal was not simply to win the debate, but to help build an international consensus without making enemies of opponents. She had remained on message, but was off track nonetheless. She had to recalibrate.

South Africa and Britain meanwhile settled on one last tactic to pull victory from the jaws of defeat. They decided to ask that India's claim be sent to the International Court of Justice (ICJ) for review, where it would be determined whether or not the complaint violated Article 2 (7) of the UN Charter. The South Africans had rounded the corner only to find themselves in their starting position. Their case stood or fell on the principle of domestic jurisdiction. Britain brought the United States and Sweden on board. South Africa withdrew its original resolution in favour of this new one and was delighted to find that it had considerable support in the joint committee for this move. The Indians were concerned about a loss, but here their earlier performance paid off. Madame Pandit had successfully charmed and convinced many. France and Mexico jointly rode to the rescue, producing their own resolutions essentially backing the Indian position, asking the General Assembly to consider the actions of South Africa as a violation of the UN Charter. Madame Pandit withdrew the Indian resolution in favour of the Franco-Mexican one in what she pointedly noted was a 'spirit of compromise'. It was a close vote on 30 November, but India pulled it off in the end.[39] South Africa would be judged by the entire General Assembly.

Still regretting her harsh cross of Nicholls, Pandit went over and shook hands with General Smuts for emphasis.[40] This was about policy, not personal recrimination.

On the evening of 7 December, Smuts spoke in favour of South Africa's position. He pointed out that the vote had been close in committee and that those favouring the Indian position there represented less than half of all UN member states. He pleaded with the Assembly to reconsider the committee vote and send the matter to the International Court for an opinion.[41]

When Smuts had finished, it was India's turn to speak. Anticipation was at a fever pitch as the Assembly waited with bated breath for Madame Pandit's closing statement. She was the focus of everyone's attention, even attracting the fashion columnists, who called her the 'center of attraction'.[42] It would have been a nerve-wracking moment for anyone. Poised and determined, Madame Pandit said: 'It is too late now to argue that fundamental violations of principles of the Charter are matters of domestic jurisdiction of Member States. If this was the case, the Charter would be a dead letter and our professions about a world free from inequalities of race, free from want and free from fear are empty mockery.'

Bringing the full force of the vision laid out by Nehru and Gandhi to bear, she continued: 'I want to carry the Assembly with me in these matters which, I submit, are common ground. If I do, as I must, unless the 54 nations assembled here place on the Charter a meaning and a significance far below what its words convey, what its spirit demands, and indeed what we have asked the world to accept . . . , then the issue . . . rests with us, the nations of the world assembled, who have taken upon themselves the defence of the law of ethics and morality . . . '

The room was mesmerized. Her words more powerful than they had dared imagine, Pandit simply had everyone spellbound.

She finished: 'We are the trustees of the future, architects of the new world . . . , and it is only on the foundation of justice that we can erect a new world order . . . Mine is an appeal to conscience, to the conscience of the world which this Assembly is. I will say no more.'[43]

The room was hers. The audience gave her the warmest of ovations.[44]

The next day, the Assembly voted overwhelmingly in India's favour: Madame Pandit had secured a two-thirds majority. The momentousness of the occasion was not lost on anyone. The event was heralded as an 'Asian victory', the triumph of the world's dispossessed and aggrieved, the first of its kind.

But Madame Pandit had a promise to keep to an old man back in India. She quickly went over to General Smuts to ask for his forgiveness if she had stepped over the line at any time during the debate. She later recounted that 'He took my hands in both of his. [And said] "My child . . . you have won a hollow victory. This vote will put me out of power in our next elections, but you will have gained nothing."' Privately, he conceded that what was going on in South Africa was not to his liking, and that more radical forces would soon make matters worse. He was proved correct. Smuts lost the next general election and The Asiatic Land Tenure and Indian Representation Act became apartheid.[45]

The larger war for racial justice in South Africa was not yet over, and a new global alliance in which India participated would have to continue the fight for decades.[46] But for now, the battle was won.

DECLARING HUMAN RIGHTS UNIVERSAL

The General Assembly vote opened a world of possibilities. The debate and its result went beyond anything that the Indians had hoped for or expected.[47] Nehru, more than anyone, concluded that imagination was the only limit to what could now be created. He needed to consolidate his ideas into a concrete plan of action. If moving past nation states had been a vaguely articulated objective up to that point, the successful assault on Article 2(7) crystallized the means by which this might be achieved. Human rights had been the crowbar with which the steel gate of state sovereignty had been pried open, if only just. Expanding and codifying human rights was the next logical step. And, serendipitously, this turned out to be the next major issue that the United Nations planned to tackle, thanks to the forceful leadership of Eleanor Roosevelt, the former first lady of the United States. The Human Rights Commission would meet in three separate sessions over the next two years, first in early 1947, again in late 1947, and finally in mid-1948. The product of their efforts, the Universal Declaration of Human Rights, would be released shortly after the last session, in late 1948.

Between late December and early January, Nehru thought carefully about what he wanted to achieve. He had to be careful, knowing fully well that there were many powerful forces—both people and countries—that would resist fundamental changes in the way the world operated. The contest over South Africa had proved that. Moreover, only one country had been the target of that campaign; as more countries felt threatened, the more fierce the opposition would be. In that sense, the South African question was but the warm-up act.

Towards the end of January 1947, Nehru had pretty much settled on a way forward. But he would unveil his grand designs slowly, in bits and pieces, sharing the full scope with only a handful of his closest compatriots, among them Madame Pandit and Mahatma Gandhi.

The first full session of the new United Nations Human Rights Commission was scheduled for 27 January. Speaking to the Constituent Assembly in India five days before, Nehru laid out a roadmap for the country's leadership: 'The only possible real objective that we, in common with other nations, can have is in the objective of co-operating in building up some kind of world structure, call it "One World", call it what you like. The beginnings of this world structure have been laid down in the United Nations Organization. It is feeble yet; it has many defects; nevertheless, it is the beginning of the world structure. And India has pledged herself to cooperate in that work.'[48] By this point, One World had become a common euphemism for a global parliament of some kind, though the contours of such an institution remained contested. A global parliament is exactly what Nehru had in mind, one that would bring all the world together. But while many other advocates of this policy, including Einstein, were ordinary citizens, Nehru actually had the means at his disposal to make things happen at the political level.

The same day that he spoke in the Constituent Assembly, Nehru sent an official letter via the Indian embassy in Washington DC to India's just-named representative to the Human Rights Commission, Hansa Mehta. Mehta was a Gujarati Brahmin and a feminist, and the daughter of a famous legal scholar and policymaker, Sir Manubhai Mehta. Hansa Mehta had the year before served on the UN Sub-commission on the Status of Women, where her performance was met with considerable acclaim. She had great success on the Sub-commission, convincing her colleagues to adopt verbatim three paragraphs from a charter she co-drafted for the All-India

Women's Conference in mid-1946.[49] This was the kind of skill that was needed to push through Nehru's agenda.

The letter primarily dealt with the question of 'nationals and non-nationals', arguing on the one hand that rights had to 'necessarily differ' between these two groups, and on the other that non-nationals had to be treated 'alike'. Nehru's concerns here stemmed from the South African question—what responsibility do states have to globally dispersed peoples? How was citizenship to be defined? Nehru was focused on these questions, and his early answer was that peoples had to submit to the laws of the state in which they chose to live, but had to be treated equally with all other peoples in that state. The guarantor of equality and justice was not a competing state or a country of origin. Rather, it was the United Nations, which would now serve as a meta-constitutional authority.[50]

Combined, the letter and Nehru's speech served as the opening volley in his quest to build a world that moved past the nation state and empire model that had grown out of the Treaty of Westphalia. Yet, to those reading Nehru at the time, and to many scholars since, his exact goal remained murky, just as he had intended. Nehru's *Autobiography* and his *Discovery of India* both seemed to make clear that he wanted a sovereign nation state for India.[51] And, in fact, he did.

Was this a case of sheer hypocrisy, the gander asking for something he wished to deny the goose? Or was it even worse: silver-tongued rhetoric that masked more base motives, following in the footsteps of a Churchill or a Smuts?

For Nehru himself, at least, the answer to both questions was no.[52] His principle was actually quite simple, and straightforward: 'no group should be deprived of any right which others possess'.[53] The world in which he lived was one in which colonized people everywhere were denied the right to their own sovereign states, the governing formation of their political masters. This had to be overturned. No one could be denied the right to a sovereign nation state if this is what was available to others. Yet the nation state was also an institution that Nehru felt 'degraded and enslaved'. This could not—must not—be the end of the journey. So, he had to fight for everyone to be free of colonial control, for there to be independent peoples in their own states. But then, he had to convince everyone to concede at least some authority to a larger, external, democratic council, that could place a check on the otherwise unlimited power of sovereign states. He believed it was this course, and this course only, that would propel humanity to live in 'larger freedom'.

The language of rights stood at the foundation of democratic discourse, and so a world parliament necessarily had to be built constitutionally around rights. But these were rights not guaranteed by a state—not defined by citizenship—and were applicable to everyone everywhere. Human rights.

Nehru knew fully well just how tricky the terrain was that he hoped to navigate. Responding to a letter from Einstein a few months later, he noted that when India had fought against South Africa's policies the year before, it had 'stood on the broader plane of human rights for all in accordance with the Charter of the United Nations'. He then candidly confessed that 'national policies are unfortunately essentially selfish policies . . . If it so happens that some international policy fits in with the national policy of the country, then that nation uses brave language about international betterment. But as soon as that international policy seems to run counter to national interests or selfishness, then a host of reasons are found not to follow that international policy.' By advocating independence and the creation of new nation states, Nehru knew that he, as much as anyone else, would soon be caught in the confines of the current system. He told Einstein, and reminded himself at the same time: 'I have no doubt that [India] shall play a progressively more important part in international affairs. What that part will be in future I can only guess. I earnestly hope that we shall continue to adhere to the idealism which has guided our struggle for freedom. But we have seen often enough idealism followed by something far less noble, and so it would be folly for me to prophesy what the future holds for us. All we can do is to try our utmost to keep up standards of moral conduct both in our domestic affairs and in the international sphere.'[54]

If he clung too tightly to his ideals, he risked not actually being able to accomplish them. If, on the other hand, he succumbed to realpolitik, his high-minded statements could be for naught.

Nehru had already passed the first test of his balancing skills when, the year before, he had supported the creation of the Security Council. The Council was by far the most powerful arm of the United Nations, with the ability to sanction member states. But comprising as it was of only a few permanent members, each of whom wielded a veto, the Security Council reeked of Old World politics, where Great Powers decided the fate of all. Many countries from the south and the east, especially, viewed the Council with disdain and urged reform. Cuba made the most explicit attempt, proposing in late 1946 to organize a conference to reformat the structure of the United Nations in a more equitable manner. Australia followed up with the idea to restrict the use of the Council veto, allowing its application under very narrow circumstances defined by the UN Charter.

Nehru, acutely cognizant of what had happened after 1919, was absolutely determined to see the United Nations succeed. And on that basis, he rejected both the Cuban and the Australian proposals. 'The old League of Nations failed,' Nehru noted, 'because it had no machinery for quick decision or action.'[55] Moreover, the Great Powers were reluctant to fully participate then, making the League weak and ineffective.[56] 'Profiting by that example, the United Nations Organisation has established some machinery for rapid decision, the Security Council, and has aimed at having effective sanctions.'[57]

'India attaches the greatest importance to the continuance of the U.N.O. and to the need of the Great Powers cooperating within it; for that reason, however much she might dislike the use of the "veto" except on very rare and special occasions, she would not support any proposal which might serve to intensify the present tension between the Great Powers or result in the withdrawal of any of them from the United Nations.'[58] Nehru emerged a shrewd and savvy politician. In the short term, he had to strategically compromise in some areas, provided they did not contradict his greater principles, so that his long-term goals might be met.

With respect to human rights (in January 1947), Nehru had every confidence in Mehta, but he also felt personally involved with what was taking place in her commission. Mehta's letter was amended with instructions to deal with questions at her discretion, but to consult the government on all matters of importance.[59] Mehta took this directive very seriously, announcing in the very first meeting of the Human Rights Commission in which any substantive action was moved that, as a matter of vital procedure, members be allowed to consult their respective governments on the 'highly important and intricate questions involved'.[60] She was the first member to speak at length on any major subject.

Opening the Commission earlier that same day, assistant secretary general for social affairs, Henri Laugier, reminded the members to be mindful of the significance of the task before them. No other element of UN action, he said, had 'more power or wider scope' than the Human Rights Commission. He added: 'The action taken in the case of South Africa established a precedent of fundamental significance in the field of international action . . . [for] out of these debates the general impression had risen up that no violation of human rights should be covered up by the principle of national sovereignty.'[61]

Mehta clearly had a strong hand to play. Madame Pandit had given the Indian team enormous credibility and a reserve of goodwill. The question was how they would use their political capital.

Mehta did not wait long. Aiming to take control of the debate, she released in the seventh meeting a complete draft resolution on human rights. Arguing that human rights had to become 'integral' to the Charter and the 'fundamental law' of the UN, her framework ended with a striking call to make the United Nations Security Council the primary enforcer of any alleged violation. It was the Council that would investigate charges of human rights abuse and be responsible for setting things right.[62]

The implication was immediately clear. This was a radical redefinition of 'security' and the Council meant to defend it.

Mehta was playing with fire. Nehru had been especially careful to avoid invoking its change, as when he rejected the Cuban and Australian proposals, since that might have upset the delicate balance of compromises that allowed the United Nations to turn the page from the League of Nations.[63] Simultaneously, he believed that the General Assembly, representing the full membership, should be further empowered.[64]

Nehru immediately concluded that Mehta had miscalculated. When he had heard of her plans to release the draft resolution he had cabled to warn her against such a move, but it was too late. He expressed his concerns and wished that at the very least she should have waited to first discern where everyone else stood. This was still on his mind nearly a week later, when he lamented to an Indian governmental committee his failure to stop the presentation.[65]

Mehta's proposal did not get much traction, but it was not the tragedy that Nehru had feared. The Commission proceeded with its discussions. Undeterred by her misfire, Mehta went back to the drawing board, listening attentively in the meetings and asking questions as appropriate.[66] She was waiting for the right moment.

She found her opening in the second session, which met later that year. Her patience had paid off. She was asked to chair the Working Group on Implementation. This was the perfect perch, for the Group was tasked to consider how to implement and defend human rights. It was not an easy assignment by any means, not only because this was controversial territory, but also because the larger Commission had not yet decided on what was meant by 'human rights'. How to concretely decide upon implementation of principles the most basic foundational elements of which were not yet agreed upon?

To be sure, the Commission had discussed several draft proposals, including Mehta's, but none had received much enthusiasm as yet. Michael Klekovkin, the Ukrainian representative to the Working Group, was most bothered by this, and made several attempts at the start of discussions to bring the Working Group to a halt until the Commission first defined 'human rights'.[67]

Mehta, however, thought human rights to be self-evident, even if there might be some haggling on technical language and on which rights should be formally documented. For her, the larger issue was implementation: how would the UN have the teeth it needed for the world's people's rights to be protected? The straight line from South Africa shone brightly, all the more so once Mehta revealed her proposed solution.

Mehta wanted to create a special UN committee on human rights that would work in conjunction with an international court to hear cases by and against individuals, groups and states. In line with Nehru's preferences, and clearly a modification of her earlier proposal, she had the General Assembly assume responsibility for application, possibly along with an attorney general.[68]

With the skills that had served her so well in the UN Sub-commission on the Status of Women on full display, Mehta pushed hard for her proposal to be accepted. It was passed unanimously, after some technical and jurisdictional adjustments.[69] The Working Group included an observation in its final report that the 'domestic jurisdiction' of states referred to in Article 2(7) of the UN Charter, if 'rightly' interpreted, 'only covered questions which had not become international in one way or another. Once states had agreed that such questions should form the subject of a Declaration or Convention, they clearly placed them outside their "domestic jurisdiction" and Article 2, paragraph 7 became inapplicable.'[70] This was an exclamation point on an already emphatically clear statement.

Mehta took the initiative for much of this, making her intentions plain in her report back to her government following the Human Rights Commission's first session. She had said then: 'The question of implementation is very complicated and involves the problem of national sovereignty but since we [India] have raised the issue of South Africa in the General Assembly, it is for us to give the lead in this matter.'[71]

The message was lost on no one. When the full Commission reconvened to discuss the Working Group's completed report,

Alexander Bogomolov, the delegate from the Soviet Union, fiercely opposed the proposal, stating: 'This was yet another attempt to interfere in the domestic affairs of a State. Under the terms of these recommendations, the Working Group required States to accept a number of organs which would play the role of referee between nationals and their respective governments, elected in accordance with democratic principles . . . The Soviet delegation could not accept these recommendations . . . since they violated the Sovereignty of the various States.'[72] Vladislav Ribnikar, the delegate from Yugoslavia who was also an ally of Bogomolov, helpfully clarified that the implementation plan was 'a new attempt to transform the United Nations into a kind of world government, placed above national sovereignty'.[73]

During the debate on South Africa, the Soviet Union had been India's strongest ally. The United States and Britain had both sided with Smuts, though India concluded internally that the US was legitimately concerned about juridical issues. The British were not so easily forgiven. More than anyone, they appeared duplicitous, privately speaking favourably about India's concerns, but publicly helping to lead the charge against them. At the conclusion of the debate, Madame Pandit had been withering in her public criticism of Britain's behaviour.[74]

But the UK's public posture was a mask, hiding serious intramural squabbling among the British team. Many had concluded that the Indian case had merit, including their star speaker, Sir Hartley Shawcross, who was not convinced either that South Africa could hide behind Article 2(7) or that the International Court was needed to prove this.[75]

By the time the Human Rights Commission had met in its second session, Britain had come around. India was now independent and all the last-minute gamesmanship that had been taking place over the course of the previous year was over.

Britain, along with France, lent full support to the Working Group's proposal for implementation.[76] The world had been turned upside down.

In fact, the whole affair brought into dramatic relief the tensions of the Cold War and the tightrope that India had to walk. In September 1946, just as India was getting its UN delegation off the ground, Nehru observed that Russia was going to be difficult to deal with. They were 'non co-operative' and 'aggressively rude', he warned.[77] The Soviets' position in the South Africa debate had largely been posturing: a chance to humiliate the West and claim solidarity with the dispossessed at very little cost to themselves. This fact became apparent with the Soviet position in the Human Rights Commission, where they resisted the implementation scheme with all their might, though it was but the logical expansion of the principle applied to South Africa.

But India also made assiduous efforts to engage the communist country. Nehru was specific and adamant in his September instructions: '[O]ur attitude must be one of bringing together different Powers and not of adding ill-feeling for each other . . . In the critical situation of today we should not encourage, or be parties to, a kind of mass attack on Russia in the United Nations General Assembly.'[78] Now that the West was more openly supportive of India's plans, the delegation had to be all the more sensitive about alienating the Soviets, since the backing of one side usually meant the knee-jerk opposition of the other.

The issue was moot, however. Implementation, particularly of the kind approved by the Working Group, was premised on the notion of justiciable rights, rights with the power of law, actionable, in the form of an international covenant. This had been on the table, and had received strong support from the UK. But the Iron Curtain was too hard to pierce. Cold War hostility prevented agreement on a covenant, and the delegates had to compromise. There would be a declaration of human rights. The focus of the third session, these rights would be universal, applicable to all, no matter where they might be, but would only have suggestive, moral force.[79]

It was less than India had hoped for. But there were more innings to be played. This was going to be a drawn-out match and India was in it for the long haul. To make this plain, Nehru flew to Paris in December 1948, where the General Assembly was meeting, to address the body himself. On the eve of the General Assembly's vote on the Universal Declaration of Human Rights, Nehru echoed his sister's words from two years ago: 'The Charter of the United Nations has laid down . . . the principles and the purposes of this great organization . . . The objectives are clear; our aim is clear . . .'[80]

But his was a 'sober' assessment, not the rousing call to action of Madame Pandit.[81] He had to take stock of the difficult challenge the Cold War presented: '[Y]et, in looking at that aim, we lose ourselves often . . . We have got into a cycle of hate and violence, and not the most brilliant debate will get you out of it, unless you look some other way and find some other means.'

Gandhi's statements made at the outset of the San Francisco Conference, and his charge that the UN must not be a mere debating society, echoed in Nehru's ear as he paraphrased them. He hoped to summon the spirit of the Mahatma to inspire those assembled with the courage to act. The world should not be afraid of the future, he admonished. 'That is the lesson which my master taught me.'[82]

5 India International

Towards a Union of India

As momentous as were the unfolding events in the United Nations, they were matched by drama half a world away. For India was decolonizing at precisely the same moment. It was a first in the modern, non-Western world, and heralded a new dawn for many. As the San Francisco Conference highlighted, what happened to India was of concern to peoples all over the globe, particularly people of colour and those who remained under colonial control, for they saw it as a harbinger of their own fate. Nehru, more than anyone, was keenly aware of these sentiments, of the great hope that a newly independent India represented, and this redoubled his commitment to global solidarity, to linking what was happening in India with a larger Afro-Asian cause, and to building a more peaceful world for all. For him, India was a template for what could be possible in the new, post-war world. It was a massive, heterogeneous polyglot of a place, the planet in miniature. If he wanted to realize his dream of semi-sovereign states federated in a global parliament built on human rights, then India had to lead the way.

But Nehru was not the only force shaping India's future. The British saw three primary groups representing distinct voices and visions: the Indian National Congress, led by Gandhi and Nehru; the Muslim League, led by Muhammad Ali Jinnah; and the Indian princely states, hundreds of semi-autonomous principalities governed by monarchies. While there were many other political figures and organizations pursuing various agendas in the region, including a vibrant communist movement, the imperial centre either lumped them into one of the other groupings or else purposefully chose to marginalize them.[1]

In early 1946, the British sent a delegation to India to explore options for what a newly independent territory (or territories) might look like. Their Cabinet Mission Plan attempted to balance the goals of the Congress, the League, and the princes with their own ambitions. Nehru, as head of the Congress, accepted the Plan only to the extent that it established independence as a near-term goal and created a Constituent Assembly to draft a constitution for the new country. He maintained that India had to be free to adapt or change the Plan as it saw fit, and that it was simply preposterous for the British to imagine that they could continue to dictate terms for a soon-to-be independent region.[2]

For Nehru, this was an obvious and essential position to take, since his vision for the planet's future was radically different from that advanced by a British empire that saw a world of new nation states as the sole possible outcome of nationalist movements. But others, particularly Jinnah, saw conspiracy in Nehru's actions, an effort to delegitimize their own aspirations.

The Muslim League, which knew nothing of Nehru's internationalist ideas, had originally accepted the Plan. They were stunned by the proposition that the Mission's ideas would not be accepted as the basic premise for moving forward, and therefore decided to stay out of the newly formed Constituent Assembly. Jinnah, who was advocating something he called 'Pakistan', was actually angling for a better negotiating position. Ironically, his Pakistan was not the nation state that came into existence shortly thereafter, but rather a complex design meant to bring parity between Hindus and Muslims in a newly conceptualized India.[3] But he too was keeping his cards close to his chest and would not reveal his objectives openly. His decision kept the Muslim League out of the Assembly and out of the main discussions on the future of India.

This confounded the plans of Hamidullah, the nawab of Bhopal, and the leader of the Chamber of Princes, the organization that represented princely states at the all-India level.[4] Hamidullah saw the princes as the third force in the negotiations, a balance to both the Congress and the Muslim League. He had hoped to use their disagreements in the Constituent Assembly for leverage, to increase the lot of the princely states.[5]

These regions were semi-autonomous monarchies that comprised roughly two-fifths of the colonial subcontinent. There were approximately 600 'princely states', though this term encompassed a great variety of regions. Some states were very large, either geographically or by population (or both), and were economic powerhouses; others were hardly much more than small landlord holdings. There were approximately a hundred states of importance, led by the big five: Baroda, Mysore, Jammu/Kashmir, Gwalior and Hyderabad. The last of these was the largest and the most powerful, located in central–south India.

The head of Hyderabad, Nizam Osman Ali Khan, was one of the richest men in the world, and remains to this day one of the richest people of all time.[6]

With the Muslim League out of the equation, Hamidullah had to figure out a new course of action. The problem was Nehru. He was a prominent critic of the ruling monarchs, who were known as princes in deference to the British crown, to which they were subservient. Nehru was a staunch democrat and despised them, most of whom he saw as capricious, self-serving autocrats, with hugely varying capabilities and notions of governance.[7] Since Nehru now led the Constituent Assembly, and was unequivocally its leading visionary, Hamidullah assumed that the Assembly would be stacked against the princes.

The nawab's hackles were further raised by a resolution that Nehru brought before the Assembly in mid-December 1946, just days after the South Africa question had been resolved in India's favour in New York. The resolution declared that the purpose of the Assembly was to craft a constitution for a 'Sovereign, Independent, Indian Republic'.[8] Many of the princes had believed that they would soon take over completely sovereign kingdoms of their own, and they saw Nehru's statement as an affront to their authority.

Nehru stood before the Constituent Assembly a few weeks later, once they reconvened after a short break, to address the princes' concerns and clarify the declaration. Sovereignty, he explained, rested with the people, and, by his reckoning, was simply a euphemism for democracy.

All states, or groups of them, he noted, would be autonomous, except for certain matters that would be controlled by the Centre, where they would be represented. The Indian state would not interfere in internal matters, provided all freedoms and protections guaranteed by the Centre were met. So 'constitutional monarchies' could easily be a part of the new Indian Union, provided this was the type of government the people in such regions chose.[9]

South Africa clearly echoed across the Indian landscape. Nehru did not try to hide the link he saw between the organization he was trying to build in India and the one he was trying to build on the world stage. For this was the very same speech in which he had unveiled his roadmap for India's dealings with the United Nations, calling on his country-mates to build One World. And this was the same day that he sent a letter to Hansa Mehta discussing issues of citizenship and instructing her to seek government counsel on matters of importance in the Human Rights Commission.

But few grasped the implications of Nehru's speech. Hamidullah, for one, could not get past Nehru's comments on sovereignty, which he understood rather straightforwardly to mean Central governmental interference in the internal affairs of princely states. He eyed Nehru with tremendous suspicion, and concluded that the princes' best bet might be to stay out of the Constituent Assembly altogether. This was not an option open to him, however. Hamidullah was Muslim, and many of the powerful princes in the Chamber he led were Hindu. Quite a few of the Hindu princes viewed Hamidullah warily, assuming, wrongly, that he was in cahoots with the Muslim League and its call for Pakistan because of his religion. The nawab was aware of these conspiracy theories, and knew that if he tried to stay out of the Constituent Assembly, he risked facing open revolt from his members.[10]

He therefore concocted a complex ploy. He would agree to discuss with the interim government the possibility of the princes joining the Constituent Assembly. But once in the meeting, he would lay down a set of preconditions to which the government could not possibly agree. This would then allow Hamidullah to lay the onus for any failure of negotiations squarely at the feet of the interim government, and in turn, he thought, significantly strengthen the hand of the princes.[11]

The States Negotiating Committee of the Chamber of Princes met with the States Committee of the Constituent Assembly on 8 February 1947. The nawab of Bhopal led the princes' delegation, while Nehru helmed the Assembly's team. The air was acrid from the start.

Just prior to the meeting, Hamidullah released a list of three demands: he wanted Nehru and his associates to agree that monarchy, with all of its attendant powers, would be allowed to continue in the new India. Additionally, the borders of all princely states would be maintained, and princely lines of succession continued.[12]

Nehru had, of course, already conceded to the idea that monarchy would have to be allowed to continue in some states in independent India, though with the caveat that the people of such states would have to democratically approve of it.[13] The other two conditions, however, were simply out of the question.[14] Everything was going exactly as Hamidullah had planned. He now had to convince everyone in the room of his sincerity. It was a task that required Shakespearean skills.

Hamidullah hammed it up to the best of his ability, pointing to his willingness to participate in the Assembly but also his obligations to his membership. He took affront to each response from the Assembly's negotiating team, and the meeting quickly dissolved into a grinding back and forth.

The Chamber's committee kept raising concerns about what place princely states would hold in independent India, while the interim government's team repeatedly pointed out, with growing exasperation, that such questions were exactly what the

Constituent Assembly had been created to consider. The only matter before the negotiating teams, the government representatives argued, was to agree on how princely states were to be represented in the new Assembly. This led to a number of bitter exchanges and the meeting had to be adjourned later that day without anything of substance being accomplished.[15] Hamidullah was very pleased with himself.

But many in the room could see the crocodile in the dry tears he had shed. Several princes, disturbed by Hamidullah's machinations, hastily organized a conclave with leaders from the Congress that evening to assure them of at least their potential support and to strategize on ways to move things along the next meeting.[16]

The next morning, Hamidullah maintained the character he had assumed the previous day. He began the meeting by disingenuously noting that the group had disbanded the night before so that deadlock might be avoided, though of course deadlock was exactly what he had sought. This time, however, Nehru was prepared. Armed with the knowledge gathered from the secret strategy session, Nehru dropped the combative posture he had taken earlier. In its place, he opened with the most conciliatory of speeches, reiterating his position, and that of the Congress, that monarchy would be allowed to continue in the new India. Should the question of 'territorial readjustment' arise, a euphemism for the border issue, all parties concerned would be consulted. Finally, Nehru stated that he and the Congress accepted entirely the Cabinet Mission's position that princely states would retain all subjects and powers other than those that they ceded to the Indian Union.[17]

Nehru had done the unexpected. He had for the most part accepted, seemingly, all of Bhopal's demands. Most of the princes were charmed by Nehru's speech and the very different, positive tone that he had set for the new day.[18] Hamidullah stood alone.

Nehru went a step further. He acknowledged openly his long-standing criticisms of the princes: 'I think the [princely] States are anachronisms in India as they are and I propose to say so in the future. But I do not think my place in the Constituent Assembly is a place to say that and I do not propose to say that.' Disarming in his honesty, but also reassuring in his promise to hold back in the Constitution-making forum, Nehru created a welcoming space for open discussion and disagreement, and most of his opponents in the room were completely won over.

Nehru then turned candid: 'That has nothing to do with my future of India or of the world. I believe in a World Order. I believe in all manner of things and I am going to speak about it.'[19]

For Nehru, the issue with princely states represented an isomorphic mirror to what was happening at the United Nations. He had to deal with cantankerous leaders with whom he did not often agree. He had to accept opinions and styles of governance at odds with his own. And he had to try to rise above such matters altogether, assuming a position of trusted statesman able to bridge differences. In this, at least in the Indian setting, he was largely successful, emerging as the tallest of 'tall men', the most influential visionary and political actor of his age.[20]

The nawab was momentarily thrown off balance by Nehru's statements, but he was by no means down for the count. He tried to regain his footing by pushing back, refocusing attention on his three preconditions to force a fissure between his own position and that of the government's. 'The Constitution and the territorial integrity and succession in the States, I hope shall not be interfered with by the Union.'

Nehru responded: 'It is not a question of interfering with the Constitution. I suppose certain fundamental rights are part of the Union structure. Presumably, they will apply to the whole of India. A certain guarantee of individual rights will be provided for in it. Today the Human Rights Commission is meeting in New York. Our representatives are there. The conception today is there are common individual rights which should be guaranteed the world over. Naturally I presume we shall accept any world charter to that effect.'[21]

This was a meeting with only a select number of Indian elites. Nehru felt free–compelled actually–to unveil some of the details of his vision to them, to lay the groundwork needed to persuade them to support his plans. After all, he would need their support if he was to present a united Indian front to the rest of the world, which he needed to do if he had any hope of leading other countries to the promised land of One World.

What he told the room was simple. The Constitution would protect the fundamental rights of all individuals in the Union. But what these rights were and what impact they would have would have to correspond with what the United Nations decided.

Hamidullah did not understand any of this. He only wanted to get Nehru to disagree with him, to reject his proposals in some way. He had to have an excuse to hold the princes back from the Constituent Assembly and to thereby increase their bargaining power. He tried again to push Nehru's buttons by rejecting the notion that the Union government could interfere in the domestic affairs of Indian princely states. 'I accept that fundamental rights recognized all over the world are to be the rights of our people too, but it does not rest with the Centre to deal with these matters.'

Nehru didn't bite. Instead, he used the opportunity to further clarify his intentions: 'The matter can go to the U.N.O. What is the U.N.O.? It is developing into a world republic in which all States, independent States, are represented and to which they may be answerable on occasions, for instance South Africa over the South African Indians' question, even though this was a domestic question because the Indians there are South African citizens.'

He continued: 'we should like the [princely] States' representatives to join the [Constituent Assembly's Fundamental Rights] Committee which has been formed . . . but which will probably draw up certain fundamental rights more or less the same as the Human Rights Charter may determine.'[22]

India would have to internalize international human rights, helping to streamline, legitimize, and legalize the new world charter. The domestic state would be bound to the international. It was the logical next step from South Africa.

But it also had import on the future of any princely state. As General Smuts had learned to his dismay, no state could hide behind the principle of domestic jurisdiction any longer. The South Africa resolution illustrated for Nehru how best he could deal with princely territories for which he had little love. Princely states, which would be autonomous units in an Indian union, would have their powers curtailed not only by whatever authority they signed over to the Central government, but also by fundamental rights guaranteed by a domestic charter. No matter what state rulers said, the fundamental rights of all people would be protected, and not even disagreements with the Indian Centre could abrogate these rights, since they would actually be guaranteed by the United Nations as well. Effectively, the days in which princes wielded unlimited authority in arbitrary fashion would be over.

While Nehru brought the results of the South Africa debate to bear on princely states in his meeting of February 1947, he was also using his encounter with the princes—his experience in facing down their opposition and wooing them—as a template for how he might handle world leaders in the fight for international human rights and the creation of One World, assuaging egos, winning friends, and bringing people with whom he did not agree to the table.

Hamidullah understood the references to South Africa only in the narrow context of the relationship between princely states and the new government of India. 'I should not be misunderstood if I say that after this point is conceded [that the Union will have jurisdiction over matters of fundamental rights], authority cannot be given to the Union to interfere in the internal situation in the States on the plea of fundamental rights.'

Nehru opted for transparency in the follow-up exchange:

> Jawaharlal Nehru: So far as fundamental rights are concerned, if any authority intervenes, it may not be the Union as such. Possibly the Supreme Court might or might not. It is judicial rather than an executive procedure. It is a common Court for the whole of India, provinces and States, and States can play as much part in that Court as any other part of India.
>
> The Chancellor: That again if only the States have accepted the authority of the Supreme Court and that is a matter for discussion.
>
> Jawaharlal Nehru: The present tendency is to go beyond the Supreme Court to the International Court, whether it is the Court of Justice at the Hague or the U.N.O. to which we belong. It is a dynamic conception which is developing and many people think in terms of the International Court or Assembly exercising more and more powers to control national rivalries. I do not really know what will happen even to the International Court. Therefore the exact powers in

> regards to fundamental rights will have to be discussed by us carefully so that a common basis, a common agreement, may be arrived at. What that basis is is a matter for discussion.[23]

While acknowledging that the future remained fluid, and that the precise configuration of rights and judiciary bodies had yet to be agreed upon, Nehru here fleshed out the nature of his own dream. The nawab repeatedly requested assurances that 'the Union' would not interfere in the internal affairs of princely states. Again and again, Nehru said as much. And the reason he was able to do so lay in the fact that he saw judicial powers outside of the realm of the Union.

Within India, fundamental rights would be discussed in a sub-committee that would report their findings back to the Constituent Assembly. But, whatever they said, the Assembly would more or less ultimately draft rights in accordance with the world charter coming from the United Nations. These rights would apply to everyone everywhere, in all states of the world, and in all their sub-states as well. India would be constitutionally required to implement these international human rights domestically. Its new Supreme Court would have the responsibility and the authority to enforce the new rights doctrine, and no state boundary or principle of sovereignty or independence could shield wrongdoing. The Court was going to be in some kind of relationship with an international justice system, possibly focused on the International Court of Justice in the Hague or on the UN General Assembly itself.

This basically did the trick. Hamidullah was out of ammunition. He continued to quibble but his defeat was now clear.

One of his compatriots in the Chamber of Princes, Sir C.P. Ramaswami Aiyar, the highly respected dewan (prime minister) of the prestigious princely state of Travancore, had his interest piqued, however, by the discussion of fundamental rights. He brought up the fact that there were essentially two different kinds of rights, those that were enforceable–justiciable–and those that were more 'noble aspirations'. The distinction had a bearing on how such rights might constitutionally be conceived.[24]

Nehru took the opportunity to express his disappointment that Hansa Mehta, a week before, had released her proposal for a declaration of human rights. Nehru was bothered (as seen in the last chapter) by what he perceived as Mehta's strategic mistake. In light of his aim to expand the power of the United Nations based on the results of the South Africa question, he thought it best to wait and see where everyone else stood.

But Nehru had also objected to Mehta's reliance on the Security Council for implementation, instinctively preferring instead to have the General Assembly take charge of such issues. He told her so directly in a telegram he sent her immediately upon the release of her proposal.[25] Nehru found Aiyar's well-meaning comments to be provocative, and though he did not say anything more of substance on this matter in the meeting, he brooded on the issue of implementation. Aiyar had astutely figured out that this was the most pressing matter. Hansa Mehta would take up the matter several months later when she would chair the Working Group on Implementation and use that position to advance the post-South Africa possibility of world government.

The major disputes in the meeting of 9 February ended with this discussion of fundamental rights. Hamidullah had been outmanoeuvred and the princes, for the most part, were persuaded to join the Constituent Assembly. Follow-up meetings, to discuss the precise details, were scheduled for March.[26]

But a few days after the February meetings, the British declared their intent to fully transfer power by June of 1948. This created a new sense of urgency. Nehru and his associates urged the princes to act fast and seat delegates at the forthcoming April sessions of the Constituent Assembly. As a body, the Chamber of Princes could not act so swiftly, requiring a series of further approvals that would take more time to secure. But some individual states leapt at the opportunity and immediately sent representatives.[27]

Among these was the princely state of Bikaner, which opted to send K.M. Pannikar, the state's dewan, as its emissary. Pannikar had participated in the negotiating committees and was resolutely in favour of princely participation in the Assembly. He was placed in the Fundamental Rights Sub-committee.[28] Nehru had been persuasive.

A trusted and able representative of the princely states was now going to help to delineate fundamental rights. Pannikar saw this task as one of the two most important in the entire Constituent Assembly, along with the Principles of the Constitution committee.

He was right, although not completely. Nehru certainly saw the work of the Fundamental Rights Sub-committee as among the key elements of Indian Constitution-making. But he also planned to see that the rights that the Indian state incorporated were in line with those produced and approved by the United Nations. This in turn would mean that all great walls of jurisdiction would fall. By participating in the Fundamental Rights Sub-committee, Pannikar would provide a princely stamp of approval for this process.

Pannikar took his role seriously and in his first Constituent Assembly proceedings on fundamental rights, he tried to find common ground between some of the concerns both Hamidullah and Nehru had expressed in the February discussions. He came up with a scheme to allow for two tracks of rights, one 'general' that would apply to the whole of India and the other to be enforced by the provinces and (princely) states. These moves were immediately rejected by the Sub-committee in favour of 'uniform' rights that would not distinguish between region and Centre.[29]

Pannikar only managed to get involved in the Sub-committee's work in April, though the body had been created in late February. Pannikar was approved in March, but by the time he took his seat, the sub-committee was already near the end of its deliberations. Shortly thereafter, it submitted a final report to the larger advisory committee, which in turn moved the entire Constituent Assembly to consider the proposal. The Assembly adopted the fundamental rights clauses for the most part in May 1947, though discussions continued until December 1948.[30]

Nehru and his associates had been trying to involve the princely states from the very outset, and here Hamidullah's plans backfired completely. Though he had been trying to strengthen the voice of princely states in their negotiations, the result was that they had little say insofar as representing any kind of 'princely states' agenda. Even someone such as Pannikar, who was greatly admired, could make little difference given the time constraints, a product of the nawab's very manoeuvrings.

The die was thus cast and there would be no jurisdictional recourse for princely states through the Constitution, as the fundamental rights clauses did not accommodate Pannikar's alternatives. Hamidullah's fears had been borne out, though he shouldered a fair amount of the responsibility. Dusk was settling in for the old monarchies.

FORGING ASIAN RELATIONS

Even as Nehru enveloped the idea of the Union of India within the framework of international human rights, he simultaneously sought to involve the entire region in a conversation on the place and purpose of such rights. In March and April of 1947, Nehru held what he called the Asian Relations Conference in New Delhi. He brought together representatives from across free Asia at this meeting. Inaugurating the Conference, Nehru said: 'We have arrived at a stage in human affairs when the ideal of that "One World" and some kind of world federation seems to be essential though there are many dangers and obstacles in the way.'

'We should work for that ideal and not for any grouping which comes in the way of this larger world group. We therefore support the United Nations,' he stated. '[I]n order to have "One World", we must also in Asia think of the countries in Asia co-operating together for that larger ideal.' As in the States Negotiating Committee, Nehru was occupied with questions of sovereignty, inter- and intra-state relations, and cooperative democracy.

What concerned Nehru most was migratory people. Following closely on the heels of the South Africa debate in the UN, Nehru was thinking through the issues of 'external' Indians.

As a new era dawned, he wondered how people who had been scattered all over the globe by colonialism related to one another. To which country did such populations owe allegiance? From which were they due citizenship? To which could they appeal for justice?

South Africa had brought many of these questions into relief. But while India was the underdog in the fight against Smuts and his allies, this positional lack of strength did not always hold true. That is, people from the Indian subcontinent were spread throughout the world, pushed and pulled by a variety of colonial and economic circumstances. In the context of this Conference, 'external' Indians lived in many parts of Asia, as did 'external' Chinese. Both India and China were behemoths compared to many of their neighbours. 'External' Indians, as well as 'external' Chinese, gave many of the Conference participants pause, since they raised concerns about smaller states accidentally running afoul of their larger brethren, who might act to protect 'their' people.

As a trust-building measure, Nehru gave up all of India's claims on its 'externals' at the meeting. He added that 'external' populations were also not owed anything by the Indian state. The Conference participants were happy with this promise.[31]

Nehru's gesture was possible because he was confident that the human rights of 'nationals and non-nationals alike' would be guaranteed by the United Nations. As Mehta pointed out in 1947 in the first major speech by any representative in the Human Rights Commission, 'during the past one hundred years, four million Indians had been transplanted to various parts of the world . . . As a result of this transplantation, numerous cases of denials of rights in law and equality and complicated questions of nationality and citizenship had arisen . . . Such problems had to be solved within the meaning of the terms of reference of the Commission on Human Rights and the principles of the [UN] Charter.'[32] Rights were going to be guaranteed for all by the United Nations, on the basis of being human, rather than on the basis of being citizens of nation states or subjects of empires. This, in turn, would maximize freedom, allowing people to move and live where they pleased, secure in the knowledge that they would always be afforded basic protections.

Nehru hoped to lead the way by giving up any claim on

'external' Indians, and helping balance the relationship between small and large states. He anticipated others would follow his lead, advancing step by step to a more integrated, more free, more peaceful and more just global community.

Gandhi endorsed this worldview at the close of the Conference. 'Did I believe in One World?' he asked rhetorically. 'Of course I believe in One World. And how can I possibly do otherwise?'[33]

The Midnight Hour

But as soon as the Conference came to an end, Nehru was forced to put his grandiose international dreams on hold. Matters closer to home would now demand his attention.

At the same time that they announced their intention to leave India by 1948, the Attlee government in Great Britain decided to replace Lord Wavell as viceroy of India, in order to best implement the transition. Lord Louis Mountbatten was named his successor. Mountbatten was a cousin of the British emperor (King George VI). Many of the princes of India were overjoyed by the appointment of the debonair Mountbatten, with his flashy smile and royal lineage, for they saw in him a sure-fire friend.[34] Once again, their poor judgement was revealed.

Mountbatten arrived in India in March 1947 and immediately concluded that Britain had to leave India as soon as possible, a decision that was in line with the wishes of the Attlee government. He therefore pushed the date of independence up dramatically, from June of 1948 to August of 1947, leaving just a few months to lay a solid foundation for the transfer of power.[35]

If issues seemed urgent in February, they now suddenly took on an acute intensity. One question burned in everyone's mind: What would the region look like after the British left?

Jinnah and the Muslim League had been pushing for something they called Pakistan, and this had generated a tremendous amount of debate throughout the subcontinent. Jinnah, a secular politician, was primarily concerned with the question of the minority, of how to prevent the region's millions of Muslims from becoming a permanently out-voiced block in a new governmental set-up. His solution was to create a Pakistan and a Hindustan, one the centre of Muslim political aspirations and the other its Hindu counterpart, and both of these would comprise a Union of India.[36]

Whether or not this was actually a tenable construction, Jinnah certainly did not desire the partition of British India into two new nation states. But the British were in a hurry to leave. With the Muslim League having rejected participation in the Constituent Assembly, and with the Cabinet Mission Plan in tatters, Mountbatten felt that the only viable alternative was this very idea. It would create a Pakistan, fulfilling the demand of the League, and it would partition the country, a formula that had been advanced by several senior, respected members of the Indian National Congress, including C. Rajagopalachari and Sardar Vallabhbhai Patel, as the only answer to the League. It seemed like a compromise that would at least meet everyone halfway. He was tragically misinformed.

Jinnah fought tooth and nail to prevent the kind of partition that Mountbatten had in mind, having rejected similar offers previously. In June of 1947, Mountbatten informed him that the decision for partition had been made. Jinnah again rejected the offer and Mountbatten responded that he would lose Pakistan altogether and probably for good if he turned his back on this opportunity. Jinnah responded that he was at peace with the potential consequences of his rejection.[37]

But the high commands of the Congress and the Muslim

League did not reflect the passions of many people on the ground. The idea of Pakistan had caught the hearts of many of the Muslim League's rank and file, not privy to Jinnah's secret plan, and a new nation state was something that generated quite a bit of interest. Conversely, a Hindu nationalist movement that had been bubbling since the 1920s hardened its position in the forties. Its members rejected the idea of partition, but for their alternative looked west to the model provided by Hitler and Mussolini. Leading Hindu nationalist intellectuals and activists like B.S. Moonje, V.D. Savarkar and M.S. Golwalkar wanted either to purge India of all non-Hindus, or to make such peoples second-class citizens of a Hindu state. These kinds of ideas generated considerable fear among minority communities and the two sides fed off of one another to build up a frenzy of animosity.[38]

Mountbatten saw no way out and wanted to extricate the British from an increasingly tense and bitter situation. He forced Jinnah to accept the idea of partition and announced the final decision in early June.[39] Tensions between various ethnic groups, and generally between Hindus and Muslims, boiled over. Violence, which had been flaring up across the region in pockets, now became a more regular, if still somewhat contained, occurrence.

With the League–Congress dispute resolved, and with it the Hindu–Muslim and minority questions, if to no one's liking, the remaining issue had to do with the princely states. Nehru had all but forgotten about them when he was prodded into action by declarations of independence from various rulers. Nehru brought the issue up in July of 1947 with Mountbatten, who, along with his wife Lady Edwina, had become fast friends with the head of India's interim government.[40]

Mountbatten worked closely with Sardar Patel and his

associate, V.P. Menon, on the princely states matter. Patel was a senior member of the Congress high command and the other of Gandhi's two lieutenants. If Nehru comprised Gandhi's ideological 'left' hand, Patel was his 'right'. His politics lingered between the traditional and the reactionary: he had sympathy for aspects of the Hindu nationalist cause, favoured a strong nation state, and had no compunction about using military or police power as needed.[41] As he took over various affairs in the new government, he became known as the 'iron man of India'.

With weeks to go before Independence, there was little time for detailed planning. Mountbatten gave princely states the choice of joining the new Union of India or the new state of Pakistan, or of declaring independence. If they chose to join one of the new countries, he further 'asked' them to accede only with regard to foreign affairs, defence and communication.[42] In this, his solution closely mirrored the one that Nehru had promised over the course of his negotiations earlier that year.

Most states understood they had little say in the matter, and each joined the country with which they were contiguous. Nehru's plans, though impacted by Partition and the violence, nonetheless continued to move forward on track.

A few weeks later, at 12 a.m. on the 15th of August 1947, India and Pakistan achieved independence from Great Britain and became the first non-Western post-colonial countries in the modern world.[43] Speaking in the chambers of the Constituent Assembly during the preceding hour, Nehru was at his most eloquent, and his most inspiring: 'Long years ago we made a tryst with destiny, and now the time comes when we shall redeem our pledge, not wholly or in full measure, but very substantially. At the stroke of the midnight hour, when the world sleeps, India will awake to life and freedom.'

He continued: 'At the dawn of history India started on her

unending quest . . . Through good and ill fortune alike she has never lost sight of that quest or forgotten the ideals which gave her strength . . . And so we have to labour and to work, and work hard, to give reality to our dreams. Those dreams are for India, but they are also for the world, for all the nations and peoples are too closely knit together today for any one of them to imagine that it can live apart. Peace has been said to be indivisible; so is freedom, so is prosperity now, and so also is disaster in this One World that can no longer be split into isolated fragments.'

To the press, he added: 'It is a fateful moment for us in India, for all Asia and for the world. A new star rises, the star of freedom in the East, a new hope comes into being, a vision long cherished materializes. May the star never set and that hope never be betrayed!'

Ending, he looked steadily forward: 'The future beckons to us. Whither do we go and what shall be our endeavour? To bring freedom and opportunity to the common man, to the peasants and workers of India; to fight and end poverty and ignorance and disease; to build up a prosperous, democratic and progressive nation, and to create social, economic and political institutions which will ensure justice and fullness of life to every man and woman . . . To the nations and peoples of the world we send greetings and pledge ourselves to cooperate with them in furthering peace, freedom and democracy.'[44]

This was Nehru at his best. He was honest about his vision, mentioning One World, but remained vague on what that materially meant.[45] This was not the place for policy specifics. Instead, he celebrated what had been accomplished while being mindful of the challenges that lay ahead.

Gandhi was in no mood to celebrate Independence in the form in which it arrived, a partition accompanied by mass violence. He kept away from the public jubilation. Nehru did not have that luxury and felt compelled to acknowledge the success that had been achieved against the old order. But he too was brooding over the many shortcomings of the moment.[46] His mood was captured by Faiz Ahmad Faiz, a progressive poet who penned 'Dawn' in August 1947. Faiz wrote in Urdu: *Chale chalo ke voh manzil abhi nahin aii* (Come, let us keep moving for we have not yet reached our destination (the promised dawn).

The concerns that both Gandhi and Nehru felt were compounded when, shortly after the transfer of power, violence in the region exploded into full-scale inter-ethnic conflict. It was particularly fierce in the eastern city of Calcutta. Gandhi, who for the most part had sat out the preceding weeks, and who had generally been regarded as in decline, was snapped out of his torpor. In his 'finest hour', the Mahatma strode into the midst of the carnage and declared a fast unto death until the violence stopped. The killing initially went on unabated, but within a few days, the Mahatma virtually single-handedly was able to restore a semblance of sanity. As Calcutta, and the state of Bengal more generally, came back to some normalcy, Gandhi travelled to Delhi and, a few months later, declared another fast aiming to bring harmony between all communities. His efforts had a huge impact. With groups and individuals across the political spectrum signing peace pledges, mass violence ended, and Gandhi called off his fast.[47]

The total deaths stemming from Partition ranged somewhere between 500,000 and 1.5 million people. It was a gruesome reality that tarnished the moment of post-colonial freedom. But it also made all the more remarkable Gandhi's achievement. The love of one old man was enough to halt the hate of millions.

Nehru, of course, was not sitting on the sidelines. He busied himself making speeches and drawing attention to Gandhi's plight.

When the immediate threat of violence diminished, Nehru was more convinced than ever that his larger goal of One World was the only way out, not only for Indians and Pakistanis, but for people everywhere. He intensified his efforts to push that agenda forward, though he feared that the inauspicious start to Independence may have irredeemably harmed India's standing in the world. In the months after Independence, he worked with his UN team as Hansa Mehta took over the Working Group on Implementation and successfully pushed through her framework.

DARKNESS BEFORE THE DAWN

But India's implementation scheme went nowhere. Human Rights Commission members decided that the idea of implementation at this stage was putting the cart before the horse; they had to first concur on what 'human rights' meant, on how they would be defined, before they could agree on how those rights could then effectively be carried out and defended. As the work of the Commission rolled into 1948, the growing bitterness between the Soviet bloc countries and the Western powers, soon to explode in the Berlin Blockade, made negotiations increasingly tough.

Matters were a little better where India was concerned. While virtually every princely state had passed quietly into the night by merging with the nation state with which they were contiguous, three had not. The tiny state of Junagadh, on India's west coast, declared for Pakistan, and the premier principality of Hyderabad, squarely in the middle of India, declared itself independent. And Kashmir, which sat between India and Pakistan, could not choose.

Hyderabad's population was mostly Hindu, while its leader, the nizam, was Muslim. Inversely, Kashmir had a large Muslim population, while Maharaja Hari Singh was Hindu. Both states roiled with communal tensions, as external religious nationalist groups contributed to ill feelings.

Patel rejected as existential threats to the new India the decisions of both Hyderabad and Junagadh, which also had a Muslim ruler with a majority Hindu population. V.P. Menon attempted to negotiate with Junagadh, which also began to see popular protests over its decision. Eventually, Junagadh reversed its decision and merged with India. A plebiscite held in 1948 to confirm the will of the people resulted in a vote of 91 per cent in favour of the Indian merger.[48]

But Hyderabad and Kashmir would not be resolved so easily. The nizam was unwilling to change his mind, and faced increasingly grisly scenes of Hindu–Muslim violence in the state. In Kashmir, Pakistani tribesmen, with the tacit approval of their government, crossed over into Kashmiri territory to push the maharaja to join their country. The maharaja panicked and acceded to India on the condition that that was the will of the people. India sent in troops, engaging in its first war with Pakistan.[49]

For Nehru, the Indian state had to succeed above all, or else there would be no end to the old order. Independent India represented a culmination of Gandhi's campaigns, and a rejection of imperialism. If India disintegrated, which was considered a very real possibility in these early years, then the hope that it represented–the possibility of freedom and justice in the context of colonialism–would be lost. Nehru could not allow that to happen. As Nehru said later that year with respect to Hyderabadi independence, 'it would make Indian independence a mockery . . . The whole of South India would

Press Information Bureau of India, courtesy of the Gandhi Photos, Digital Collection, University of Hawaii

Gandhi with Sir Stafford Cripps, New Delhi, 1942

Press Information Bureau of India, courtesy of the Gandhi Photos, Digital Collection, University of Hawaii

Nehru, Gandhi and Khan Abdul Ghaffar Khan ('Frontier Gandhi') at the Asian Relations Conference, New Delhi, April 1947

UN Photo/Marvin Bolotsky

Hansa Mehta with Eleanor Roosevelt at the UN Commission on Human Rights, 1949

Department of State, courtesy of Harry S. Truman Library

Prime Minister Nehru's procession is cheered by crowds in New York City, October 1949

Department of State, courtesy of Harry S. Truman Library

Prime Minister Nehru with Madame Pandit and US President Harry Truman, October 1949

Department of State, courtesy of Harry S. Truman Library

Nehru with Albert Einstein, 1949; Madame Pandit can be seen in between them

UN Photo/Marvin Bolotsky

Madame Pandit after her election as president of the UN General Assembly, standing between Dag Hammarskjöld and Canada's Lester Pearson, 1953

UN Photo/AI

Nehru addressing the UN General Assembly, 1956

be in jeopardy . . .' He noted that nowhere else in the world did one independent nation exist fully surrounded by another.[50] Successful independence for India was only one step in a larger movement to a better world, but it was nonetheless an essential step.

Most did not understand the prime minister's nuanced views. India's response to Kashmir and Hyderabad challenged the ideals that Nehru advocated, and he came under criticism for it. Nehru managed to brush off the attacks related to Hyderabad. This was Patel's bailiwick, and he was the one person with the stature to stand equal to the prime minister. When the Indian army marched into Hyderabad at the end of 1948, they quickly dispatched one of the militias propping up the monarchy, the Razakars, and brought Hyderabad into the Indian Union. Nehru had resisted efforts to use force throughout the year, instead advocating that Hyderabad turn over matters of foreign affairs, defence and communications to the Indian centre, falling back to the proposals floated in early 1947.[51] So, despite the police action, Nehru managed to avoid charges of hypocrisy.

Kashmir, on the other hand, represented a true challenge to his beliefs. Shortly after Independence, Nehru had rejected a defence plan drawn up by his commander-in-chief. 'Scrap the Army! The police are good enough to meet our needs,' he had reportedly said, echoing elements of the approach Gandhi had laid out just prior to San Francisco (see Chapter 3).[52] But faced with the situation in Kashmir, Nehru quickly changed his mind, and India found herself at war with Pakistan mere months later, a hot conflict which would continue through 1948. Nehru, a native Kashmiri, simply could not imagine India without it. Eleanor Roosevelt would later observe that though 'he was a man of great physical and moral courage . . . His remarkable intellectual abilities did not free him entirely of prejudices'.

Nehru was 'completely emotional', 'suffered a stoppage of all reason', and 'contradicted the high ideals he normally expressed' when discussing Kashmir.[53]

Gandhi's death at the hands of an assassin in late January 1948, shortly after the success of his second great fast for peace, added to the grim atmosphere. It was a terrible personal loss for Nehru. His love and admiration for Gandhi was genuine and deep. In the weeks and months that followed, Nehru grappled with what Gandhi meant–to politics, to India, to humanity.

India International

Gandhi's greatest innovation had been his development of the principle of satyagraha. In his various campaigns, Gandhi had insisted that his many admirers, and legions of followers, commit themselves to the way of truth. To do this demanded that they personally take on tasks meant to confront the evils–the untruths–in their own lives. Gandhi subjected himself to these same conditions, what he called his 'experiments with truth', trying out various dietary restrictions, taking vows of silence for periods of time, forcing himself to refrain from sexual activity, and doing assorted chores, like cleaning latrines, once reserved for reviled and oppressed groups. Through these acts, he sought to live truthfully, and, in doing so, to gain both the moral power and the physical courage to persuade opponents to see the untruth in their actions and bring about radical change.[54]

Nehru, in his nascent dealings in the international arena, saw the applicability of Gandhi's lessons. National states, as they engaged with one another, essentially took on the status of individual actors. It followed that a state that 'experimented with truth' would have the ability needed to dramatically alter the landscape.

He decided on a bold move. He had to make his vision of One World public. He wanted his message to reach both a domestic audience and a larger global one. He would have to make two separate, and different, presentations. On 8 March, a little over a month after Gandhi's assassination, Nehru rose in the Legislative Session of the Constituent Assembly and made his pitch. 'I think . . . you will find that there has been a miserable failure in the foreign policy of every great power and country,' he began.

Then, the events of the past few months weighing heavily on his mind, he turned momentarily wistful: 'owing to the unfortunate events that have happened in India since the 15th of August 1947, anything we did in the world outside lost weight or lost weight for a time . . . Indeed, potentially we counted for a great deal, though actually we need not have counted for much. But . . . those events suddenly brought down our credit in the international domain tremendously. It affected the United Nations when they met last October [1947] to consider the [follow up to] the South Africa issue.'

India's failure to contain violence and live up to its ideals had actively hindered the advancement of the South African cause, which was at the foundation of all of Nehru's internationalist plans. How then to move forward? First and foremost, Nehru argued, India had to remain free of bloc alliances. Only by keeping an independent mind, and voice, though ready to compromise in dialogue, could India remain effective in the world. And the world needed an effective and idealistic India.

Nehru now painted his path forward: '[T]he United Nations, in spite of its failings and weaknesses, is something that is good. It should be encouraged and supported in every way, and should be allowed to develop into some kind of world government or world order.'

With that, he turned to the question of Indian leadership. How could India lead the world, particularly morally, when it had so obviously come up short in its nascent independent life? Nehru was cutting: 'I do not wish to enter into any comparisons with other countries, and certainly we have done nothing in India to merit leadership of anybody. It is for us to lead ourselves; then only can we lead others properly and I do not wish to place the case of India at any higher level.'

The setup was perfect. 'I am . . . in spite of being Minister in charge of External Affairs, not interested in external affairs so much as internal affairs at the present moment. External affairs will follow internal affairs. Indeed, there is no basis for external affairs if internal affairs go wrong.'

The Gandhian move was complete. India had to act righteously inwardly if it wanted to outwardly affect the world and its people in a positive way.

'That being so, the fact remains that we stand for certain things. Now, when we come into contact with the external world, do we stand for them or not?'[55] It was a clarion call. Would his fellow legislators hear?[56]

He ended by addressing head-on the obvious criticism of his vision. 'The world, however, is in a pretty bad way and it is easy enough for people to tell me, "Oh, you talk idealistically, you should be practical". May I remind the [Assembly] that we have seen, these many years, the results of persons and things being very practical? I have had enough of this practicalness, which leads to incessant conflict and which leads to all the misery and suffering that we have seen. If that is the meaning of being practical, the sooner we are not practical, the better.'[57]

His speech, meant also to address the concerns of a number of critics, was front-page news the next day.[58] Now he needed to figure out a way to get his message across outside of India.

The opportunity arose a few weeks later, when he had the chance to speak on a popular and influential American radio show. The University of Chicago's Roundtable programme was aired throughout the United States under the auspices of the National Broadcasting Corporation (NBC). It focused on topical issues of the day and had the clout to attract leading intellectuals and public figures. Nehru accepted an invitation to speak about world government on the 4th April broadcast, beaming his message by shortwave from the All-India Radio offices in New Delhi.[59]

He polished and condensed the speech he made in the Constituent Assembly, streamlining and simplifying his message. He was at his most inspiring: 'Tortured humanity hungers for real peace, but some evil fate pursues it and pushes it further and further away from what it desires most.' What was this great desire, this way out for tortured humanity that would bring real peace? 'We talk of World Government and One World and millions yearn for it. Earnest efforts continue to be made to realize this ideal of the human race, which has become so imperative today.'

With his intentions plain, he now tried to explain the problem as he understood it: 'And yet those efforts have thus far proved ineffective, even though it becomes ever clearer that if there is to be no world order then there might be no order at all left in the world . . . Mahatma Gandhi made an outstanding contribution not only to the freedom of India but to the cause of world peace. He taught us the doctrine of non-violence . . . as an active and positive instrument for the peaceful solution of international differences . . . He applied moral values to political action and pointed out that ends and means can never be separated, for the means ultimately govern the end.'

Again, he realized the lofty nature of his appeal and tried to pre-empt any criticism: 'All this may seem fantastic and impractical in the modern world . . . And yet we have seen repeatedly the failure of other methods and nothing can be less practical than to pursue a method that has failed again and again.'

He now turned as specific as possible: 'I have no doubt that a World Government must and will come, for there is no other remedy for the world's sickness. The machinery for it is not difficult to devise. It can be an extension of the federal principle, a growth of the idea underlying the United Nations, giving each national unit freedom to fashion its destiny according to its genius, but subject always to the basic covenant of a World Government.'

And, at last, he made clear his position on human rights, the primary mechanism through which India had been advancing One World in the previous year and a half. 'We talk of rights of individuals and nations, but it must be remembered that every right carries an obligation with it. There has been far too much emphasis on rights and far too little on obligations; if obligations were undertaken, rights would naturally flow from them. This means an approach of life different from the competitive and acquisitive approach of today.'

This was, of course, Gandhi's view. Only by emphasizing a sense of shared kinship and moral duty to others—other people, other communities, other states—could true justice be achieved. For Gandhi, as for Nehru, rights flowed from such obligations. Their view stemmed from a notion of humanity that was neither jaded nor pollyannaish. Everyone had the *potential* to be good, even if they were seriously compromised by ill-advised actions. Such actions could be challenged, and overcome, by campaigns that emphasized universal kinship and duty. This had been the basis of Gandhi's idea of satyagraha. Nehru was extending the principle to order all of the world's affairs.[60]

He summed up his case: 'Today fear consumes us all—fear of the future, fear of war, fear of the people of the nations we dislike and who dislike us . . . Let us try to get rid of this fear and base our thoughts and actions on what is essentially right and moral, and then . . . the dark clouds that surround us may lift and the way to the evolution of a world order based on freedom will be clear.'[61] To make sure there was no mistaking his intentions, Nehru had the Roundtable include in the published transcripts of the broadcast a supplement containing the draft covenant and declaration of human rights, as well as the United States' Federalist Paper XV. It was written by 'founding father' Alexander Hamilton, whose papers generally, and XV in particular, celebrated the US Constitution and the superiority of union over confederation. [62]

Nehru had laid his cards, if not quite all of them, on the table. With the Human Rights Commission gearing up for its third session, he hoped that his words would have a positive effect. And indeed, as the Commission picked up its work later the following month, the idea of international rights with legal power, the framework needed to create the foundation for One World, remained a viable option.

To underscore his point of view, Nehru welcomed Edward T. Clark to Delhi on 16 April. Clark was the vice-president of the World Movement for World Federal Government, born out of the August 1947 Montreux Convention and the precursor to the World Federalist Movement. Nehru gave him a letter that indicated his clear support: 'I have no doubt in my mind that the only way for the solution of the world's major problems is for some kind of world Government to develop . . . I welcome therefore, every attempt that is made to educate and direct public opinion to this end . . . So far as India is concerned, we have repeatedly expressed our opinion in favour of the development of an international organization or some kind of world Government which gives full autonomy to its various national units and which at the same time removes the causes of war and conflict.'[63]

Regardless of Nehru's actions, it quickly became clear that the Human Rights Commission could not resolve the issues and tensions created by legally binding rights in the short time allotted. The Covenant of Human Rights–where rights would be justiciable and therefore enforceable–would be pushed off until a future meeting. For now, the Commission could only agree on a non-justiciable declaration of universal human rights.

Nehru was not discouraged. In July, just a few weeks after the Commission had completed its third session, India's ambassador to the United States, Asaf Ali, published an article entitled 'India's Role in One World'. As an official representative of the country, Ali's piece had to reflect the policy of the External Affairs Ministry, which was led by Nehru. Ali put India's agenda in the clearest of terms. 'Perhaps the nearest description of the world we hope for,' he said, 'would be the knitting together of all human relationships and activities as well as the natural resources of this planet into one economic and ethical fabric with a view to obtaining the maximum good of mankind with the fullest individual and collective freedom.'

What did this mean for political realities on the ground? 'The first prerequisite of achieving such a result, in my opinion, is the definition and final acceptance by all human beings of fundamental human rights. So long as this foundation is not well and truly laid, and so long as fundamental human rights are not beyond the pale of controversy, it will be futile to think of achieving one world.'

If human rights could be agreed upon and deployed, what did India want to see? 'One world will require a world government, with all its requisite organs for executive, deliberative, and judicial functions. This means that the absolute sovereignty of each nation will have to undergo an agreed modification, and some of the powers exercised by individual nations will have to be pooled and delegated to the federal world government. The extent of such federal powers will naturally be the subject of negotiation between various nations and powers in order to establish cooperative peace and collective progress.'

Ali devoted the rest of his article to summarizing history, noting the sunset of the League of Nations and the new horizon of the UN. He lamented the slow pace at which the UN was developing, and devoted much space to India's unique role in helping One World to come about. Because it sat at the crossroads of the world, and stood for a larger revival of the entire East, India could help people choose between a bifurcated planet full of fear, and a united one full of hope.[64] Nehru's vision was, at last, made plain for all to see.

In November, Nehru personally addressed the United Nations General Assembly in Paris, a few weeks before its final vote on the Commission's declaration.[65] He reiterated the case he had made in his two speeches earlier that year, admonishing his fellow UN delegates to keep themselves open to alternative political paths and not give in to fear of the future. The *Indian Express* newspaper, at the time based in Madras in South India, came out strongly in support of Nehru's overall vision, but also lamented Great Power politics and the fierce resistance to change.[66]

Nehru had good reason to be persistent. The idea of a covenant was resuscitated in early 1949 and the Human Rights Commission was asked by its administering council to now consider proposals to make the covenant a reality.[67]

A few weeks prior to the meeting of the fifth session of the Human Rights Commission, where the matter of the covenant would be taken up, Hansa Mehta made a point-by-point comparison of the new Indian Constitution with the Universal Declaration of Human Rights the UN had passed at the end of 1948.[68] The Constitution was near the end of the approval process, though it was not there yet, but the chapters on fundamental rights had already been ratified. Mehta opened her comparison by noting that the Human Rights Commission had yet to begin work on the covenant, which would be a legal document. The Indian Constitution, though, was legally binding and enforceable, and thus it would be significant to see how it stacked up against the rights now deemed universal by the United Nations.

In the initial meeting of the Working Group on Implementation, as members were discussing the relationship between domestic and international jurisdictions, and the potential pitfalls with which such a relationship was fraught, Mehta had observed that 'it was clear that the provisions of the [human rights] Conventions would have to become part of the national law of signatory states.'[69] Here she was able to establish that India had done just that. It was precisely a demonstration of the 'Gandhian spirit' that Nehru had called for in his speech to the Constituent Assembly a little over a year before. India had inwardly 'experimented with truth', its still evolving status allowing for great latitude in what was even conceivable, much more so than in any of the long-standing nation states of the West.

Mehta's analysis revealed that the Indian Constitution, exactly as Nehru had foretold in February 1947, measured up well against the Universal Declaration, incorporating and legalizing its most salient features. Most significantly, she concluded her comparison by noting that 'Article 40 in the constitution is very important. It deals with the promotion of International peace and security and covers part of the preamble of the Declaration. It says "The State shall endeavor to–(a) promote international peace and security; (b) maintain just and honourable relations between nations; (c) foster respect for international law and treaty obligations in the dealings of organised people with one another; and (d) encourage settlement of international disputes by arbitration."'

Essentially, these lines implied that the state was accountable to international authority. It was the codification of everything Nehru had been saying–and fighting for–since he took over the interim government. Article 40 of the draft Constitution (what would become Article 51 in the final, official version) appeared in the Directive Principles of the new Constitution. These principles, according to Article 37, were not enforceable by any court, as they were non-justiciable rights, an ironic situation certainly. But the Indians, particularly Mehta, had taken effective steps to see to it that the Directive Principles were key elements of the Constitution, clarifying that 'the principles therein laid down are nevertheless fundamental in the governance of the country and it shall be the duty of the State to apply these principles in making laws'.[70]

This was the Gandhian sense of obligation, now applied to the architecture of the state. Mehta made sure that this point was impossible to miss, alluding to Nehru's earlier speech. She concluded that the new Constitution 'made the civil rights justiceable [sic] . . . With regard to the other rights they form the positive contents of what the state must do for the individual. While the constitution emphasizes the duty of the state it does not refer to the duties of the individual . . . [But] Article 29(1) of the [Universal] Declaration . . . says: "Everyone has duties to the community in which alone the free and full development of his personality is possible." Rights and duties . . . go together. Those who do not fulfill their obligations have no right to ask for their rights. The duties are therefore implied in the rights . . . '[71]

This Indian idea of human rights as described by Mehta in 1949 was the clearest indication of Nehru's intent to operationalize his vision of One World, for it straddled the conceptualization of positive and negative rights that mirrored the Cold War worldviews of the United States and the Soviet Union.

By 1948, the post-war consensus on the need for international human rights, growing out of the Nuremberg trials (where prominent Nazis were prosecuted after the war) and an awareness of the magnitude of Nazi sin, had begun to factionalize over what exactly those rights meant. The West, led by the United States, generally favoured negative rights, rights that were civil and political and focused on the individual. These were the rights that were privileged in the United States' Bill of Rights and in France's Declaration of the Rights of Man. The Soviets and many colonized people throughout the world tended to approve more of positive rights, social and economic rights that usually required the active intervention of government.[72]

The Indians saw both as worthy. This further highlighted their view that the polarization of the world was unnecessary. By incorporating both positive and negative rights into the Constitution, Nehru hoped that India could materially reveal the shared road that all humanity could travel together.

By emphasizing India's views on human rights, and its willingness to obligate itself to a democratic international organization, Nehru hoped to serve as a beacon for the other nations foundering in the sea of Cold War ideologies. He hoped to turn this light on the Human Rights Commission and show them a way forward for the covenant they were now charged to create. It was in this international covenant that all of Nehru's hopes now lay.

6 Towards a Better Future

The Arc of the Covenants

In late 1949, as the Human Rights Commission began to deal with a covenant of human rights in earnest, Nehru made a trip to the United States, accompanied by his daughter and future prime minister, Indira, and his sister, Madame Pandit, now India's ambassador to Washington. Up until early that year, Madame Pandit had been serving as ambassador to Moscow, though Gandhi had informed her shortly before he died in January 1948 that she would soon be transferred to the United States.[1] Pandit's position in the capitals of the two superpowers reflected the signal importance that Nehru attached to bridging relations between the two sides of the world. Pandit's diplomatic and debating skills were unmatched, and she enjoyed a reputation on the international stage that was equally unparalleled. Her appointments were meant to reflect the status that India accorded both the Soviet Union and America: it held them in comparably high regard. This was, of course, a political move as much as anything else, since the point was to build trust among foes.

Nehru and the others toured the US extensively in 1949, visiting New York, Washington, Boston, Chicago, Knoxville, Los Angeles and San Francisco, as well as parts of rural America. This was a victory lap of sorts, retracing many of the steps that Madame Pandit had taken in 1945. This time, Earl Warren, still California's governor, had his picture taken with the Nehrus.[2]

Pointedly, Nehru visited Hyde Park and paid his respects at FDR's grave. He also visited Wellesley, Harvard and the University of Southern California, and was awarded an honorary degree at Columbia by General Eisenhower. At Princeton, he paid a private visit to Albert Einstein, and the two made productive use of their first and only face-to-face meeting.[3]

The American press swooned. *The New York Times* declared him a 'welcome visitor', and lavished praise.[4] The US was, of course, keen to woo India as an ally in the Cold War. But Nehru's personal reputation soared above all else, as his charms and good looks, like his sister's, captivated almost any who crossed his path.

Nehru hoped to turn this personal charisma into meaningful results. On 13 October, he delivered an address to the US Congress. Because the House Chamber was under renovation, he had to first speak to the House of Representatives, and then deliver the exact same address moments later to the Senate, seated in a different chamber.[5] His speech echoed the high rhetoric of his 1948 radio address, and many of his earlier foreign policy statements. India's objective, he declared, was 'world peace and the enlargement of human freedom'.

He added that 'even when preparing to resist aggression [with all necessary force], the ultimate objective, the objective of peace and reconciliation, must never be lost sight of, and heart and mind must be attuned to this supreme aim, and not swayed or clouded by hatred or fear'. This reflected his state of mind perfectly. If he had been chastened by the complex, political decisions required of his office, he did not let this temper his ideals.

He underscored his goal by speaking of the need for political as well as economic rights. While the US had been an early advocate of economic rights–notably, 'Freedom from Want' was one of FDR's Four Freedoms–it was the Soviet Union that had really pushed for explicit articles in the covenant in the fifth session of the Human Rights Commission.[6] By calling for both positive and negative rights in a direct appeal to American policymakers, Nehru tried to validate both sets of worldviews and find some way to bring them into accord with one another.

That way involved applying Gandhism to India's foreign policy. Gandhi had taught a 'technique of action that was peaceful and yet effective, and yielded results which led us not only to freedom but to friendship with those with whom we were till yesterday in conflict'. The message of One World was the clear subtext.

Nehru admitted that he did not know how far Gandhi's techniques 'can be applied to wider spheres of action'. 'Yet I have no doubt,' he concluded, 'that the basic approach which lay behind that technique of action was the right approach in human affairs and the only approach that ultimately solves a problem satisfactorily.' He was interrupted several times by rounds of spontaneous applause.[7]

The speech was billed as the only 'major address' of his trip,[8] but an appearance at the end of the month was equally important.

Having chosen the University of Chicago Roundtable radio broadcast for his important international address on world government in 1948, beamed from New Delhi, he now sat down for an interview with Chicago anthropology professor Robert Redfield in the studios of that same programme.

After Nehru began with a homage to Gandhi, Redfield dove into his questions. Within minutes, he quoted a passage from one of Nehru's works in which the prime minister had said: 'There really seems no alternative between world conquest and world association. There is no middle course.' Redfield wanted to know what that association meant, and wondered why there was no other way.

Nehru summarized some of the points made by Asaf Ali in his article from the year before, arguing that science and technology had made the world a very small place. 'Unless there is full cooperation between various parts of the world, there is likely to be conflict,' he explained. The process of cooperation might not be quick, he added, but it was nonetheless necessary in the face of rapid change.

Nehru then spoke on the precise form that world cooperation might take. 'Obviously it cannot ignore the freedom of nations. It means ultimately that certain forms of sovereignty might be given over to some central authority, world authority; but, generally speaking, it would deal with world affairs, international affairs; and domestically, every country would be completely independent to follow any policy it chooses.'

Redfield was quick to decipher the meaning, and asked Nehru if he was not speaking of a world federal structure. 'Yes, if you like, you can call it "federal",' Nehru replied, 'though, to begin with, the authority of that federal structure must be very limited. Gradually, as people get used to it, it might increase.'[9]

Nehru felt strongly about his vision of One World, which all of this represented, but he knew that any kind of world government had to express the will of the people for legitimacy. His commitment to democracy was unequivocal, and Nehru knew that many distrusted the idea of such an overarching organization. The most vocal critics of world government thus far had been the Soviets, and their public reasons had to do with democratic protections and mechanisms, as Bogomolov had put it in the Human Rights Commissions' second session (see Chapter 4). The South Africa question, though, had convinced Nehru beyond all doubt that world government was necessary, as he reasserted to Redfield during the interview. But he wanted to take into account everyone's concerns, building One World with consensus, so that people could grow to trust the new institutions.

Nehru would soon test his abilities to build faith in new institutions. As his tour of the United States drew to a close, the date neared for India's new Constitution to be put into effect. On 26 January 1950, India would officially become a republic, and the system that had grown out of years of debate and discussion from divergent quarters would become the law of the land. With it came the expectation and burden of democracy. Nehru was determined to live up to these expectations, and within months appointed a chief election commissioner, and enacted legislations authorizing elections. The elections would not take place for almost another two years, but the wheels were turning at blazing speed, and people were, in fact, satisfied. The time frame, which on first appearance may seem very long, was actually quite a short one, considering the magnitude of the undertaking: 176 million people had to vote, and 85 per cent could not read or write in any meaningful way. It was a task of mind-blowing proportions.[10]

But even as he concentrated on this epic endeavour, the first time in the world's history that such a large number of people would be mobilized and organized to express their political preferences, Nehru had to retain his focus on the events unfolding in the Human Rights Commission. For just as the election process was being set up in India, the Commission began to face a serious fracture over rights. The debates during the sixth session, which met from March to May 1950, began to centre on whether rights should be placed within a hierarchy, with some rights being considered more fundamental, a prerequisite to, other rights. The fissure split civil and political rights from economic and social rights to an extent, though everyone still agreed both were important. The Commission was running out of time as it finished working on a set of articles, primarily civil and political, for a draft covenant, and thought that a series of covenants would be necessary. The Commission kicked the issue back up to the Economic and Social Council, its mother body. The Council by and large agreed with the Commission's decisions but sent the matter to the General Assembly for direction. The Assembly, in turn, directed that there should be one covenant, inclusive of all rights, including economic and social.

Nehru followed all of these developments closely, and grew concerned that polarizing Cold War ideologies were forcing each side to retreat into trenches. India took decisive action in the seventh session of the Human Rights Commission, which met from April to May 1951. Delegates began to draft and consider articles of economic and social rights for the once-more singular covenant. They also began to develop methods of implementation of these new articles. But as the session drew to a close, Hansa Mehta, still India's representative to the Commission and now holding the position of second vice-chair, moved that the covenant be split into two, one for civil and political rights, and the other for economic and social rights. Because the decision to include all rights in one binding document came from the General Assembly, she recommended that the matter again go up the chain of command and be reconsidered. (The Human Rights Commission was a subsidiary of the Economic and Social Council, which in turn was an organ of the General Assembly; each body–assembly, commission, and committee–had their own schedule for sessions.)

Her reasoning was that 'economic, social, and cultural rights though equally fundamental and therefore important, form a separate category of rights from that of civil and political rights in that they are not justiceable [sic] rights . . . [and] the method of their implementation is, therefore, different.'[11] As the summary annotation on the covenants noted, 'Those in favor of drafting two separate covenants argued that civil and political rights were enforceable, or justiciable, or of an "absolute" character, while economic, social, and cultural rights were not or might not be; that the former were immediately applicable, while the latter were to be progressively implemented; and that, generally speaking, the former were rights of the individual "against" the State, that is against unlawful and unjust action of the State, while the latter were rights which the State would have to take positive action to promote.'[12] Mehta clarified that by 'justiciable rights, she meant those rights for the violation of which governments could be sued. Governments could not be sued for failing to carry out economic, social and cultural rights, since the responsible party might well, for example, be employers.'[13]

What was going on here? India, which had devoted all of its energies to bringing people together, to creating One World, had essentially acknowledged the bifurcation of the world, and appeared willing to enshrine those differences into the founding constitutional principles of the new world they were building.

Yet the delineation of rights between economic and social on the one hand and civil and political on the other closely mirrored the structure of rights found in the Indian Constitution itself. There, the Fundamental Rights Sub-committee had likewise come to the conclusion that differences in implementation between justiciable, 'negative' rights, and 'positive' rights that were mandates on the state, meant that rights had to be grouped differently (see Chapter 5). Some belonged to the standard articles. These were 'legal' civil and political rights. Other rights, the economic and social rights for which the state had to act, had to be placed under the Directive Principles. In the Indian sub-committee, Mehta had stressed that these rights were 'nonetheless fundamental' and were the 'duty' of the state to apply.

So, the division that India proposed in the UN, of a covenant on civil and political rights, and a covenant on economic, social and cultural rights, in this context had its origins in the actions that India had taken domestically. But the harsh realities of the Cold War, and the dangers of a polarized world, were clear to everyone, especially to Nehru, who had spent all his energy trying to counter this trend. Splintering the covenant, even for genuine concerns regarding methods of implementation, nonetheless ran the risk of exacerbating a major ideological rift, and inflaming Cold War tensions rather than calming them.

Such a result was not at all what Nehru had in mind, of course. But he had come to have a nuanced understanding of unity. Nehru's idea of the universal stemmed from Gandhi's, and what they emphasized was kinship, an innate bond that all people shared. But in beliefs and the practice of customs and culture, Gandhi and Nehru were always most sensitive to the idea of difference, to the beauty that lay in the panorama of human ways of living, provided those differences did not impinge on others. Indeed, Gandhi's entire ethical framework was built around the principle of obligation to 'the other'.[14] This meant that he recognized and affirmed the things that differentiated humans from one another, whether by race, or class, or gender, or custom, or nation while simultaneously affirming the primordial link between them and rejecting all forms of discrimination and domination. In his many speeches on One World, Nehru was always careful to recognize the differences in ways of living that humans preferred, and he was adamant that any world system had to allow for such difference, so that each person and community could live according to their 'genius', as he put it in his 1948 radio address.

Splitting the covenant into two recognized that there were separate genealogies for civil and political, and economic and social rights. As India officially put it, it affirmed that the two stood 'on an entirely different footing'.[15] At the same time, India and everyone else agreed that 'the enjoyment of civil and political freedoms and of economic, social and cultural rights are interconnected and interdependent . . . [And] when deprived of economic, social and cultural rights, man does not represent the human person whom the Universal Declaration regards as the ideal of the free man.'[16]

From India's perspective, the Gandhian ideal had gone global. Two covenants allowed the world to accept that there were two notions of human rights, and to validate this difference. In the act of this validation, 'the other' would also be endorsed and supported. In practical terms, this meant that the respective opinions and worldviews of the Soviet Union and the United States, and their respective allies, of East and West, would be respected, their underlying value systems applauded, and all brought together to serve the whole of humankind.

As Nehru had observed repeatedly, the Cold War was built on fear and mistrust, with capitalist and communist each viewing the other with suspicion. Two covenants allowed the best of both systems to be articulated and appreciated, and the differences that divided the world to be laid out. But since these differences were 'interconnected and interdependent', the creation and approval of two covenants would, while maintaining the principle of difference, create harmony by bringing the two systems into beneficial conversation.[17] The new, global society that emerged would, in Wendell Willkie's terms, be 'free alike of the economic injustices of the West and the political malpractices of the East'.[18]

Mehta's initiative drew fire from the Soviet delegation. The Commission's deliberations were quite tense by this point, as suspicions of Cold War machinations ever lingered in the air. The Soviet response was particularly aggressive, as they sought to play up the hidden hand of the United States and the United Kingdom.[19]

Mehta could not let this stand, for she saw this as an utter distortion of India's position and goal. She indignantly and rigorously defended her purpose. She drew an explicit comparison with the Indian Constitution, where both kinds of rights had found a home. Then she explained that 'homogenous rights should be grouped together. If civil and political rights were embodied in one instrument, and economic, social and cultural rights in another, the peoples of the world would understand more clearly the nature of the differences between them.' She concluded that, as heirs to Gandhi (and the Buddha), the Indian delegation obviously had a strong commitment to human rights.[20]

Despite her protests, the Commission roundly rejected India's proposal. But when the single covenant was sent up to the

Economic and Social Council for review, the Council opted to send it on to the General Assembly to reconsider the idea of two covenants.[21] India held seats in both the Council and the General Assembly. In the debate on whether there should be one or two covenants, India took the lead again, and through a series of parliamentary manoeuvres and amendments, they ensured that there would indeed be two. While on this particular issue India voted alongside the United States and against the Soviet preference for one document, on a variety of other matters, such as the issue of self-determination, the alignments were very different, suggesting that these were not, in fact, alliance-based votes. Supporting the victorious case for two covenants were the delegations from China, Brazil and Venezuela, among others.[22]

Just as these events were unfolding, K.M. Munshi, a famed Indian legal scholar who had been instrumental in the drafting of the country's new Constitution, gave a speech in Bombay marking the anniversary of the Universal Declaration of Human Rights. He summed up the situation: 'After the fall of the League of Nations, the world again clamored for a world organ, and the United Nations Organization was founded. Though divided under the influence of the two great power blocs, it is a forum where words replace weapons and the world's conscience . . . becomes the arbiter . . .

'This is where India comes in, as a protagonist of the power of moral force. We have only the weapons of [a] man of peace [Gandhi]; a sense of fairness, a burning desire for peace and a faith in One World.

'We have been friendly with both Russia and China. We are associated with the U.S.A. and the Commonwealth . . . We can, therefore, mobilize the incalculable moral opinion . . . and form the conventions of world self-rule.'[23]

But the debate over the two covenants in the General Assembly only underscored how rancorous things had become. Nehru knew that any more progress on human rights would require careful strategy, and so in 1952 he decided to move his A-team back to the UN. Madame Pandit was once again called on to lead India's delegation to the General Assembly for its late 1952 seventh session.

MADAME PRESIDENT

Madame Pandit had won plaudits in Washington for her work as ambassador, as she had in Moscow earlier. Her posting always tore down old walls. She was the first woman to represent a foreign power in the United States.[24] Reflecting widespread public opinion, the American press raved. One Washington paper reflected on her efforts at San Francisco and claimed that it would be a 'sure thing that she would be a success in her new office'. After all, the paper reminded its readers, she had both 'beauty and brains'.[25] An Indianapolis report called her 'India's most brilliant woman', whose 'distinguished oratory to the United Nations is known in the United States'. They hoped that she and her brother would 'open a new bridge to United States–Soviet amity'.[26] Her appointment in the US had received nationwide coverage, with stories appearing from Alabama to Florida.[27] Quoting Pearl Buck, *The Washington Post* said that she 'is so beautiful that one must first become accustomed to the fact'. Quoting a reporter who witnessed her in action in the UN in 1946, the *Post* added 'It is a joy to listen to her, to watch her snatch points from her platform opponents in debate. Seeing her in action, one understands better the spirit that has upheld both herself and her distinguished brother.'[28]

The American press continued to venerate her throughout

her tenure as ambassador, even as she took tough and unpopular stands defending the Soviet Union and now communist China in a variety of instances.[29] Her diplomatic skills were unrivalled. In 1949, the student body of the Vogue School of Fashion Modeling named her one of the Ten Model Women of the world, lauding her for intelligence.[30] A year later, Eleanor Roosevelt declared that Madame Pandit was 'the most remarkable woman she had ever met', quite a compliment from a woman of such accomplishment as herself.[31]

But even as she wowed the US, Madame Pandit kept a close watch on the United Nations. She reasserted in 1951: 'I have great faith in the United Nations. I feel that the UN is our only hope.'[32]

Just as the debate over the two covenants was beginning in the sixth session of the General Assembly later that year, Madame Pandit had announced that she planned to step down as ambassador to the United States. She was leaving to launch a 'truth campaign' and hoped that 'East and West will join together for world freedom and economic stability and the elimination of the threat of war'.[33] Just a few days before, she had spoken to the World Assembly of Youth, a UN-affiliated organization focused on the role of young people in rights campaigns and governance issues. There she had called for worldwide support of human rights. Now, 'for the first time in history,' she exhorted, 'a conscious, coordinated effort is being made to translate that respect [for the individual] into people's lives, in political, economic, and social terms . . . We are standing at the crossroads of civilization where there is no room for the might of one (nation) or the glory of another.' The 'time will come,' she concluded, 'when through tolerance and mutual cooperation a pattern of life will be formed.' Through that, the 'blessed reality' of world peace at last would come.[34]

Before Madame Pandit turned to the United Nations though, she and her brother had to face at last the monumental event they had dreamt of for so long: India was about to hold elections, over the months of January and February 1952. Nehru threw himself into the process, travelling 25,000 miles by air, sea and land, speaking directly to almost 20 million people. About 60 per cent of those registered to vote came to the polls, a staggering 176 million people.[35] Eleanor Roosevelt, during a visit to India the next month, marvelled at the entire enterprise, and commended Nehru for his 'remarkable campaigning'.[36]

Nehru was richly rewarded for his efforts, his Congress party walking away with nearly 75 per cent of all seats in the new Parliament.[37] Nehru's prestige and power was now backed by a huge popular mandate. It was a vindication of his vision, and a testament to his tremendous political skills.

Back at the United Nations, hope was building that the Human Rights Commission would complete its work during its eighth session, held in late spring 1952. Although they worked with all due but deliberate speed, this turned out not to be possible. Several items having to do with implementation and some related matters could not be addressed in time and the Commission had to request permission to complete its work during its ninth session in 1953. By this point, Hansa Mehta was simply exhausted, and felt that she had contributed everything she could to the cause of human rights. She stepped down from her six-year service on the Commission. Her departure diminished India's capabilities, as her replacement, Kamaladevi Chattopadhyay, though a Gandhian activist with several plaudits to her name, only lasted one session and disrupted the continuity of thought and purpose that Mehta had been able to maintain.

The Human Rights Commission brought the covenants to

near completion, but was again unable to attend to some lingering matters. They would be given one more year.

Now, fortune seemed to smile on India's efforts. As the General Assembly opened at the end of 1953 for its eighth session, India put Madame Pandit up for president of the Assembly. She won and became the first woman to hold that post. It was a tribute to her talents, and the esteem with which she and India were held. She was supported in secret ballot by the Commonwealth, the US and the Soviet delegations.[38]

Nehru's plans seemed to be coming together. Indeed, the universal admiration he evoked never seemed greater, as people and politicians venerated him for his integrity and penetrating thought. So extraordinary was Nehru's reputation by this point that even Churchill, who had been returned to power in Britain's 1951 election, sought out the Indian prime minister's advice on world affairs.[39] If anything was emblematic of Nehru's stature, it was surely this—India's old nemesis and staunch advocate of British imperialism asking Gandhi's heir for policy insight.

But even as Nehru was moving his chess pieces into position, the board was changing before the grandmaster's eyes. The Assembly did everything in its power to hasten the completion of the covenants, even transmitting draft resolutions on the remaining issues to the Human Rights Commission. The Commission, for its part, also strove to meet its obligations, and successfully completed its work at the tenth session.[40] The International Covenants on Civil and Political Rights, and Economic and Social Rights were now complete. All that remained was formal adoption by the United Nations and ratification by member states. But the animosity of the Cold War proved too much, with fear and doubt lurking behind every action. The conflict in Korea—a result of a split in the peninsula stemming from the post-war settlement—as well as the armistice that ended the war in 1953 had exacerbated the fractious atmosphere. Nehru felt the pressure from all sides, and knew that he had to take dramatic action if he was to counter it.

THE SPIRIT OF BANDUNG

In April of 1955, India helped to organize a summit of free states throughout Asia and Africa. Essentially, the meeting brought together representatives from the entire part of the globe not subsumed by Cold War alliances. India co-organized the event with a number of its regional neighbours, including Pakistan and Indonesia. The event, the Asian–African Conference for International Order, was to be held in an Indonesian city, and soon came to be known eponymously as the Bandung Conference.[41]

In his major address at the Conference, Nehru drew attention to a comment made by the prime minister of Burma, who said that the meeting had attempted 'to arrive at common opinion and common outlook' by overcoming differences. Nehru saw things another way. While lauding the achievements of the Conference as 'great,' because there was general agreement on all resolutions, he emphasized that 'much greater has been the background of all of those agreements. We had to wrestle with our differences. We are not yes-men sitting here to say "yes" to this country or that, not even to one another.'

Nehru stressed on the principle of difference, and suggested that achievement in international relations had to rest on the recognition and affirmation of difference. Nehru made clear moments later that what was on his mind was what was going on in the UN, and in the Human Rights Commission. 'Of course, Europe and Asia and America are all dependent on one another. It is not right to think in terms of isolation in this modern world which is moving towards the ideal of One World.'[42]

A few days later, in a speech to India's lower house of Parliament, the Lok Sabha, he was unequivocal: 'Each major decision of the Conference happily refers to the United Nations and to world problems and ideals. We believe that from Bandung our great organization, the United Nations, has derived strength. This means in turn that Asia and Africa must play an increasing role in the conduct and destiny of the world organization.'[43]

Nehru's faith in an international human rights charter and the creation of One World was unshakeable. This was most evident in the fate of 'external' Indians, the issue that had received significant attention at the Asian Relations Conference in 1947 (see Chapter 5). Conversely, the issue did not come up at Bandung at all, reflecting the fact that India had been true to its word and had not, as a matter of foreign policy with any other country, brought up concerns related to migratory populations. [44] The reason was simple. This was the purview of the United Nations, and the new covenants on human rights.

Some members of the United States' establishment were very skeptical about Bandung. Nehru went out of his way to assuage their fears, repeatedly stating his affection for America and Europe, if not for colonial policies and warmongering. 'We want to be friends with the West and friends with [the] East and friends with everybody,' he noted.[45]

Nehru hoped that the West would trust him. For now, it was the Soviet side that most needed his attention, for they had been repeatedly spurned in the UN and were particularly upset about the split of the covenant of human rights into two, which the Soviets saw as an American conspiracy to devalue economic and social rights. Nehru thought the Soviet position was misinformed, both factually, since it was India that had led the fight to split the covenant, and politically, since India believed that the creation of two covenants was in fact essential to the legitimacy of both.

In June 1955, Nehru journeyed to the Soviet Union, where, as in the United States, he was met with rapturous audiences. Reuters reported that the reception was the 'biggest outburst of enthusiasm' since the celebrations marking the end of World War II. Nehru's arrival was front-page news, accompanied by praise of his message of 'peaceful co-existence'. The crowds thronged and threw flowers at his motorcade, which wound slowly through them rather than making the hasty dash usual in Moscow.[46]

Nehru was all praise for his hosts, bending over backwards to extend a hand of friendship and win their trust. While personally he had affinity for some Soviet policies, and was especially grateful for their consistent public stands against imperialism and racism, this had not stopped him from fighting against many of their positions. Nowhere was this more clear than in the Human Rights Commission where, time and again, the Soviets angrily denounced Indian objectives.

From the outset until 1953, most of this resistance stemmed from Stalin's political proclivities. Stalin was wary of any interference in his internal affairs, not least because he maintained a ruthless, iron grip on the state. Nehru's vision of transparent states accountable to a united world government chartered around actionable human rights certainly ran counter to Stalin's preference for authoritarianism and secrecy. Stalin's successor, Nikita Khrushchev, seemed different, somewhat more open-minded and liberal.

Nehru saw this as a strategic moment when people of goodwill and vision could finally bring about permanent peace. He made every effort to show how much he admired and respected the Soviet people.

His efforts were a huge success in the Soviet Union. But the West reacted frostily. A United Press report could not contain its disdain, writing that Nehru's visit amounted to staged diplomatic exhibitionism. The Russians, they went on, reacted hysterically to the Indian prime minister, who failed to challenge his hosts on any of their domestic abuses.[47]

The hypocrisy was startling, since Nehru had been accorded the same reception wherever he travelled. The US press and people had gone equally agog in 1949. And Nehru then, as in 1955, muted his criticism of his host's shortcomings, in the former case related to US racial policies.

But the bad blood between the bi-polar power blocs ran deep. The United Press report only highlighted the difficulty of the challenge Nehru faced. He could not simply superficially call for a new global community. Rather, he had to transfuse his commitment to One World to both people and politicians across the East and West. Only global agreement on its necessity could bring One World into being.

Nehru's efforts in wooing the Soviets bore immediate fruit, as Khrushchev announced plans to reciprocate and visit India later that year. The Russian press gave the visit extensive coverage, with both *Pravda* and *Izvestiya* reporting on details of travel and speeches. Khrushchev was accompanied by Soviet Premier Nikolai Bulganin, assuring that the trip was given priority in Soviet policy.

Nehru welcomed the delegation to Delhi by citing Gandhi and saying that the Mahatma 'called on us to free ourselves from hatred and coercion, to be friends with everyone and at the same time to hold to our convictions and principles. We make so bold as to use this approach even with regard to those who do not agree with us . . . It is in this spirit that the people of India approach the great Soviet people, seeking friendship and cooperation.'[48]

In his official report to the Supreme Soviet upon their return to Moscow, Bulganin noted that the trip to India 'surpassed all our expectations'. A million people greeted them in Delhi, and three million turned out in Calcutta, which made the deepest impression on the Soviet leaders. Bulganin was especially effusive in his praise of Nehru, calling him 'an outstanding statesman of our epoch'. And, importantly, he asserted that the trip 'confirmed again and again . . . the principle of peaceful coexistence among states with different social and political systems'.[49]

While there could be no doubt that Nehru had effectively warmed relations with the Soviets, there were signs of trouble on the horizon. Even while praising India's role as 'initiator and outstanding participant' in the Bandung Conference, Bulganin in a speech to the Indian Parliament reinforced his view that 'national interests' had to be guaranteed.[50] In his report to the Supreme Soviet, he emphasized that the Indo-Soviet agreement following the visit confirmed 'devotion' to sovereignty and territorial integrity, and particularly 'noninterference in each other's internal affairs for any economic, political, or ideological motives'.[51]

The Indian reason for signing this agreement, which in its endorsement of state sovereignty stood at odds with Indian aims at the UN, stemmed in part from the fact that the Communist Party of India, under direction from the Soviet Union, had unsuccessfully tried to overthrow the Indian government in the early years of its existence.[52] What was significant from Nehru's point of view was that this was a bilateral accord, and did not necessarily impact changes wrought at the global level by UN policy.[53] To the Soviets, this was a distinction without a difference, and they saw the agreement as a new willingness on the part of India to support the Soviet position in favour of strong state sovereignty in international relations.

In part, the Soviets could be forgiven for their misunderstanding, for Nehru had made much of his concept of Panchsheel, or Five Principles, at a reception for Khrushchev and Bulganin, building off of an initial speech he had given in the Lok Sabha on the subject in September, shortly before their arrival. Panchsheel was meant to serve as the foundation for 'peaceful-co-existence' between all peoples. The Five Principles were territorial integrity and sovereignty, non-aggression, non-interference in internal affairs, equality and mutual benefit, and peaceful co-existence.

Panchsheel had originated as an agreement in 1954 between India and China, stemming from the crisis in Tibet over Chinese territorial claims and Indian sanctuary given to the Dalai Lama. The original agreement was explicit that it was a bilateral agreement and was about 'mutual' non-aggression.[54] For Nehru, Panchsheel reflected the equality of all states and the respect that each had to hold for the other. One state could not, and should not, tell another how to live. It was again the principle of difference that underlay the policy. He said: 'The conception of Panchsheel means that there may be different ways of progress, possibly different outlooks, but that, broadly, the ultimate objectives may be the same . . . truth is not confined to one country or one people.'[55]

The only ethical way forward, in true Gandhian fashion, was to recognize and honour these differences while simultaneously trying to bring harmony between them. The twin covenants on human rights symbolized this method and would herald an incipient form of One World.

For the most part, the Soviets and most other observers missed the nuances in Nehru's intentions. Khrushchev was completely taken by the adulation he received in India, and played to the crowds' deeply felt anti-imperialism by harshly criticizing the West. Nehru took exception in a closed-door Congress session to some of the Soviet comments, especially anything that made a direct attack on particular Western countries.[56] The attacks went against the grain of everything Nehru was trying to achieve.

But Khrushchev's comments were little more than an impolite, and impolitic, slip-up. For the most part, the world was talking about Non-alignment and the Panchsheel. Bandung and the Soviet visits were considered great achievements, and India basked in the glow of foreign policy success.

COLD WAR COLLISION

But this was to prove an ephemeral spring as the icy gusts of the Cold War soon returned with a vengeance. In the latter half of 1956, two seemingly unrelated events would again move the world to crisis.

In July, Egypt nationalized the Suez Canal. Egypt and Britain had disagreed on the fate of the Canal zone from the early 1920s, when Egypt had become independent. By the '40s, it was Britain's largest overseas military base. Egyptians demanded that the Suez be demilitarized and, when Britain dragged its feet, brought the matter before the United Nations. The Arab war with the new state of Israel in 1948–49 added to the combustible situation.

Meanwhile, a treaty that they had signed with Egypt regarding rights and privileges related to the Suez was set to expire in December 1956. Britain believed that this was merely a technicality and that they would maintain their special hold on the Suez in perpetuity.

But the Free Officers Revolution in 1952, which brought the socialist Gamal Nasser to power, had changed the situation in Egypt dramatically. Nasser wanted complete independence for Egypt and saw the British presence as lingering colonialism.

Cold War events in 1956 related to Egypt's recognition of communist China and US retaliation led Nasser to nationalize the company that ran the Canal. Britain, along with France and Israel, resented this move, which they saw as both a military and commercial threat.[57]

Nehru saw the great danger that the mounting anger represented. Western sabre rattling aroused anti-colonial passions not only in Egypt, but throughout the newly independent worlds of Asia and Africa. Nehru cautioned against threats of force and thought that a just and equitable solution could be reached.[58] He threw himself personally into the conflict and tried to mediate between the aggrieved parties, even offering to send Indian forces into Egypt as part of a UN operation to maintain peace. His efforts were greatly appreciated by Britain's Left, and by the United States. So Nehru was all the more shocked, and hurt, when Britain, in alliance with France and Israel, invaded Egypt soon thereafter.

To make matters worse, at exactly the same moment, the Soviet Union invaded Hungary to suppress an uprising against Moscow's control. For all of Nehru's outreach efforts the previous year, he still had remarkably poor communication channels behind the Iron Curtain. On top of this, the Indian ambassador to Moscow, in a moment of it-can't-be-worse timing, had taken ill and was out of commission, and he was the only reliable source available. Nehru simply did not understand what was going on in the Soviet satellite. So when the US came calling, asking if India would support bringing the invasion up at the UN, Nehru pleaded ignorance.[59]

Nehru's sterling reputation took a hit because of his delay at this crucial juncture. The Indian diplomatic establishment immediately began to send strong signals that Nehru had to take an unequivocal stand against the invasion, or risk eroding his credibility.

For Nehru, the Soviet invasion was an egregious bolt of bad luck. The Soviets and the United States had actually agreed that the British-led invasion of Egypt was unacceptable, and Nehru needed them on board to maintain pressure on the Suez aggressors. Additionally, Nehru had recognized a significant shift in Soviet attitudes under Khrushchev. Earlier in 1956, Khrushchev had famously denounced Stalin's purges and distanced himself from his predecessor's style and predilections.[60]

Nehru had really been hoping for adoption of the international covenants, and he saw the Soviets, not the West, as the greatest challenge to passage. The twin invasions in late 1956 clearly made progress on human rights unlikely. But, as the secretary general of the Ministry of External Affairs, N.R. Pillai, pointed out in a top-secret note, Nehru needed to act on Hungary 'with a view to deciding our attitude in the light of the principles we have been advocating'. Inaction was undermining India's integrity, and its high-minded foreign policy.[61]

By early November, Nehru was persuaded and began to take a more critical view of Soviet actions. His Moscow ambassador now recovered, Nehru began a flurry of diplomatic activity to try to calm the situation.

The most damaging blow came next. The cause was the head of India's delegation to the United Nations, V.K. Krishna Menon. When Madame Pandit became president of the General Assembly in 1953, she had had to dissociate herself from her country's delegation, since she now had to preside equitably over the entire assembly. The vacancy was filled by Menon, who had served with Pandit in the delegation. Menon was an acrimonious figure, and very ideologically driven. He held animus for the West, and the United States in particular. Madame Pandit barely concealed her contempt for the man.[62] But Menon was a highly regarded intellectual, and Nehru enjoyed sparring with him. By 1954, in a fateful move, Menon had used his bond with the prime minister to replace Madame Pandit as Nehru's prime counsel on international relations.[63]

Nehru's faith reinforced Menon's own high impression of himself, and he acted with authority, often disregarding proper diplomatic procedures and channels. So just as Nehru was beginning to privately and publicly critique the Soviet invasion, Menon, as a limb moving of its own accord, spoke in the UN against any criticism of the Soviet Union. When a motion came up to condemn the Soviet use of force, India abstained, Menon infamously declaring that Hungary was an 'internal matter'.

Many of India's friends were aghast, most disturbed by the unmistakable double standard that had just been applied to the Western and Soviet alliances. All of Nehru's nuances were lost. Nehru's reputation as honest broker, as the giant among statesmen and -women, was severely damaged.

Nehru expressed his disapproval of Menon's actions immediately by telegram, and days later spoke in the Lok Sabha demanding Soviet withdrawal and expressing his support for Hungarian self-determination. But it was too little, too late.

Madame Pandit, now the high commissioner in London, warned her brother that the situation was dire and very bad news for India's diplomatic health.[64] The utopia that had seemed so near their grasp in the aftermath of World War II, and for which they had worked so assiduously, seemed to be slipping through their fingers.

TOWARDS A BETTER FUTURE

Nehru decided that he had but one course open to him. He had to take his message directly to the world's people.[65] So, a few weeks later, he decided to use his marquee speech in the UN General Assembly as a final, stirring rallying cry for One World. He titled his speech 'Towards a World Community'.[66]

The world, he warned, faced a stark choice. On the one hand, 'we have what is called a cold war . . . But the idea of the cold war is the very negation of what the United Nations stands for . . . Cold wars mean nourishing the idea of war in the minds of men.'

The Cold War, he noted, had recently led to two extraordinary developments: Egypt and Hungary. Compensating for Krishna Menon's gaffe, and making clear his own position, he explicitly condemned both as 'very important and very unfortunate happenings'. But both, he argued, had oxymoronically been heartening, since they also revealed just how potent global action actually was. 'The one big thing that has emerged is that world opinion represented in the United Nations Assembly, and elsewhere, is today a strong enough factor not to tolerate what it considers wrong.'

Because the people of the world united in opposition to the invasions, an important precedent was created. 'Every country, weak or strong, will have to think twice before it does something which enrages world opinion. That itself shows the development of some kind of a conscience of the world.' The language powerfully evoked Madame Pandit's stirring speech to the same assembly back in 1946.

'I submit to you,' he went on, 'that this idea of the cold war is essentially and fundamentally wrong. It is immoral. It is opposed to all ideas of peace and cooperation. Therefore, let us be clear in our minds as to what the right way is.'

Turning to the horizon, he soulfully argued: 'We must look ahead. The only way to look ahead assuredly is for some kind of a world order, One World, to emerge.'

Nehru now tried to be specific. First, he confessed that there 'is plenty of hatred and bitterness in the world today . . . We cannot become angels . . . ' The solution lay in the tools that Gandhi had given to humankind. Our 'actions in a larger way as individuals and as nations might perhaps be so controlled, without giving up a single principle or opinion that we hold, as not to make the path of reconciliation difficult.' To put it another way, the 'means are as important as ends. If the means are not right, the end is also likely to be not right, however much we may want it to be right.'

So, he concluded, 'The means should always be peaceful, not merely in an external way in the non-use of armaments, but in the approach of the mind. That approach will create a climate of peace which will help greatly in the solution of our problems.'

The world had to approach the situation in Egypt and Hungary with 'understanding and sympathy' even as it rejected aggression. Neither the UN nor anyone else should address the matter with 'anger or with the desire to humiliate anybody', for those methods would, when all was said and done, only make matters worse.

While non-violent action was thus the only option, Nehru urged the world to take several other concrete steps. He called for disarmament, and the removal of all national armed forces from foreign soil, even if those forces were there by agreement of the two countries concerned. The placement of external militaries, he charged, never involved only the countries concerned in the exchange. Instead, everyone was negatively impacted, since the military presence heightened fear and furthered arms expansion.

Finally, Nehru called on the nations of the world to abide by the principles of independence as defined by the UN Charter. What did this kind of independence mean? 'The countries that are dominated by another country should cease to be so dominated.' While that was straightforward, this did not mean that any state could do whatever it pleased. 'No country, or at any rate very few countries in the world, can be said to be independent in the sense that they can do anything they like. There are restraining factors, and quite rightly. In the final analysis, the United Nations itself is a restraining factor in regard to countries misbehaving or taking advantage of their so-called independence to interfere with the independence of others. Every country's independence should be limited in this sense.'[67]

Nehru was warmly received. His talk was front-page news in *The New York Times* the next day.

Almost a year later, the Soviet Union introduced a resolution in the UN General Assembly that adopted Nehru's Panchsheel platform to help promote the peaceful co-existence of states. India was heartened by the proposal, but put forward a slightly modified version, in conjunction with Yugoslavia and Sweden. The primary difference between the two proposals was that the Indian-sponsored version noted that simple co-existence, living together side by side, was not enough. Rather, states had to actively 'strengthen international peace' and develop cooperative relations.[68]

During the debate that followed, virtually all of the concerns that Nehru had raised in his 1956 speech were considered. The Soviets and the Western allies discussed their grievances with each other openly, and sometimes fiercely. In the end, though, the Soviets withdrew their measure in deference to the three-power proposal, and the Assembly then voted unanimously to adopt the Resolution. Both the Soviet Union and the United States were most supportive of the plan. For Nehru, this proved that in 'the final analysis, there is a great deal in common between these apparently rival great powers'. He hoped that if 'the spirit underlying the resolution actuates the Governments concerned, a very great deal of progress would be made'.[69]

His hope restored, Nehru continued to advance his cause. This culminated in his final 'impassioned plea' to the UN General Assembly in November 1961, made against the backdrop of the just-resolved Berlin Crisis and the ongoing construction of the Berlin Wall, splitting the city into East and West halves. This time, he boiled things down to their simplest and most guttural terms. 'It is destruction or survival.'

It was not a choice between war and peace, he said. Rather, humanity had to 'co-operate or perish'. There was to be 'co-existence or no existence at all'.

As always, Nehru roused his audience and they roared their approval. He received a standing ovation.[70]

He had done everything in his power to make real the better world that so many desired. It was now in the hands of all of earth's people to decide on the future they wanted.

EPILOGUE

Nehru never lived to see his dreams realized. In late 1962, he sadly observed: 'We were living in a world of illusion . . . [W]e were getting out of touch with reality in the modern world and we were living in an artificial world of our own creation. We have been shocked out of it.'[1] What sparked this final collapse of his idealism was the Sino-Indian War, which had ended weeks before. China, which Nehru had long considered a friend and ally, had unexpectedly invaded India and easily breezed through the subcontinent's defences, incompetently helmed by Krishna Menon. Then, just as suddenly, they withdrew their forces.[2]

The primary impetus for the war had to do with Chinese unhappiness with popular support in India for Tibet and its spiritual leader, the Dalai Lama, to whom India had given refuge. China began to send signals with maps that showed Chinese possession of Indian territory, but Nehru thought the whole thing a misunderstanding that could be easily resolved. The whole affair was a cruel blow.

But China was merely the straw that broke the camel's back. For Nehru had made no headway on his grand vision for the world. The international covenants on human rights remained stalled. And just prior to the Chinese invasion, the Cuban Missile Crisis brought the Cold War archenemies 'eyeball to eyeball', and everyone else to the brink of nuclear holocaust. The world seemed bent on conflict, and in his last days, Nehru finally gave in.[3]

Critics everywhere spent 1962 and 1963 blasting Nehru's policy of Non-alignment. Neutrality was naive and foolish, they called out in chorus.

His other way rejected, Nehru concluded that he had to reconfigure India for the world as it was and as it was going to remain, not as he wished it to be. Months after stating his disillusionment, the sixteenth amendment to the Indian Constitution was passed, retroactively adding in specific language throughout the document to preserve and maintain 'the sovereignty and integrity of India'. The amendment represented the antithesis of everything for which Nehru, and Gandhi, had fought for two decades.[4] Nehru had allowed a dystopic realism to replace his high-minded idealism. The following year, he died a broken man.

But even as her brother was giving in to despair, Madame Pandit kept the faith. In a dramatic speech in 1962, coinciding with her brother's more morose postmortem on the Sino-Indian war, she gave an impassioned defence of Nehru's policies and actions, and urged her audience to believe once again.

She criticized the cynical opposition to Non-alignment as entirely misguided. Opponents of 'Nehrutrality', as they derisively called it, mistook Non-alignment for an uneven neutralism that leaned towards the Soviet Union. The tilt, they charged, revealed the inconsistencies and absurdities of a bankrupt policy. But these critics, Madame Pandit charged, did not understand Non-alignment at all.

What everyone missed, she explained, was that Non-alignment was merely 'an aspect of India's foreign policy', a just means to a just end. 'Inter-dependence, rather than isolation, is the key-note of India's policy.' The actual 'objectives of this foreign policy are peace and enlargement of human freedom'.

These goals had been articulated as early as September 1946, when Nehru explained that India's foreign policy would have several defining features. 'These features were: 1. Full participation in international conferences . . . 2. Close contacts with other nations and co-operation with them in the furtherance of world peace. 3. Non-alignment with power groups. 4. Belief in the indivisibility of peace and freedom. 5. Special concern for emancipation of colonial and dependent countries. 6. Opposition to racialism. [and] 7. Claim for equality and honourable treatment for the people of India anywhere in the world.'

All of this was guided by the eighth feature: 'Belief in the ultimate evolution of "One World" based on closer co-operation and absence of exploitation.' Ever since Nehru first laid this out, the 'policy with these features has . . . been the avowed foreign policy of this country.' Non-alignment, in this context, was (and remained) 'a challenge to the concept of a bi-polar world'.

'The cold-war approach to international politics leads to the adoption of an attitude which visualises the world as being divided into two rigidly demarcated and solidly consolidated power blocks . . . Non-alignment attacks the very basis of this attitude . . . ' Military solutions could not address international problems in any lasting way, she went on, and therefore were no solution at all. Instead, the 'U.N. provides a means to find this solution. It is therefore necessary to strengthen the U.N.'

'If on the forum of U.N. or at other international gatherings,

Indian representatives were found to vote sometimes with representatives of the Anglo-American Block and at other times with representatives of [the] Soviet Block, this is not because of a desire on the part of India to keep balance between her relations with the two blocks, but because of her commitment to certain principles and objectives which require her to vote in a particular way, irrespective of whether that vote sided with one block or the other.'

The principles of Panchsheel would then help to maintain peaceful international relations. 'It is along these lines that India has during the past 17 years or so attempted to translate its foreign policy on concrete issues.'

Madame Pandit then took aim at realists. 'Criticism is very often expressed that in the pursuit of idealistic objectives the framers of India's policy have sacrificed national interest. While it is true that the policy of every country has to serve the cause of national interest, the problem of defining national interests continues to pose difficulty.' India's policy was realistic, she argued, and the critics were the ones who were not.

Quoting Nehru, she said, 'Some people may think of the interest of their country regardless of other countries, or take a short-distance view, and others may think that in the long-term policy the interest of another country is as important to them as that of their own country.' The notion that the other–the other country, the other state, the other community, the other person–had to be respected, and that it was bound to the self in a universal bond of kinship was, of course, vintage Gandhi, now applied to foreign policy.

'Realism also dictates the necessity of appreciating the changed character of world politics, and the role of power and the new ways of security. With the changed character of world politics security may have to be sought not only from military strength but also from policies and political processes.'

Finally, she turned to the Chinese invasion. 'That the policy of non-alignment has not prevented the Chinese aggression is a fact. But that need not necessarily be considered as a failure of that policy, for after all that was not the function of Non-alignment only.' Indeed, if anything, the Chinese conflict underscored the success of Non-alignment, and the need for an even greater pursuit of India's larger goal of a peaceful, democratic world community. 'In so far as the countries of the Western Block have come to our aid and many countries of the communist Block have also sympathized with us, the issue of Sino-Indian conflict has not become a cold war issue.'

Non-alignment helped India to reach out to people across the globe, and to be on friendly terms across blocs, reducing tensions and promoting amicable international relations. 'In view of these facts, it would be difficult to say that the policy of non-alignment has failed.'[5]

Madame Pandit's rousing defence hit home for some. In 1966, S. Radhakrishnan, the president of India, in association with a number of prominent figures, published a book of essays honouring Mahatma Gandhi. It was entitled *Mahatma Gandhi and One World*. Some of the writers included long-time Gandhian veterans like J.B. Kripalani, a former president of the Indian National Congress, and Kakasaheb Kalelkar, a philospher from Gandhi's home state of Gujarat.

In his piece, Radhakrishnan said: 'It is a change in the minds of men that has to be brought about. We are still believing in the nation State and in the right to use force to have our own aims realized. These are things which have us by the throat.

'Though . . . we call ourselves members of the United Nations, our loyalties are to our own nation States; they are not to the world as a whole, not to humanity as a whole. We must break away from the past . . . Nationalism is not the highest concept. The highest concept is world community.'

'The concept of One World must be implemented in every action of every nation, if that One World is to be established.' It, he concluded, 'is the purpose of Providence'.[6]

Radhakrishnan's essay was based on a speech he had delivered at the UN in 1963. The other contributors, all the Mahatma's friends and associates, then expanded on the premise and explained how and why One World represented Gandhi's dream.

Kamaladevi Chattopadhyay, who had replaced Hansa Mehta for one year on the Human Rights Commission, explained it most succinctly. Gandhi, she said 'believed in sovereignty in terms of an authority which directed the national community through democratic process, that is, "consent". The relationship between States, also, therefore emerged from a mutual identity, common interest and purpose basic to all human existence. Military or similar alliances and expansionist actions are ruled out. The emphasis is on the "right conduct" between fellow States.'

She ended by quoting Gandhi. 'I would not like to live in this world if it is not to be One World.'[7]

Over the next few years, Madame Pandit would continue the fight, defending the policy vision she, her brother and Gandhi had struggled to achieve for so many years, and urging audiences worldwide to embrace the goal of genuine international cooperation.[8] In one of her last major addresses on the subject, she noted that the 'past years have been difficult ones for those who labored for peace–it seems often that one is fighting a losing battle, but it is at just such times that we need courage'. Quoting the legendary secretary general of the United Nations, Dag Hammarskjöld, Madame Pandit concluded poetically: 'When the morning freshness has been replaced by the weariness of midday, when the leg muscles quiver under the strain; the climb seems endless and suddenly nothing will go quite as you wish–it is then that you must not hesitate.'[9]

*

Despite Madame Pandit's best efforts, India began to drift away from its founding inspiration almost immediately after Nehru faded. Most disturbing was the fact that Nehru's daughter, Indira Gandhi, led as Indian prime minister the charge for a new, more harshly defined nationalism that prized sovereignty and a muscular foreign policy. Madame Pandit fought against these trends, growing increasingly distant from her niece and eventually breaking with Mrs Gandhi over the dictatorial powers she assumed during her declaration of Emergency between 1975 and 1977.[10]

But while India ceased to champion the cause of One World, events have unfolded in the ensuing decades that have vindicated the integrity and strength of the original vision. The International Covenants on Civil and Political, and Economic, Social, and Cultural Rights were adopted by the General Assembly in 1966, and came into effect in 1976. The vast majority of the world–over 160 countries–are parties to both covenants.

Mechanisms for the implementation of human rights include a Human Rights Committee, created and empowered by the International Covenant on Civil and Political Rights. More recently, in 1993, the United Nations created the Office of the High Commissioner for Human Rights. The high commissioner holds the rank of undersecretary general, and is answerable directly to the secretary general.[11] Together with the International Court of Justice and the newly created International Criminal Court, the Committee and the high commissioner represent virtually all aspects of the Framework for Implementation that Hansa Mehta had proposed and championed as Chair of the Working Group on Implementation in the second session of the Human Rights Commission back in 1947.[12]

More broadly, the creation of the European Union stands as testimony to the promise of supra-national integration. Increasing economic interdependencies likewise speak to the limits of the old order of nation states. And so, the dream lives on.

But the world of the twenty-first century, of course, is not the one that Nehru had faced, and the problems are not the same either. Catastrophic climate change; transnational, globalized terrorism committed by both state and non-state actors; jingoistic nationalism and its twin, xenophobia; pandemic public health concerns; the inability to create sustainable development agendas—these are the problems the world now confronts.

Nor is the United Nations the organization that Nehru and his allies had hoped for. It is large and unwieldy. There are 192 member states, and their representatives all too often seek only to protect the narrow interests of their own government, many of which do not represent the interests or wishes of their people. The bureaucracy does not attract the best and the brightest. The organization as a whole is beholden to Great Power politics, and particularly to the whim of the United States, at least in terms of its core peace and defence arm, the Security Council. And, in terms of its primary mission of maintaining peace and security, the UN is a body that has failed, the charred corpses of those who have died in Vietnam, Cambodia, Iran and Iraq, Bosnia, Afghanistan and countless other places, all standing as grim testimony to the UN's weakness.

And so it is tempting to say that the UN is an organization that perhaps should be abandoned, joining its predecessor, the League of Nations, on the dust heap of history. But with what alternative would we be faced? Without the United Nations, in some version or another, we would be left with the unbridled whims of nation states and other networked actors, creating the kind of environment that gave rise to both the First and the Second World Wars. Regional alliances or organizations like the G20, the partnership of developed and emerging economies, while producing useful space for dialogue and action, also ultimately face any number of limitations, not least that they are even less representative and just as susceptible to many of the problems currently plaguing the UN.

The challenges we face, as those of Nehru's time, intricately intertwine the global and the local. The international element remains fundamental to solving humanity's problems. And for all its shortcomings, the UN has done much that is good, leading the way, however haltingly or circuitously, on human rights, climate control and a host of other critical issues. So, if the United Nations remains key to future progress, yet is hampered by organizational flaws and Machiavellian motivations, what path does the world take moving forward?

Global climate change and enduring poverty pose profound challenges. Violent weather and rising water levels caused by warming seas and melting ice caps pose existential threats to many countries and peoples. Migrant and displaced populations moving due to distress caused by disaster, or poverty, and related public health menaces are huge burdens to bear.

No country can solve problems of such magnitude on its own. For the world in so many ways has never been more borderless. The stand of one country on climate change will have environmental repercussions throughout the planet. The recent financial crisis (2008–11) stemming from derivative markets and multinational banks based mainly in the United States has reverberated throughout the world, and bad policy and contagion make for continued economic instability. Unless all countries and peoples act in concert, such threats cannot be contained.

The United Nations has tried to address many such internationally interconnected issues, whether in the form of the Kyoto Protocols and follow-ups such as the Cancún meeting to address global warming, or with respect to the Millennium Development Goals, or the new Responsibility to Protect (R2P) initiative. But for all its good intentions, the UN remains far from major accomplishment on even one such project. Cancún, while 'realist', does not in any way alter our course–we remain headed towards catastrophic climate change in the near future. The Millennium Development Goals, ranging from halving world poverty to implementing universal primary school education to stopping the spread of AIDS, look to go unmet. And R2P, while a major step forward, seems sadly utopian in the era of Sudan and Katrina and any number of more mundane instances where states have failed to protect their people from harm.[13]

Much of this failure stems from a leadership vacuum. Many countries have dragged their feet on climate change issues, while some developed countries have resisted living up to their funding commitment to the Millennium Development Goals. R2P has been applied selectively even as some powerful countries have tried to revise norms regarding torture.[14]

Many countries are using this moment to jockey for positions of power, but this is a self-interested approach by means of which none of the aforementioned problems can possibly be addressed. And the world *needs* these problems to be solved, and soon. And for that, the world *needs* the United Nations to succeed, for its own sake as much as for any greater moral principle.

The United Nations must have an efficient and capable bureaucracy; it must have the resources to carry on its work; and it must transcend its members' propensity to act solely on the basis of state interest. Countries must commit to sending the most skilled and accomplished to serve in the international institution. And all efforts to suitably fund the UN should be made, while simultaneously advancing mechanisms of transparency and accountability.

Ultimately, the United Nations must become more democratic. As some prominent scholars have recently argued, there needs to be 'layered cosmopolitan perspectives' that account for local, regional and national formations.[15] How precisely this might be done is a matter of debate. Proposals include weighted voting schemes and the creation of a new, democratically elected global parliament.[16] We—all of us—must examine these proposals carefully and take a stand in support of a plan that balances the voices of states with voices of people grouped together under a number of varied rubrics. Only by making the UN more responsive and representative can the international institution live up to the dreams of its creators and the needs of our time.

Nehru's words echo across the decades: 'All this may seem fantastic and impractical in the modern world . . . And yet we have seen repeatedly the failure of other methods and nothing can be less practical than to pursue a method that has failed again and again.'[17]

NOTES

PREFACE

1. Ayesha Jalal, *Democracy and Authoritarianism in South Asia: A Comparative and Historical Perspective* (Cambridge: Cambridge University Press, 1995); Ayesha Jalal, *The State of Martial Rule: The Origins of Pakistan's Political Economy of Defence* (Cambridge: Cambridge University Press, 1990); Dipesh Chakrabarty, Rochona Majumdar and Andrew Sartori, eds, *From the Colonial to the Postcolonial: India and Pakistan in Transition* (New Delhi: Oxford University Press, 2007); Yasmin Saikia, *Women, War and the Making of Bangladesh: Remembering 1971* (Durham, North Carolina: Duke University Press, 2011); Joya Chatterji, *The Spoils of Partition: Bengal and India, 1947–1967* (Cambridge: Cambridge University Press, 2011); Sarah Ansari, *Life after Partition: Migration, Community and Strife in Sindh, 1947–1962* (Karachi: Oxford University Press, 2005); and Ramachandra Guha, *India after Gandhi: The History of the World's Largest Democracy* (New York: HarperCollins, 2007). Jalal clearly leads the field here by over a decade. Chakrabarty's volume contains contributions from a number of historians. This list is only meant to be emblematic of the growing trend.
2. This is most clearly and persuasively argued in Partha Chatterjee, *Nationalist Thought and the Colonial World: A Derivative Discourse?* (Minneapolis: University of Minnesota Press, 2004, first published 1986). Gandhi's views are generally surmised from a reading of his

famous 1909 tract, *Hind Swaraj*; online at: http://www.mkgandhi.org/swarajya/coverpage.htm. Nehru's vision is often drawn from his *An Autobiography* (London: John Lane, 1936); online at: http://www.questia.com/PM.qst?a=o&d=74007923; and his *Discovery of India* (New York: John Day, 1946).

3. Roger Normand and Sarah Zaidi, *Human Rights at the UN: The Political History of Universal Justice* (Bloomington: Indiana University Press, 2007); Mary Ann Glendon, *A World Made New: Eleanor Roosevelt and the Universal Declaration of Human Rights* (New York: Random House, 2002, first published 2001); Johannes Morsink, *The Universal Declaration of Human Rights: Origins, Drafting & Intent* (Philadelphia: University of Pennsylvania Press, 1999); Henry J. Steiner, Philip Alston and Ryan Goodman, *International Human Rights in Context: Law, Politics, Morals* (New York: Oxford University Press, third edition, 2008); Elizabeth Borgwardt, *A New Deal for the World: America's Vision for Human Rights* (Cambridge, Massachusetts: Harvard University Press, 2005).
4. Guha, *India after Gandhi*, especially pp. 161–78.
5. This is a bit different from the otherwise nuanced view advanced in one of the definitive textbooks on post-colonial Indian government and policy. Robert Hardgrave and Stanley Kochanek describe Non-alignment as 'a pragmatic policy of independent action' that 'by no means precluded an activist stance in the Indian self-interest'. See Robert Hardgrave and Stanley Kochanek, *India: Government and Politics in a Developing Nation* (New York: Harcourt Brace, fifth edition, 1993), pp. 392–96. Mithi Mukherjee rejects the idea of a Gandhian influence on Indian foreign policy, instead viewing Non-alignment as a legacy of empire. See Mithi Mukherjee, '"A World of Illusion": The Legacy of Empire in India's Foreign Relations, 1947–1962', *The International History Review* 32 (2), June 2010, pp. 253–71.

1. THE WORLD AT WAR

1. David M. Kennedy, *Freedom from Fear: The American People in Depression and War, 1929–1945* (New York: Oxford University Press, 2005), pp. 465–515, especially pp. 493, 495, 500–08.
2. I am grateful to my colleague, Jonathan Rosenberg, for clarifying this point.
3. Kennedy, *Freedom from Fear*, pp. 381–425.
4. His attacks on Roma ('Gypsies') would come later.
5. In Germany, this built on a problem that had begun in 1928, when

American banks pulled short-term loans as a result of the then Wall Street boom. I thank my colleague, Benjamin Hett, for clarifying this point for me.

6. Kennedy, *Freedom from Fear*, pp. 1–380.
7. Who started the fire, and for what purpose, remain under debate to this day. A forthcoming book by Benjamin Hett argues persuasively that the Nazis set the fire themselves as part of a conspiracy to consolidate their power.
8. Kennedy, *Freedom from Fear*, p. 502.
9. http://www.americanrhetoric.com/speeches/fdrthefourfreedoms.htm
10. Gandhi's speeches and writings in 1938 and 1939 talk of Hitler as a starkly violent person, but nonetheless a human being who might be transformed. Gandhi wrote directly to Hitler on 23 July 1939 appealing to him 'for the sake of humanity' not to proceed with war to achieve his objectives. *The Collected Works of Mahatma Gandhi* (CWMG), vol. 76, pp. 156–57; http://www.gandhiserve.org/cwmg/VOL076.PDF. Later that year, he noted that 'it seems as if Herr Hitler knows no God but brute force and . . . will listen to nothing else.' Letter to Jivraj Mehta, 5 September 1939, ibid., p. 312. Nonetheless, '[e]ven if Hitler was so minded, he could not devastate seven hundred thousand non-violent villages. He would become non-violent in the process.' Gandhi's discussion with executive members of Gandhi Seva Sangh, 25 October 1939, CWMG, vol. 77, p. 41; http://www.gandhiserve.org/cwmg/VOL077.PDF. Even as late as May 1940, Gandhi notes: 'I do not believe Herr Hitler to be as bad as he is portrayed. He might even have been a friendly power as he may still may be.' Letter to Lord Linlithgow, CWMG, vol. 78, p. 253; http://www.gandhiserve.org/cwmg/VOL078.PDF.
11. Gandhi, 'How to Combat Hitlerism', CWMG, vol. 78, pp. 344–45. I am grateful to my student, Alex Abell, for his astute observations on some of the material in this paragraph.
12. Benjamin Zachariah, *Nehru* (London: Routledge, 2005, first published 2004), p. 11.
13. Nehru's unease mirrored that of many others of the Mahatma's admirers. Indeed, the Congress itself was split on the decision and several senior leaders resigned (temporarily) in protest. Abroad, even as ardent a friend as Betrand Russell, the great English philosopher and pacifist, who had served as president of the India League of England and championed Indian independence, wrote that Gandhi's stand was a threat to India and to England. War, in this case, was

necessary, he argued. Bertrand Russell's letter, *The New York Times*, 5 August 1942, p. 18.

14. 'Text of Resolution Offered by Gandhi', *The New York Times*, 5 August 1942, p. 6. See also http://www.ibiblio.org/pha/policy/1942/420427a.html.
15. The Quit India Resolution endorsed by the All-India Congress, August 1942 [R/3/1/355]. British Library online: http://www.bl.uk/reshelp/findhelpregion/asia/india/indianindependence/transfer/transfer1/index.html.

2. INDIA IN NEW YORK

1. During her tenure as minister, she once faced down an angry mob that had gathered outside her home. She had no security, on the grounds the protest was a democratic right, and the mob had surrounded the house and broken all the windows. Pandit suddenly stormed outside, stood on a chair, and welcomed a conversation with them. Violence was their privilege, she told them, but would only backfire. The crowd dispersed, and she received a letter of apology several weeks later. Vijaya Lakshmi Pandit, *The Scope of Happiness: A Personal Memoir* (New York: Crown Publishers, 1979), pp. 141–43.
2. The Nehrus' mother, Swaroop Rani, collapsed in January 1938 at the end of a party, as she was reaching out to give her daughter Nan a loving, farewell hug. She had had a stroke and died within a few hours. Swaroop Rani's older sister of ten years died immediately after the funeral from grief. Pandit, *The Scope of Happiness*, pp. 144–45.
3. Letter from Gandhi to Chiang Kai-shek, 14 June 1942, CWMG, vol. 83, pp. 25–28; http://www.gandhiserve.org/cwmg/VOL083.PDF.
4. Nicholas Mansergh, E.W. Lumby and Penderel Moon, eds, *The Transfer of Power, 1942–7* (London: Her Majesty's Stationary Office, 1971), vol. 2, no. 235. Secret telegram from Seymour to Eden, includes summary of communication from Chiang Kai-shek to Gandhi, pp. 351–52.
5. Speech at the All-India Congress Committee Meeting, Bombay, 8 August 1942, CWMG, vol. 83, pp. 201–06.
6. Pandit, *The Scope of Happiness*, p. 167. Nehru wrote the letter on 12 April and sent it to Roosevelt via Colonel Louis Johnson, the former American assistant secretary of war. The message was conveyed the next day and Roosevelt replied via Colonel Johnson on the 15th. He thanked Nehru for his letter and assured him of American support

against Japanese aggression. That same day, Colonel Johnson was also informed, in a message clearly meant for Nehru, that FDR had personally tried to put pressure on Churchill to 'prevent the breakdown of negotiations' with Cripps. Letters and documents from February–April 1942, some marked 'Secret and (Strictly) Confidential', declassified by the US State Department in 1995. Europe Files: India, 1942; Summner Welles Papers; Franklin D. Roosevelt Library, Hyde Park, New York.

7. For Pandit's point of view on the famine, see Pandit, *The Scope of Happiness*, pp. 169–73. Amartya Sen has famously analysed the 1943 famine to argue that food was actually available but shortages were created by hoarding and its impact on the market. Amartya Sen, *Poverty and Famines: An Essay on Entitlement and Deprivation* (New Delhi: Oxford University Press, 1999, first published 1981). Prices were already high because India was supplying food, and other materials as well, to the British war effort. The result was induced poverty—food was simply too expensive for most people to afford. The British government in Bengal was slow, inefficient and incompetent in their response to the disaster. Madhusree Mukerjee has argued in a meticulously researched new book that Churchill's racism prevented him from seeing Indians deserving of help, and he denied requests for assistance, diverting food resources to a post-war stockpile for Europe. Additionally, his decision to drastically cut shipping in the Indian Ocean area resulted in widespread shortages in India; fearing an impact on the war effort, British officials began to purchase food grain on the market at any price, triggering hyperinflation. See Madhusree Mukherjee, *Churchill's Secret War: The British Empire and the Ravaging of India during World War II* (New York: Basic Books, 2010). See http://madhusree.com for an excellent rebuttal of criticisms of the book.
8. Description taken from the banner of *India Today*, a bulletin of the India League of America. In Folder: India 1942–45, Box 50, The Sidney Hertzberg Papers, NYPL Manuscripts.
9. As tabulated by the inflation calculator: http://www.dollartimes.com/calculators/inflation.htm.
10. Pandit, *The Scope of Happiness*, pp. 185–87.
11. Confidential memo of conversation between Lord Halifax and NAACP secretary, 24 April 1942, 'Race Relations in the International Arena, 1940–1955', Papers of the NAACP, Part 14, Series A, Group II, Reel 9.
12. Ibid., correspondence between NAACP secretary and numerous others,

including Pearl Buck, Wendell Willkie and Eleanor Roosevelt, many 'private and confidential'.

13. Ibid., Walter White to Clare Booth Luce (personal and confidential), 5 June 1942.
14. Ibid., Pearl Buck to Walter White, 12 June 1942.
15. Ibid., Walter White to Pearl Buck, 15 June 1942.
16. Ibid., Walter White to Clare Booth Luce (personal and confidential), 5 June 1942; White to McIntyre, 1 July 1942.
17. M.S. Venkataramani and B.K. Shrivastava, *Quit India: The American Response to the 1942 Struggle* (New Delhi: Vikas Publishing, 1979), pp. 317–19.
18. The list of places Willkie visited may be found here: http://www.usfamily.net/web/timwalker/sitedocs/tour.html. See also the inside of the book cover to Wendell L. Willkie, *One World* (New York: Simon and Schuster, 1943).
19. Luce to Willkie, 1942 correspondence, Box 113, Folder 5 and Box 115, Clare Booth Luce Papers, Folder 6, LOC.
20. Kenton J. Clymer, *Quest for Freedom: The United States and India's Independence* (New York: Columbia University Press, 1995), pp. 103–07; Venkataramani and Shrivastava, *Quit India*, pp. 316–20.
21. Letter from Walter White to President Harry S. Truman, 10 August 1947, 'Race Relations in the International Arena, 1940–1955', Papers of the NAACP, Part 14, Series A, Group II, Reel 12.
22. Venkataramani and Shrivastava, *Quit India*, pp. 320–23; Willkie, *One World*, particularly pp. 15, 140.
23. 'Text of Willkie's Address to the Nation Renewing His Plea for a Second Front', *The New York Times*, 27 October 1942, p. 8.
24. Luce to Willkie, 1942 correspondence, Box 115, Folder 6, Clare Booth Luce Papers, LOC. Cf. Robert A. Divine, *Second Chance: The Triumph of Internationalism in America during World War II* (New York: Atheneum, 1967), pp. 72–73. Divine notes that an estimated thirty-six million Americans listened to Willkie's speech.
25. October 1942 Folder, Official file: Box 4040, Wendell Willkie, 1941–45, Franklin Delano Roosevelt Papers, Franklin D. Roosevelt Library, Hyde Park, New York.
26. Venkataramani and Shrivastava, *Quit India*, pp. 321–35; John S. D. Eisenhower, *Allies: Pearl Harbor to D-day* (New York: Doubleday, 1982), pp. 195–96.
27. Eisenhower, *Allies*, pp. 195–96. See also Borgwardt, *A New Deal for the World*, p. 83; and Clymer, *Quest for Freedom*, pp. 105–07.

28. Willkie, *One World*.
29. Clymer, *Quest for Freedom*, p. 106. In the same moment, Nehru read Pearl Buck's *Asia and Democracy*. See Nehru's *Prison Diary*, 28 December 1943, in S. Gopal, ed., *Selected Works of Jawaharlal Nehru* (New Delhi: Orient Longman, 1972), first series, vol. 13, pp. 322–23. Writing to his daughter Indira on 29 February 1944, Nehru remarked about Willkie's book, which he was sending to her, that 'in the context in which it is written and considering the author's background, it is really a remarkable book and I found it exhilarating. The concept of one world hanging together, all inter-linked, is still quite difficult enough for most people, in the East or the West, to grasp, even though they may hold advanced ideas. Even when it is partly grasped intellectually, there is no emotional appreciation of it. Yet I think this is the basic idea of our present-day world and unless we imbibe it, our other ideas are apt to be airy and without reality.' *SWJN*, first series, vol. 13, p. 364.
30. Marika Sherwood, 'India at the Founding of the United Nations', *International Studies* 33 (4), 1996, p. 413, especially n. 21.
31. Pandit, *The Scope of Happiness*, pp. 186–87.
32. Ibid., p. 189.
33. Ibid., p. 190.
34. Ibid., pp. 191–92.
35. Pascal James Imperato and Eleanor M. Imperato, *They Married Adventure: The Wandering Lives of Martin and Osa Johnson* (Rutgers: Rutgers University Press, 1999), pp. 194–95.
36. Ibid., pp. 196–97, 214.
37. Pandit, *The Scope of Happiness*, p. 192. These kinds of views are illustrative of what Edward Said has famously called Orientalism. See Edward W. Said, *Orientalism* (New York: Vintage Books, 1994, first published 1978). For more on migrant South Asian communities in North America, see Karen Isaksen Leonard, *Making Ethnic Choices: California's Punjabi Mexican Americans* (Philadelphia: Temple University Press, 1994); and Karen Isaksen Leonard, *The South Asian Americans* (Westport, Connecticut: Greenwood Press, 1997).
38. India League Pamphlet, 1945, India League of America, 1944–59, Box 39, Folder 7, Henry Luce Papers, LOC; Vera Brittain, *Envoy Extraordinary: A Study of Vijaya Lakshmi Pandit and Her Contribution to Modern India* (London: George Allen, 1965), pp. 66–67; 'India Is Visualized Seizing Independence', *The New York Times*, 27 January 1945, p. 4.

39. Opening remarks by Vijaya Lakshmi Pandit, leader of the Indian group, in T.A. Bisson and Bruno Lasker, eds, *Security in the Pacific: A Preliminary Report of the Ninth Conference of the Institute of Pacific Relations* (New York: Institute of Pacific Relations, 1945), pp. 11–12.
40. *India Today* (a publication of the India League), January 1945, p. 4. Sidney Hertzberg Papers, Box 25, Folder: India League of America Papers 1945, NYPL Manuscripts.
41. Pandit, *The Scope of Happiness*, pp. 197–98.
42. Keith Jeffery, *The Secret History of MI6* (New York: Penguin, 2010), p. 450.
43. Clymer, *Quest for Freedom*, p. 191.
44. 'India Is Visualized Seizing Independence', *The New York Times*, 27 January 1945, p. 4.
45. India Independence day programme, 26 January 1945, Pearl Buck Papers, 'PSB India League of America', Warren Sherk Collection, Randolph College Archives.
46. 'India Is Visualized Seizing Independence', p. 4.
47. Sherwood, 'India at the Founding of the United Nations', p. 414.
48. 'Gives Assurance on India', *The New York Times*, 30 January 1945, p. 8. See also Clymer, *Quest for Freedom*, pp. 208–09.
49. '$1,915,309 Donated to Assist Children', *The New York Times*, 31 January 1945, p. 23. Cf. pamphlet 'India League of America, 1944–1959', Box 39, Folder 7, Henry Luce Papers, LOC.
50. Letter from Pearl Buck to Henry Luce, 29 November 1943, 'American Relief for India, 1943–1945', Box 24, Folder 2, Henry Luce Papers, LOC. For more on Buck, her husband, Richard Walsh, and others and their fight against the Indian famine, see this folder generally.
51. Letter to Nehru, 25 August 1942, 1942 correspondence, Box 113, Folder 5, Clare Booth Luce Papers, LOC.
52. Nehru to Clare Booth Luce, 22 July 1945, 'Correspondence with Nehru', 1945, Box 119, Folder 11, Clare Booth Luce Papers, LOC.
53. List of guests, Pandit dinner on 3 February 1945. 'Entertainment, Party Lists', 1940–50, Box 56, Folder 17, Clare Booth Luce Papers, LOC.
54. Entry for 'America's Town Meeting of the Air', in John Dunning, *On the Air: The Encyclopedia of Old-time Radio* (New York: Oxford University Press, 1998), pp. 30–31. Some information also gleaned from reading through the transcripts published as *Town Hall*.
55. Robert Rhodes James, *Robert Boothby: A Portrait of Churchill's Ally* (New York: Viking, 1991), pp. 146–47.

56. *Town Meeting: Bulletin of America's Town Meeting of the Air* (collected as *Town Hall*), vol. 10, no. 44, 1 March 1945. I also listened to a sound recording of the original broadcast in the Library of Congress. I am grateful to Karen Fishman who was particularly helpful and generous with her time in helping me locate the recording, and in finding additional material related to the broadcast. She also pointed me to the Dunning volume.
57. FO 371/44561 C437369, National Archives, UK, pp. 28–32.

3. Showdown in San Francisco

1. The idea for a post-war world organization of some kind originally came from Churchill, who raised it at the 1941 Atlantic Conference. But it was FDR who thought most carefully about the idea and spent years developing a concrete vision for such an institution. In 1942, Roosevelt began with the notion of the 'Four Policemen'—the Great Powers—to straddle the globe each within their own sector to maintain peace. But Secretary of State Cordell Hull, working with Leo Pasvolsky and soon-to-be Secretary of State Edward Stettinius, challenged the president as early as July of the same year to think differently. Hull and his allies came up with plans on which both Dumbarton Oaks and eventually the UN Charter itself were based. Willkie's activities helped create conditions for thinking about a world organization in a new way. Leon Gordenker, 'American Post-war Planning: Policy Elites and the New Deal', in Robert A. Garson and Stuart S. Kidd, eds, *The Roosevelt Years: New Perspectives on American History, 1933–1945* (Edinburgh: Edinburgh University Press, 1999), pp. 173–89. FDR publicly broached the idea in April 1943, months before Tehran. John Allphin Moore and Jerry Pubantz, *Encyclopedia of the United Nations* (New York: Facts on File, 2002), pp. 257–60; entry on Franklin D. Roosevelt.
2. http://www.doaks.org/about/the_dumbarton_oaks_conversations.html
3. Martin Gilbert, *Road to Victory: Winston S. Churchill, 1941–1945* (Boston: Houghton Mifflin, 1986), vol. 7, pp. 1,170–75.
4. Churchill quoted in Gilbert, *Road to Victory*, p. 1,183. No source given for quotation.
5. Ibid., p. 1,199. No source given for quotation. See also pp. 1,198–99 generally.
6. Ibid., pp. 1,187–88, 1,190–91.

7. Telegrams between Gandhi and Madame Pandit, 22 and 26 February 1945, CWMG, vol. 85, p. 422; http://www.gandhiserve.org/cwmg/VOL085.PDF.
8. The Big Three released a statement following their discussions at Yalta in which they stated that they made a distinction between the people of Germany and Nazism and militarism. Elimination of the latter two would lead to a 'decent life' for Germans and 'a place for them in the comity of nations'. Gilbert, *Road to Victory*, pp. 1,210–11.
9. 'Statement to the Press', 17 April 1945, CWMG, vol. 86, pp. 188–99.
10. Gandhi's was a devotion to the Other, an ethical formulation that foreshadowed the most important thought of the great twentieth-century philosopher Emmanuel Lévinas. See Lévinas, *Totality and Infinity: An Essay on Exteriority*, trans. Alphonso Lingis (Pittsburgh: Duquesne University Press, 2007); and Samuel Moyn, *Origins of the Other: Emmanuel Levinas between Revelation and Ethics* (Ithaca, New York: Cornell University Press, 2005). For more comparison of the ethics of Gandhi and Lévinas, see Ajay Skaria, 'The Strange Violence of *Satyagraha*: Gandhi, *Itihaas*, and History', in Manu Bhagavan, ed, *Heterotopias: Nationalism and the Possibility of History in South Asia* (New Delhi: Oxford University Press, 2010), pp. 142–85.
11. Interview with Ralph Coniston, before 25 April 1945, CWMG, vol. 86, pp. 222–25; http://www.gandhiserve.org/cwmg/VOL086.PDF. Strangely, it appears that Coniston never published the interview in *Collier's Weekly*; I went through every issue of *Collier's* from February to December 1945 and could not find any mention of Gandhi, though Coniston did have another piece on India appear in this period.
12. Gandhi spelt this out in response to a question about the idea of world federation posed to him a few days before the Quit India Resolution was released. Question Box: World Federation, on or before 2 August 1942, CWMG, vol. 83, pp. 155–56; http://www.gandhiserve.org/cwmg/VOL083.PDF.
13. FO 371/44560 C437369, p. 172, National Archives, UK.
14. Correspondence between Eleanor Roosevelt and Edward Stettinius, 4 and 7 April 1945. Arus, Stettinius folder, 70 Government Department 1945, Section V, Box 426, White House correspondence, Eleanor Roosevelt Papers, 1933–45, Franklin D. Roosevelt Library, Hyde Park, New York. There appears to have been no clandestine operations taken against Madame Pandit. Under a Freedom of Information/Privacy Act request I made to the Federal Bureau of Investigations (FBI), I discovered no files to indicate that the FBI was

acting in any way against the Indians. J. Edgar Hoover, the FBI's director, was aware of her trip, at least by January 1946, but appeared dismissive of any concerns or objections raised in some critical correspondence. The files I have seen were from January 1946, and were marked 'Secret' and appear to have been declassified in 1987, though they were still redacted.

15. Pandit, *The Scope of Happiness*, p. 197.
16. 'India Stands for Equality, Leader Tells Baltimoreans', *Baltimore Afro-American*, 7 April 1945, pp. 1, 20.
17. Ibid.
18. See Sherwood, 'India at the Founding of the United Nations', pp. 421–22.
19. DuBois, as quoted in Jonathan Rosenberg, *How Far the Promised Land?: World Affairs and the American Civil Rights Movement from the First World War to Vietnam* (Princeton: Princeton University Press, 2006), p. 156. See also pp. 156–57, 160–64; and Sherwood, 'India at the Founding of the United Nations', pp. 417–18, 421.
20. 'Indian Woman Twists the Tale of British Lion', *Chicago Daily Tribune*, 27 April 1945, p. 6. It is not clear how many plants there were. Sherwood ('India at the Founding of the United Nations', p. 426) notes that a General Hawthorne gate-crashed Pandit's press conference and asked 'awkward questions', and was driven out. She also points to another version of this story to indicate that a stenographer with the British Indian delegation heckled Pandit, but was discovered and run out of the room. The *Tribune* recounted a similar story, saying that a Mr K.A. Kahan, with a black goatee, was the perpetrator. Whether both Hawthorne and Kahan were present, or whether their identities were mixed up, is unknown.
21. 'Two Spokesmen of Freedom Denounce Reds and British', *Chicago Daily Tribune*, 29 April 1945, p. 10.
22. Eagan to Pandit, 30 April 1945, Pandit Papers, II Inst., Subject File I, p. 2, Nehru Memorial Museum and Library (NMML). (A citation note: page numbers for NMML files are handwritten. Occasionally, these numbers are not consecutive, or are missing. Where a page number is visible, I have cited it, but with the caveat that it may or may not correspond to proper placement of the document within the file.)
23. 'Statement to the Press', 4 May 1945, CWMG, vol. 86, pp. 303–05; http://www.gandhiserve.org/cwmg/VOL086.PDF.
24. 'India Self Rule Issue Pressed by Mrs. Pandit', *Chicago Daily Tribune*, 5 May 1945, p. 8.

25. 'Mrs. Pandit to Submit Memorial to United Nations' Delegates', *The Indian Express*, 10 April 1945, p. 5.
26. Pandit memo to the secretary general of the United Nations Conference, 2 May 1945, Pandit Papers, II Inst., Subject File I. pp. 9–10.
27. 'Statement to the Press', 4 May 1945, CWMG, vol. 86, pp. 303–05; http://www.gandhiserve.org/cwmg/VOL086.PDF. The Nobel- and Oscar-winning Irish playwright George Bernard Shaw also came to Gandhi's defence; ibid.
28. Letter from Hiss to Pandit, 11 May 1945, Pandit Papers, II Inst., Subject File I, p. 13. Hiss would go on to notoriety a few years later when he was accused of being a covert communist and a Soviet spy during the Second Red Scare led by Senator Joseph McCarthy. The accusation, prosecution and conviction remain controversial to this day. See Susan Jacoby, *Alger Hiss and the Battle for History* (New Haven: Yale University Press, 2009).
29. Pandit statement, 10 May 1945, Pandit Papers, II Inst., Subject File I, p. 12. Eden was saying that he had no regrets and had nothing for which to apologize–that he did not stand there in a 'white sheet'. The Ku Klux Klan was the pre-eminent, violent white supremacist organization in the United States whose members often wore white sheets.
30. 'Charge Halifax Effort to "Gag" Indian's Speech', *Chicago Daily Tribune*, 15 May 1945, p. 2. Republican Earl Warren would go on to become the legendary chief justice of the United States Supreme Court, leading the court to the definitive, progressive decisions it took in the 1960s. See Jim Newton, *Justice for All: Earl Warren and the Nation He Made* (New York: Penguin, 2006).
31. Ibid. The largest stain on Warren's career was his support for the internment of Japanese Americans. See Ronald Takaki, *Strangers from a Different Shore: A History of Asian Americans* (New York: Little, Brown, and Co, updated and revised, 1998, first published 1989.)
32. Letters from Rochester to Pandit and Warren, 15 and 26 May 1945, Pandit Papers, II Inst., Subject File I, pp. 15, 18–19.
33. Statement by Pandit, 20 May 1945, Pandit Papers, II Inst., Subject File I, p. 17.
34. Sherwood, 'India at the Founding of the United Nations', p. 425.
35. In general, Churchill was more concerned with having the Americans on his side than the other way around. Roosevelt used this, and his personal friendship, to his advantage to press Churchill on the colonies.

Churchill immensely disliked the pressure. Truman had a much colder relationship with Churchill overall. I am grateful to my colleague Benjamin Hett for clarifying this point for me.

36. http://www.un.org/en/documents/charter/chapter11.shtml
37. UK Foreign Office, *A Commentary on the Charter of the United Nations*, Cmd. 6666, Misc. no. 9, 1945, p. 11. Presented by the Foreign Affairs secretary to Parliament. Cf. Kenneth Robinson, 'World Opinion and Colonial Status', *International Organization* 8 (4), 1954, especially pp. 475–76.
38. Excerpts from speeches at the Scottish Rite Auditorium, 28 May 1945; and letter from Frida Huge to Pandit, 29 May 1945, Pandit Papers, II Inst., Subject File I, pp. 20–21.
39. *Voice of India*, May 1945, published by the Committee for India's Freedom, 'Race Relations in the International Arena, 1940–55', Papers of the NAACP, Part 14, Series A, Group II, Reel 9.
40. 'Peace Parley Called a Spur to War in East', *Chicago Daily Tribune*, 5 June 1945, p. 3.
41. Letter from Nehru to Pandit, 27 February 1945; Nayantara Sahgal, *Before Freedom: Nehru's Letters to His Sister* (New Delhi: HarperCollins, 2000), p. 455.
42. Letter from Nehru to Pandit, 24 July 1945, ibid.
43. See Chapter 2 for Madame Pandit's encounter with New York City mayor Fiorello LaGuardia.
44. 'The Day in Washington', *The New York Times*, 1 November 1945, p. 12; Pandit, *The Scope of Happiness*, p. 197.
45. 'Nehru's Sister, in U.S., Defends Bose As Patriot', *Chicago Daily Tribune*, 26 November 1945, p. 2.
46. 'Vijaya Pandit Demands Aid of U.S. in India', *Chicago Daily Tribune*, 6 December 1945, p. 19.
47. 'Nehru's Visit to Karachi', *The Indian Express*, 2 January 1946, p. 5.
48. 'Britain's Anti-Indian Propaganda in America', *The Indian Express*, 29 January 1946, p. 5.

4. The New Hope

1. Tony Judt, *Postwar: A History of Europe since 1945* (London: Vintage Press, 2010, first published 2005), pp. 14, 82.
2. Pandit, *The Scope of Happiness*, pp. 204–07. Quote from p. 205.
3. Jawaharlal Nehru, incomplete and unpublished review of Bertrand Russell's *Road to Freedom*, written sometime after 1919, Nehru Papers,

Writings and Speeches, NMML, Serial no. 21, cited in Erez Manela, 'The "Wilsonian Moment" in India and the Crisis of Empire in 1919', in Wm. Roger Louis, ed., *Yet More Adventures with Britannia: Personalities, Politics and Culture in Britain* (New York: I.B. Tauris, 2005). Full quotation on p. 283; citation information taken from p. 287, n. 41. Wilsonianism, Manela argues, sought to produce a world of equal, sovereign nation states. Nehru does not openly express his support for this aspect of the fourteen points and by the forties it is apparent that he in any event had rejected it. Also, it is important to note that while 1919 inspired colonized people everywhere, gave them hope, the structural edifice of the League that emerged did not address their concerns or incorporate their voices in any meaningful way. See, for instance, Neil Smith, *The Endgame of Globalization* (New York: Routledge, 2005), especially pp. 53–81; and Vijay Prashad, *The Darker Nations: A People's History of the Third World* (New York: The New Press, 2007), pp. 16–30, especially pp. 21, 27 and 28. This is why I think the mid-1940s represented the world's first true 'global moment', when people everywhere actually participated with heretofore unseen parity. The League's failure at equal accommodation additionally signalled that colonialism was far from over. Nehru's angst at this stage is also a lament over this fact, that is, a worry that the old mal-order has not been ended as much as an eulogy for the world that might have been.

4. Jawaharlal Nehru, *The Discovery of India* (New York: The John Day Company, 1946), p. 543.
5. Ibid., pp. 41–42.
6. Cf. Divine, *Second Chance.*
7. 'Future Taking Shape', Jawaharlal Nehru, *India's Foreign Policy: Selected Speeches, September 1946–April 1961* (New Delhi: Government of India, 1961), p. 2.
8. 'For a World Government', *The New York Times*, 15 September 1945, p. 11.
9. Einstein, quoted in Strobe Talbott, *The Great Experiment: The Story of Ancient Empires, Modern States, and the Quest for a Global Nation* (New York: Simon and Schuster, 2008), pp. 197–98. Einstein had long been fascinated by India, and Gandhi in particular. He had initiated correspondence with the Mahatma as early as 1931. Various other nationalists, such as Madan Mohan Malaviya, also exchanged letters with Einstein. Einstein wrote a brief testimonial to Gandhi for a book celebrating the Indian's seventieth birthday in 1939 (32 600, 601).

The following year, Nehru wrote an introduction to a similar kind of work that found its way into Einstein's hands (32 605–06). Nehru was an admirer of Einstein. There is no written record to indicate that Nehru knew of Einstein's exact comments in 1945 and 1946, but the two became close starting in 1947, though they only ever met once, in Einstein's home in 1949. See Chapter 6 of this volume. Einstein was a staunch supporter of India's internationalist efforts. Details of the Gandhi–Einstein–Nehru relationship can be found in Boxes 44 and 45, 32 600–10, 32 725–52, Einstein Papers, Princeton University Special Collections.

10. Pandit, *The Scope of Happiness*, pp. 208–09.
11. http://avalon.law.yale.edu/wwii/atlantic.asp
12. Gilbert, *Road to Victory*, p. 1,199; Paul Gordon Lauren, 'First Principles of Racial Equality: History and the Politics and Diplomacy of Human Rights Provisions in the United Nations Charter', *Human Rights Quarterly* 5 (1), 1983, pp. 4–5.
13. http://www.un.org/en/documents/charter/chapter11.shtml
14. Kenneth Twitchett, 'The Colonial Powers and the United Nations', *Journal of Contemporary History* 4 (1), 1969, pp. 167–85; Robinson, 'World Opinion and Colonial Status', especially pp. 475–76. Speaking broadly about the situation in September 1946 in an internal memo, Nehru commented that 'it appears that if any country takes up a straight and truthful attitude in consonance with the declared aims and objects of the United Nations, this is considered embarrassing . . . The whole process appears to be one of making fine heart-warming declarations of the rights of individuals and nations, and then making every effort to interpret these declarations differently, and taking away all the real substance from them . . . Questions affecting hundreds of millions of people are discussed in this opportunist and pettifogging manner and the fine impulses of peoples are prostituted by diplomats for base ends.' Memo of Jawaharlal Nehru, 16 September 1946, Ministry of External Affairs, No 1(9)-CC/1946, pp. 4–5 of the file, National Archives of India (NAI).
15. Summary of Pandit's remarks before the 143rd UN Plenary Meeting, 25 September 1948, in S.K. Madhavan, ed., *India at the United Nations* (New Delhi: APH Publishing Corp., 1999), vol. 1, p. 22. This volume is part of a collection of speeches by the Indian delegation to the UN. The speech is incorrectly dated January 1948 in the volume. See http://www.un.int/india/ind11.htm for the correct date and full record.

16. Pandit, *The Scope of Happiness*, p. 205.
17. I use 'non-Western' here in the Saidian sense.
18. June 1946 letter and pamphlet by Dr Y.M. Dadoo, Passive Resistance Council, Transvaal Indian Congress; and chair, Johannesburg District of the Communist Party. Available online at: http://www.liberation.org.za/collections/sacp/dadoo/dadoo03.php. For additional information on the reaction to the Ghetto Act, and on Dadoo, see cablegram sent by the Natal Indian Congress on 2 July 1946, S-0544-4-28, United Nations Archives (UNA).
19. Pandit Papers, II Inst., Subject File I, 'UN General Assembly Delegation of India: Memorandum on the Position of Indians in the Union of South Africa', 26 August 1946, NMML; and Carol E. Anderson, 'International Conscience, the Cold War, and Apartheid: The NAACP's Alliance with the Reverend Michael Scott for South West Africa's Liberation, 1946–1951', *Journal of World History* 19 (3), September 2008, pp. 298–99. The mandate system placed territories under the control of various Western powers, disassembling the old Ottoman empire and German colonies as well. South Africa acquired South West Africa as a mandate, that is, as a neo-colony. It moved to outright annex the territory in 1946, and to claim sovereign control over the territory.
20. Pandit, *The Scope of Happiness*, pp. 205–06. See also Lorna Lloyd, '"A Most Auspicious Beginning": The 1946 United Nations General Assembly and the Question of the Treatment of Indians in South Africa', *Review of International Studies* 16 (2), April 1990, p. 136.
21. Pandit, *The Scope of Happiness*, p. 206, and pp. 204–07 for broader context.
22. 'UN General Assembly Delegation of India: Memorandum on the Position of Indians in the Union of South Africa.'
23. Pandit Papers, II Inst., Subject File II, *Confidential Memorandum*, p. 99 of the file, NMML.
24. Ibid., p. 106 of the file.
25. Ibid., this and the above, pp. 102–03 and 109–13 of the file. See also 'Indian Case in South Africa under Articles 10 and 14 of the United Nations Charter', 'Secret' memorandum; and 'Is the Indian Question in South Africa Essentially a Matter within the Domestic Jurisdiction of the Government of South Africa?', 'Secret' memorandum, Indian Ministry of External Affairs, no. 6 (22)-CC/46, pp. 91–107, NAI. Among those contributing to India's legal team was Sir Tej Bahadur Sapru, Madame Pandit's trusted friend and her lawyer during her case

to protect her rights after her husband passed away. See Lloyd, 'A Most Auspicious Beginning', p. 134, n. 10.

26. Pandit Papers, I Inst., Speeches/Writings by Her. F, no. 4, NMML.
27. 'Colonial Freedom Is Urged by India', *The New York Times*, 26 October 1946, p. 3. See also Ministry of External Affairs, India, no. 6 (22)-CC/46, 'Secret' telegram from the leader of the Indian delegation, New York, to the Foreign Office, New Delhi, 22/23 November 1946, p. 90 of the file, NAI. (As with the NMML files, documents from the NAI contain handwritten page numbers that are confusing and sometimes out of order. I cite them with the caveat that they may or may not represent the exact location of a document within a file.)
28. Carol E. Anderson, *Bourgeois Radicals: The NAACP and the Struggle for Colonial Liberation* (Cambridge University Press, forthcoming). I am grateful to Carol for sharing her work with me in manuscript form, as a conference paper entitled 'Allies of a Kind: India and the NAACP's Alliance against South Africa's Colonialism and *Apartheid*, 1946–1951'. She cites the following in claiming South Africa's hold over the US and Britain: Mr Ross to Mr Hiss, memo, 25 October 1946, Box 21, File 'Trusteeship—Background Memos, etc.', Lot File 55D323, 'Record Group 59: General Records of the Department of State', National Archives, College Park, Maryland (hereafter 'RG 59'); John Foster Dulles to Paul Robeson, 7 December 1946, 'Papers of W. Alphaeus Hunton', Schomburg Center for Research in Black Culture, microfilm, Reel 1; Henshaw, 'South African Territorial Expansion', 4. 'Jim Crow' was the name given to the US's policies of segregation and racial discrimination. For an excellent account, see C. Vann Woodward, *The Strange Career of Jim Crow* (New York: Oxford University Press, third edition, 1974).
29. For further, intricate details on the manoeuvrings between delegations, see Lloyd, 'A Most Auspicious Beginning', pp. 131–53. The material in the preceding paragraph has been taken from pp. 136–39. Lloyd claims that all of this occurred on 29 October (p. 137), an impossibility given that cables were exchanged between Pandit and India (see endnotes 30 and 31) on 25 and 28 October celebrating their victory in the first round. Lloyd herself cites the Pandit cable and dates it 25 October (p. 138, n. 36). Cf. 'Treatment of Indians in the Union of South Africa', *Report of the Indian Delegation to the Second Part of the First Session of General Assembly of the United Nations* (New Delhi: Government of India, 1946), pp. 28–33, NMML.
30. Ministry of External Affairs, India, no. 6(22)-CC/46. Copy of cable, Jawaharlal Nehru Comrel New Delhi, p. 83 of the file, NAI.

31. Ibid., 'Important' telegram from Nehru to the Indian delegation at UNO. Includes sub-telegram from Gandhi dated 28 October 1946. Appears to be p. 84 of the file, but no page number given.
32. Pandit Papers, II Inst., Subject File II. Memorandum by the Government of the Union of South Africa on the subject of Indian legislation, United Nations General Assembly document A/167, 31 October 1946, pp. 41–42. Pp. 68–69 of the Pandit file, NMML.
33. 'Private and Secret' letter from Pethick-Lawrence to Lord Wavell, 8 November 1946. Mansergh, et. al., *The Transfer of Power*, vol. 9, document 18, p. 35.
34. Anderson, 'Allies of a Kind'. See also Anderson, 'International Conscience, the Cold War, and Apartheid', pp. 297–325. The NAACP reached out to an Anglican minister named Michael Scott—a white South African citizen and a vocal critic of his country's policies. Scott went on a fact-finding mission and came up with incontrovertible evidence that South Africa's presentation of the facts was in complete error. In 1947, Scott came to the UN and, in order to circumvent South African attempts to have the US deny him a visa, worked with Walter White and the NAACP and the India League to become part of India's delegation to the United Nations that year, where he used his position to shed light on what was going on in South Africa.
35. Pandit Papers, II Inst., Subject File II, p. 142 of the file, NMML.
36. Lloyd, 'A Most Auspicious Beginning'. pp. 139–40; '8 Lands Back India on African Issues', *The New York Times*, 22 November 1946, p. 17.
37. Pandit Papers, II. Inst., Subject File II, pp. 74–86, NMML. Quotations from pp. 74–75.
38. 'Delegates Bitter over African Case', 27 November 1946, *The New York Times*, p. 6. See also Lloyd, 'A Most Auspicious Beginning', pp. 141–42.
39. Lloyd, 'A Most Auspicious Beginning', pp. 142–45. See also Ministry of External Affairs, India, no. 6(22)-CC/46. Telegrams, some secret, between Vijayalaxmi Pandit and team and Jawaharlal Nehru, 27–30 November, 2/3 December 1946, pp. 120–24 of the file, NAI. No page number visible for the December telegram, listed as 'Secret 12548, D3059-CC/46'.
40. Lloyd, 'A Most Auspicious Beginning', p. 145.
41. 'Smuts Fights Test on Indians' Issue', 8 December 1946, *The New York Times*, p. 19. See also Lloyd, 'A Most Auspicious Beginning', p. 146. The Council of African Affairs, chaired by Paul Robeson, was

completely dismissive of the International Court of Justice solution, seeing it as a means to avoid taking immediate action on the principle of racial equality as enshrined in the UN Charter. Letter from the council to the US delegation to the General Assembly of the United Nations, 6 December 1946, Pandit Papers, II Inst, Subject File II, p. 87 of the file.

42. 'U.N. Night Session Like Opera Scene', 8 December 1946, *The New York Times*, p. 8.
43. Ministry of External Affairs, India, no. 6(22)-CC/46. 'Red Letter Day for India', Government of India Press Information Bureau, pp. 248–52, of the file. NAI.
44. 'Smuts Fights Test on Indians' Issue.'
45. Smuts' loss in the UN was only a factor in his loss, which also had to do with his focus on winning World War II. Pandit, *The Scope of Happiness*, p. 211; and Lloyd, 'A Most Auspicious Beginning', pp. 148–49.
46. Anderson, *Bourgeois Radicals*, and 'Allies of a Kind'; Lloyd, 'A Most Auspicious Beginning', pp. 149–53.
47. Ministry of External Affairs, India, no. 6(22)-CC/46, 9/10 December 1946. 'Secret' telegram from the leader of the Indian delegation, New York, to Foreign Office, New Delhi, page numbers difficult to read, but appear to be 245–46, NAI.
48. Constituent Assembly Debates of India, vol. 2, 22 January 1947, http://parliamentofIndia.nic.in/ls/debates/vol2p3.htm.
49. For details, see *Equal Rights*, vol. 32, no. 3, May–June 1946, especially no. 27, S-0544-4-28, UNA; and Hansa Mehta, Rajkumari Amrit Kaur and Lakshmi Menon, *The Indian Woman's Charter of Rights and Duties*, July 1946. Nehru had originally asked K.C. Neogy to serve on the Human Rights Commission (HRC), but Neogy withdrew a few days before the first meeting in New York, ostensibly because he wanted to be with his family in East Bengal, which was under a forecast of violence. See Jawaharlal Nehru, *Selected Works of Jawaharlal Nehru, Second Series*, edited by S. Gopal (New Delhi: Teen Murti House, 1984), vol. 1, p. 197. Hereafter referred to as *SWJN*. While there is no reason to doubt this very plausible explanation regarding Neogy, it is also possible that Nehru wanted someone with a proven ability to get committees to agree to what they wanted. Mehta clearly had that ability.
50. Letter from E.S. Bajpai, Embassy of India, Washington DC, to Hansa Mehta, containing a sub-letter from Nehru, 22 January 1947, Mehta Papers, F/No 12.

51. The most famous and respected scholarly account is Partha Chatterjee, 'The Moment of Arrival: Nehru and the Passive Revolution', *Nationalist Thought and the Colonial World* (Minneapolis: University of Minnesota Press, 2004, first published 1986), pp. 131–66.
52. Internal memos indicate that privately Nehru actually believed in the truthfulness and justice of his actions and cause. He disliked shenanigans, and strongly felt that honesty and goodwill were necessary for international (and domestic) relations. No surprise from this disciple of Gandhi. 'This whole stage play and manoeuvring [sic] behind the scenes brings little credit to any of the countries concerned . . . I see no reason why India should allow herself to be exploited in this game of greedy and opportunist Powers who say one thing and mean another. I think it is time that India should take up a straight attitude even though she might have little support in the Assemblies of Nations. I am inclined to think, however, that any country which adopts this straight attitude and speaks really in terms of the United Nations Charter without whittling them in any way, will have vast audience in the world and tremendous support.' Memo from Jawaharlal Nehru, 16 September 1946, Ministry of External Affairs, No 1(9)-CC/1946, pp. 4, 6 of the file, NAI.
53. Letter from E.S. Bajpai, Embassy of India, Washington DC, to Hansa Mehta, containing a sub-letter from Nehru, 22 January 1947.
54. Letter from Nehru to Einstein, 11 July 1947, in response to Einstein's letter of 13 June. *SWJN*, second series, vol. 3, 1985, pp. 393–96. Also available in the Einstein Papers, Princeton University Special Collections.
55. Interview with the press, 28 July 1947. Appeared in *The Hindu*, 30 July 1947, *SWJN*, second series, vol. 3, p. 370.
56. Paul Kennedy, *The Parliament of Man: The Past, Present, and Future of the United Nations* (New York: Random House, 2006), pp. 3–47.
57. Interview with the press 28 July 1947, *The Hindu*.
58. Letter to Australian high commissioner to India Iven Mackay, 30 October 1946, *SWJN*, second series, vol. 1, p. 461.
59. Letter from E.S. Bajpai, Embassy of India, Washington DC, to Hansa Mehta, containing a sub-letter from Nehru, 22 January 1947.
60. The second meeting was held on 27 January 1947 at 3 p.m., while the first was held earlier the same day, at 11 a.m. Mehta's is the first lengthy and substantial speech of the Commission. She comes out of the gate strong, in what appears to me to be an effort to set the agenda. See (the source of the quotation): E/CN.4/SR.2, pp. 3–4. See also the

whole file, as well as E/CN.4/SR.1, Folder: January–June 1947, Isador Lubin Papers, Franklin D. Roosevelt Library, Hyde Park, New York (ILFDRL). A core, or 'nuclear', version of the Commission had actually met the previous year for the first time, on 29 April 1946, on the Bronx campus of Hunter College, New York, which was the first home of the just-formed UN. UN Press Release, Meeting of the HRC, 26 April 1946, S-0991-5-15, UNA.

61. 27 January 1947, E/CN.4/SR.1, pp. 1–2, Folder: January–June 1947, ILFDRL. The 'E' number on this document is not clearly legible due to document damage. Hansa Mehta picked up on Laugier's comments on South Africa and highlighted them in her official report on the first session. Hansa Mehta, 'Report of the Human Rights Commission', 27 January–10 February 1947. Ministry of External Affairs (India)-UNI Branch, no. 5(46)-UNO-I-47, pp. 1–2, NAI.
62. HRC: 'Draft of a Resolution for the General Assembly Submitted by the Representative of India', 31 January 1947, E/CN.4/11, p. 2, Folder: January–June 1947, ILFDRL. See also 31 January 1947, E/CN.4/SR.8, p. 3, Folder: January–June 1947, ILFDRL.
63. Paul Kennedy, *The Parliament of Man*, pp. 3–47.
64. *SWJN*, second series, vol. 2, p. 485.
65. Ibid., pp. 218, 485.
66. This is apparent from the records of the first session, ILFDRL.
67. Summary records of the first–third meetings of the second session of the Working Group on Implementation, HRC, 5–6 December 1947, E/CN.4/AC.4/SR/1–3, Folder: January–June 1947, ILFDRL.
68. See summary records of the second, third, fifth, sixth and seventh meetings of the second session of the Working Group on Implementation, HRC, 5–9 December 1947, E/CN.4/AC.4/SR/2 (especially p. 3), E/CN.4/AC.4/SR/3 (especially p. 6), E/CN.4/AC.4/SR.5 (especially pp. 3–4), E/CN.4/AC.4/SR/6 (especially pp. 2–3), E/CN.4/AC.4/SR.7, Folder: June–December 1947, ILFDRL. See also UN Economic and Social Council, E/CN.4/Sub.2/27, 1 December 1947, courtesy of the Dag Hammarskjöld Library (DHL); and Briggs, 'Implementation of the Proposed International Covenant on Human Rights', *The American Journal of International Law* 42 (2), 1948. See also summary record of the seventh meeting of the second session of the Working Group on Implementation, HRC, 9 December 1947, E/CN.4/AC.4/SR.7, 5, 7, Folder: June–December 1947, ILFDRL. Cf. UN Economic and Social Council, E/CN.4/Sub.2/27, 1 December 1947, courtesy of the DHL.

69. Mehta had originally proposed that the International Court of Justice be the central body charged with power. The Committee agreed in principle but, out of concern for issues of jurisdiction and authority, backed a modification by Colonel W.R. Hodgson, the representative from Australia, to create a new International Court of Human Rights with 'binding and enforceable decisions'. Seventh meeting, p. 4. Mehta actually opposed this new court on the grounds that 'political considerations might make it difficult to enforce . . . [its] judgments'. Sixth meeting, p. 10. The International Court was accepted unanimously. The creation of a new International Court of Human Rights passed 3 for to 1 against (with India appearing the no vote). But the Group then voted unanimously for 'the principle that the proposed court should have the power to make binding and enforceable decisions'. Summary record of the seventh meeting of the second session of the Working Group on Implementation, HRC, 9 December 1947, E/CN.4/AC.4/SR.7, 6, Folder: June–December 1947, ILFDRL.
70. E/CN.4/53, 10 December 1947, United Nations Official Document System (UNODS). Also reproduced in E/600, 17 December 1947, cited in Briggs, 'Implementation of the Proposed International Covenant on Human Rights', p. 392.
71. Mehta, *Report of the Human Rights Commission*, Ministry of External Affairs (India)–UNI Branch, no. 5(46)-UNO-I-47, pp. 16–17, NAI.
72. 15 December 1947, E/CN.4/SR.38, pp. 8–9, Folder: December 1947, ILFDRL.
73. Glendon, *A World Made New*, p. 95; 15 December 1947, E/CN.4/SR.38, p. 10, Folder: December 1947, ILFDRL. Toni Sender, an observer from the American Federation of Labor, tried to play peacemaker. She declared that the Working Group had 'brought a ray of hope to the working masses', a goal the Soviets seemingly would fine laudable. She added: 'If in the important issue of implementation, national sovereignty were to become the principle, as some delegations seemed to wish, it would then follow that the Security Council and even the International Court of Justice should be abolished, since all their work might be construed as interference in the domestic affairs of States.' 15 December 1947, E/CN.4/SR.38, pp. 14–15, Folder: December 1947, ILFDRL.
74. 'Secret' telegrams from the leader of the Indian Delegation in New York to Nehru/External Affairs Department, New Delhi, 29/30 November, 2/3, 9/10 December 1946, Ministry of External Affairs, no. 6(22)-CC/46, pp. 123–24, 242–44 of the file (but page numbers not clear), NAI. See also Lloyd, 'A Most Auspicious Beginning'.

75. Lloyd, 'A Most Auspicious Beginning', p. 143. As one of the four chief prosecutors of the Nuremberg trials, Sir Hartley's views on the limitations of Article 2 (7) make perfect sense.
76. 15 December 1947, E/CN.4/SR.38, pp. 11–14, Folder: December 1947, ILFDRL.
77. Note to Foreign Secretary, 7 September 1946, *SWJN*, second series, vol. 1, p. 443.
78. Ibid.
79. See Glendon, *A World Made New*; Morsink, *The Universal Declaration of Human Rights*; Normand and Zaidi, *Human Rights at the UN*, pp. 177–96. Cf. Samuel Moyn, *The Last Utopia: Human Rights in History* (Cambridge, Massachusetts: Harvard University Press, 2010). For more on the Cold War, see John Lewis Gaddis, *The Cold War: A New History* (New York: Penguin, 2005); Rashid Khalidi, *Sowing Crisis: The Cold War and American Hegemony in the Middle East* (Boston: Beacon Press, 2009); Matthew Connelly, *A Diplomatic Revolution: Algeria's Fight for Independence and the Origins of the Post-Cold War Era* (New York: Oxford University Press, 2002); and Odd Arne Westad, *The Global Cold War: Third World Interventions and the Making of Our Times* (Cambridge: Cambridge University Press, 2005).
80. Nehru, speech before the third session of the UN, 3 November 1948, in Madhavan, *India at the United Nations,* pp. 53–55.
81. 'Nehru Seeks End to Colonial Yoke', *The New York Times*, 4 November 1948, p. 27.
82. Nehru, speech before the third session of the UN.

5. INDIA INTERNATIONAL

1. See Ayesha Jalal, *The Sole Spokesman: Jinnah, the Muslim League and the Demand for Pakistan* (Cambridge: Cambridge University Press, 1994, first published 1985), pp. 174–240; Ayesha Jalal and Sugata Bose, *Modern South Asia: History, Culture, Political Economy* (New York, Routledge, second edition, 2004), pp. 149–51; Ian Copland, *The Princes of India in the Endgame of Empire, 1917–1947* (Cambridge: Cambridge University Press, 1999), pp. 217–37.
2. Copland, *The Princes of India in the Endgame of Empire.*
3. See Jalal, *The Sole Spokesman*. Indeed, many of South Asia's leading thinkers and nationalists rejected the idea of nation states and postulated alternatives, among them Nobel laureate Rabindranth Tagore, famed poet Mohammed Iqbal, and Mahatma Gandhi. It is an

irony of history, or perhaps a testament to its force, that those who agreed on such a fundamental principle, and on so much else, could nonetheless end up in bitter opposition. See Bhagavan, *Heterotopias*; Ashis Nandy, *The Illegitimacy of Nationalism: Rabindranath Tagore and the Politics of Self* (Delhi: Oxford University Press, 1996. first published 1994). See also Manu Goswami, 'Autonomy and Comparability: Notes on the Anticolonial and the Postcolonial', *boundary* 2 32 (2), Summer 2005, pp. 201–25.

4. For more on the Chamber, see Barbara N. Ramusack, *The Indian Princes and Their States* (Cambridge: Cambridge University Press, 2004); and Ramusack, *The Princes of India in the Twilight of Empire: Dissolution of a Patron–Client System, 1914–1939* (Columbus: Ohio State University Press, 1978).
5. Copland, *The Princes of India in the Endgame of Empire*, pp. 240–41.
6. For more on princely states, see Manu Bhagavan, *Sovereign Spheres: Princes, Education and Empire in Colonial India* (New Delhi: Oxford University Press, 2003).
7. For instance, Nehru, speaking at the All-India States People Conference in February 1939, declared: 'There are about six hundred States in India . . . They differ greatly among themselves . . . The majority of them, however, are sinks of reaction and incompetence and unrestrained autocratic power, sometimes exercised by vicious and degraded individuals. But whether the Ruler happens to be good or bad, or his Ministers competent or incompetent, the evil lies in the system . . . Offspring of the British Power in India, suckled by imperialism for its own purposes, it has survived till today . . . For us in India that system has in reality been one of the faces of imperialism. Therefore, when conflict comes we must recognize who our opponent is.' Jawaharlal Nehru, *The Unity of India: Collected Writings 1937–1940* (New York: John Day, 1942), pp. 30–31.
8. Constituent Assembly Debates of India, 13 December 1946, http://parliamentofindia.nic.in/ls/debates/vol1p5.htm. The Resolution dealt with questions of borders, union powers and fundamental rights, and ended with a commitment to 'world peace and the welfare of mankind'. S. Radhakrishnan, speaking on 20 January 1947, noted that the Resolution contained a reference to fundamental rights. See http://parliamentofindia.nic.in/ls/debates/vol2p1.htm.
9. Constituent Assembly Debates of India, 22 January 1947. There were both English and Hindustani versions of this speech with slight variations between the two. See Manu Bhagavan, 'Princely States and

the Making of Modern India', *The Indian Economic and Social History Review* 46 (3), 2009, pp. 449–51.

10. Copland, *The Princes of India in the Endgame of Empire*, pp. 183–268; Bhagavan, 'Princely States and the Making of Modern India', pp. 430–31. For a brief, broad overview of the integration of princely states, see Guha, *India after Gandhi*, pp. 51–73. For a more detailed, first-person account, see the classic V.P. Menon, *Integration of the Indian States* (Madras: Orient Longman, 1985, first published 1956).
11. Copland, *The Princes of India in the Endgame of Empire*, pp. 240–41; Bhagavan, 'Princely States and the Making of Modern India', pp. 430–31.
12. Bhagavan, 'Princely States and the Making of Modern India'. See also K.M. Pannikar, *An Autobiography*, trans. K. Krishnamurthy (Madras: Oxford University Press, 1977, first published 1954).
13. Constituent Assembly Debates of India, 22 January 1947.
14. Copland, *The Princes of India in the Endgame of Empire*, p. 241.
15. 'Proceedings of the Joint Meetings of the States Committee of the Constituent Assembly and the States Negotiating Committee of the Chamber of Princes' (hereafter 'Joint Proceedings'), February–March 1947, in B. Shiva Rao, ed., *The Framing of India's Constitution: Select Documents* (New Delhi: Universal Law Publishing, 2006, first published 1967), vol. 1, pp. 644–73.
16. Copland, *The Princes of India in the Endgame of Empire*, p. 242.
17. 'Joint Proceedings', pp. 673–75.
18. Copland, *The Princes of India in the Endgame of Empire*, p. 243; Menon, *Integration of the Indian States*, pp. 72–73; 'Report of the States Committee', 24 April 1947, in Rao, *The Framing of India's Constitution*, pp. 732–34.
19. 'Joint Proceedings', pp. 674–75.
20. The 'tall men' reference is taken from Stuart Corbridge and John Harriss, *Reinventing India: Liberalization, Hindu Nationalism and Popular Democracy* (New Delhi: Oxford University Press, second edition, 2000), p. 43. For more general discussion of Nehru's influence, see pp. 25–26, 43–66; and Chatterjee, *Nationalist Thought and the Colonial World*.
21. Exchange in 'Joint Proceedings', p. 677.
22. Ibid., pp. 677–78.
23. Ibid., p. 678.
24. Ibid., pp. 678–79.
25. *SWJN*, second series, vol. 2, p. 485.
26. 'Summary of the Discussions Held at Bombay by the Rulers of Princely

States and their Ministers', March–April 1947; 'Report of the States Committee', 24 April 1947, in Rao, *The Framing of India's Constitution*, pp. 729–43.

27. 'Report of the States Committee', p. 735; Copland, *The Princes of India in the Endgame of Empire*, pp. 243–46.
28. Granville Austin, *The Indian Constitution: Cornerstone of a Nation* (New Delhi: Oxford University Press, 2000, first published 1966), p. 62.
29. Austin, *The Indian Constitution*, p. 70. See also 'Minutes of the Fundamental Rights Subcommittee', 15 April 1947, in Rao, *The Framing of India's Constitution*, vol. 2, p. 166.
30. Austin, *The Indian Constitution*, pp. 50–115, particularly pp. 62–63; Rao, *The Framing of India's Constitution*, vol. 2, pp. 21–306.
31. Analysis of the Asian Relations Conference based on Itty Abraham, 'Bandung and State Formation in Post-colonial Asia', in See Seng Tan and Amitav Acharya, *Bandung Revisited: The Legacy of the 1955 Asian-African Conference for International Order* (Singapore: National University of Singapore Press, 2008), pp. 48–67.
32. 27 January 1947, E/CN.4/SR.2, p. 3, Folder: January–June 1947, ILFDRL.
33. http://www.gandhiserve.org/information/listen_to_gandhi/lec_2_iarc/lec_2_iarc.html. Also listen to Gandhi's speech here: http://www.washingtonpost.com/wpdyn/content/story/2008/06/30/ST2008063002509.html?sid=ST2008063002509&pos=top. Gandhi, in the recording, flips One World to World One in the second phrase. In the printed version of the speech on Gandhiserve, 'One World' is not capitalized.
34. Copland, *The Princes of India in the Endgame of Empire*, p. 246.
35. D.R. SarDesai, *India: The Definitive History* (Boulder, Colorado: Westview Press, 2008), p. 309.
36. Jalal, *The Sole Spokesman*.
37. Ibid., pp. 120–21, 241–93, especially pp. 283–85.
38. For details on Hindu nationalism in late colonial India, see Manu Bhagavan, 'Princely States and the Hindu Imaginary', *The Journal of Asian Studies* 67 (3), 2008, pp. 881–915; Manu Bhagavan, 'The Hindutva Underground', *Economic and Political Weekly*, special article, 13 September 2008, pp. 39–48; Christophe Jaffrelot, *The Hindu Nationalist Movement in India* (New York: Columbia University Press, 1996, first published 1993); Tapan Basu, Pradip Datta, Sumit Sarkar, Tanika Sarkar and Sambuddha Sen, *Khaki Shorts, Saffron Flags: A Critique of the Hindu Right* (Hyderabad: Orient Longman, 1993); Marzia

Casolari, 'Hindutva's Foreign Tie-Up in the 1930s: Archival Evidence', *Economic and Political Weekly*, 22–28 January 2000, pp. 218–28.

39. Jalal, *The Sole Spokesman*, pp. 283–85.
40. Copland, *The Princes of India in the Endgame of Empire*, pp. 246–61, especially pp. 247–56.
41. For some discussion of Patel's politics, see Prakash Chandra Upadhyaya, 'The Politics of Indian Secularism', *Modern Asian Studies* 26 (4), pp. 815–53; Jaffrelot, who describes Patel as a Hindu traditionalist, in *The Hindu Nationalist Movement in India*, especially pp. 84–91; Parita Mukta, 'On the Political Culture of Authoritarianism', in Ghanshyam Shah, Mario Rutten and Hein Streefkerk, eds, *Development and Deprivation in Gujarat: In Honour of Jan Breman* (New Delhi: Sage Publications, 2003), pp. 59–73; Guha, *India after Gandhi*, pp. 137–38.
42. Menon, *Integration of the Indian States*, pp. 92–123, especially p. 109; Copland, *The Princes of India in the Endgame of Empire*, pp. 255–61.
43. The United States held a symbolic place in the post-colonial imagination for its successful rejection of European imperialism. Many people in the Indian subcontinent during the late colonial period felt affinity with the United States and its history. The presidencies of Woodrow Wilson and Franklin Roosevelt helped carry these warm feelings forward, as the idea of a League of Nations and Roosevelt's anti-imperialist rhetoric resonated with many. While all of this was true, the independence of India and Pakistan was resolutely different from that of the United States, since the former involved non-European peoples.
44. 'A Tryst with Destiny' and 'The Appointed Day', Nehru, *India's Foreign Policy*, pp. 13–16. See also Robert Trumbull, 'India and Pakistan Become Nations; Clashes Continue', *The New York Times*, 15 August 1947, pp. 1–2.
45. In many reproductions of the speech, One World is not capitalized, and so the reference is lost. The version I cite is the official version published by the Government of India.
46. *SWJN*, second series, vol. 3, pp. 179–82; Alex von Tunzelmann, *Indian Summer: The Secret History of the End of an Empire* (New York: Henry Holt, 2007), pp. 4–5.
47. David Hardiman, *Gandhi in His Time and Ours: The Global Legacy of His Ideas* (New York: Columbia University Press, 2003), pp. 184–91.
48. Guha, *India after Gandhi*, pp. 64–65. See also John Wood, 'British Versus Princely Legacies and the Political Integration of Gujarat', *The Journal of Asian Studies* 44 (1), 1984, pp. 65–99.

49. For more on Hyderabad, see Bhagavan, 'Princely States and the Hindu Imaginary'; Dick Kooiman, *Communalism and Indian Princely States: Travancore, Baroda and Hyderabad in the 1930s* (Delhi: Manohar, 2002); Margrit Pernau, *The Passing of Patrimonialism: Politics and Political Culture in Hyderabad, 1911–1948* (New Delhi: Manohar, 2000).
50. 'World Federation Vital, Nehru Says', exclusive interview with *The New York Times*, 15 August 1948, p. 24. A record of the Campaign for World Government, which noticed the interview, indicates that Nehru actually gave the 'exclusive interview' to the United Press of America. Campaign for World Government, Records of the New York Office, Box 6, Folder: Series I, correspondence, 1933–70, n.d., A. General correspondence, 1933–70, n.d., 1945–70 (2 of 4), 6.2, NYPL Manuscripts.
51. Taylor Sherman, 'The Integration of the Princely State of Hyderabad and the Making of the Postcolonial State in India, 1948–1956', *The Indian Economic and Social History Review* 44 (4), 2007, pp. 489–516, especially p. 495; 'World Federation Vital, Nehru Says'. See also Guha, *India after Gandhi*, pp. 65–71.
52. See D.K. Palit, *Major General A.A. Rudra: His Service in Three Armies and Two World Wars* (New Delhi: Reliance, 2006), p. 321. The book is actually an autobiography of sorts, with Palit representing Rudra's personal narration of his life in Palit's own words. Rudra, a colourful and long-standing military officer, recalls being told of Nehru's views by his commander-in-chief moments after the original conversation took place, and when the commander was particularly shocked and perturbed by Nehru's orders.
53. Eleanor Roosevelt, *The Autobiography of Eleanor Roosevelt* (New York: De Capo, 1992), p. 295. For more on Kashmir, see Guha, *India after Gandhi*, pp. 74–96; Mridu Rai, *Hindu Rulers, Muslim Subjects: Islam, Rights, and the History of Kashmir* (New Delhi: Permanent Black, 2004); and Chitralekha Zutshi, *Languages of Belonging: Islam, Regional Identity, and the Making of Kashmir* (New York: Oxford University Press, 2004). Despite the problems he faced in trying to meet, as he saw it, the national interest of the country he ran, Nehru never wavered in his idealistic goals. There was, of course, constant tension, as short-term political decisions chafed against the long-term vision, and opened Nehru up to charges of hypocrisy. Nehru saw no way to escape this tension, since realpolitik demanded immediate, and sometimes controversial, decisions. He was helpless to escape, since it was the system of nation states that dominated the world that created the

conditions necessary for such actions. It was only by changing the system, he felt, that he and everyone else could be freed of the confines of narrow self-interest. To an extent, this is illustrated in comments Nehru made in the Indian Parliament in 1952. There, confronted with continuing tensions in Kashmir, he made clear that he saw the UN as fundamental to any solution even to this issue. 'Having gone there [the UN] and respecting the idea of a World Organization dealing with such matters, it was but right she [India] should remain there, even though sometimes things happened which she disliked.' While he was going to advocate for India's interests, he maintained that 'the way of peace is always the better and the shorter way, however long it may seem, and the way of war is certainly the longer way and in fact no way at all to solve a problem.' Extract from Report of H.P.M.'s Speech in Parliament on 2 February 1952 (*Hindustan Times*, 13 February 1952), Ministry of External Affairs-Pak III Branch, India, no. PIII/ 52/197 44/107, NAI.

54. See Mohandas K. Gandhi, *An Autobiography: The Story of My Experiments with Truth* (Boston: Beacon Press, 1993, first published 1957); for deep insight into Gandhi's concept of satyagraha, see Ajay Skaria, 'The Strange Violence of *Satyagraha*: Gandhi, *IItihaas*, and History'.
55. Above excerpts from 'We Lead Ourselves', Speech in the Constituent Assembly (Legislative), 8 March 1948, in Nehru, *India's Foreign Policy*, pp. 29–37.
56. They did. On 20 March 1948, C. Rajagopalachari, one of the grand old figures in the Congress party, delivered a convocation address in which he spoke out in favour of Nehru's goals: 'The hope of internationalists is to attain a world federation one day wherein peace and justice could be assured for all the peoples of the world, irrespective of colour or continent or type of culture. So long as this is not attained and we have to rest content with a balanced system of national powers as a transitory substitute for the more stable equilibrium of a world federation, there is always a tendency for . . . inevitable conflict . . . What is wanted now is someone who will explain America to Russia and Russia to America . . . one who commands respect and influence and is trusted by both.' He added that India and Pakistan should 'join hands' to help themselves and the world situation. Speech excerpt enclosed with a letter dated 27 March to a representative of the Movement for World Government, Campaign for World Government, Records of the New York Office, Box 6, Folder: Series I, correspondence, 1933–70, n.d., A. General correspondence, 1933–

70, n.d. –1945–70 (2 of 4), 6.2, NYPL Manuscripts. In his letter of the 27th, 'Rajaji' noted that the organization, interested in creating a World Constituent Assembly in 1950, should contact Jawaharlal Nehru.

57. Above excerpts from 'We Lead Ourselves'.
58. 'Nehru Re-states Basis of Foreign Policy', *The Indian Express*, 9 March 1948, pp. 1, 6.
59. *Chicago Daily Tribune*, 4 April 1948, p. SW12.
60. See Dennis Dalton, ed., *Mahatma Gandhi: Selected Political Writings* (Indianapolis: Hackett Publishing Company, 1996), pp. 95–152. See also Judith Brown, 'Gandhi and Human Rights: In Search of True Humanity', in Richard L. Johnson, ed., *Gandhi's Experiments with Truth: Essential Writings by and about Mahatma Gandhi* (New York: Lexington Books, 2006), pp. 237–52.
61. Excerpts from 'A Crisis of Spirit', Nehru, *India's Foreign Policy*, pp. 182–83.
62. 'The Problem of World Government', *The University of Chicago Roundtable*, in cooperation with the National Broadcasting Company, no. 524, 4 April 1948.
63. 'Move for World Federal Govt.', *The Indian Express*, 22 April 1948, p. 4. See also Campaign for World Government, Records of the New York Office, 1917–72, MssCol 461, collections guide, NYPL, Laura Rutton, September 2006, pp. 5, 8. Nehru's speech and Clark's visit were followed closely by international members of the Campaign for World Government. Correspondence between London- and Delhi-based members indicated tremendous excitement. They also noted that B. Shiva Rao, an influential advisor who participated in both the United Nations delegations and the Indian Constituent Assembly (and who edited the authoritative collection *The Framing of India's Constitution*), was planning to convene a group to mobilize opinion in India in favour of world government. Not-to-be published letter between Norman D. Cliff and Usborne, 20 April 1948. Nehru also responded on 6 April to a letter from Usborne from the 27th of March that duplicated the invitation to Rajagopalachari (see Note 56 above), asking Nehru (and India) to participate in a World Constituent Assembly in 1950. Nehru responded that 1950 was a long way away, but he expressed his support for the idea in principle. Nehru to Usborne, 6 April 1948. Campaign for World Government, Records of the New York Office, Box 6, Folder: Series I, correspondence, 1933–70, n.d., A. General correspondence, 1933–70, n.d. –1945–70 (2 of 4), 6.2, NYPL Manuscripts.

64. Asaf Ali, 'India's Role in One World', *Annals of the American Academy of Political and Social Science*, vol. 259, July 1948, pp. 22–26.
65. Nehru, speech before the third session of the UN, 3 November 1948, in Madhavan, *India at the United Nations*, pp. 53–55.
66. 'Nehru's Warning', *The Indian Express*, 5 November 1948, p. 4.
67. Normand and Zaidi, *Human Rights at the UN*, p. 202.
68. 'Human Rights in the New Constitution of India.' Speeches by Hansa Mehta, Mehta Papers, Sub-file no. 4, 1949, NMML. The speech is hand dated 21 March. The fifth session of the HRC met from 9 June to 20 June 1949. See E/CN.4/350, UNODS.
69. Summary Record of the first meeting of the second session of the Working Group on Implementation, HRC, 5 December 1947, E/CN.4/AC.4/SR.1, 3, Folder: June–December 1947, ILFDRL. See also Briggs, 1948, pp. 391–92.
70. See Article 37 of the Indian Constitution. Available at http://indiacode.nic.in/coiweb/welcome.html. The original draft of this guide to the Directive Principles was much weaker. Hansa Mehta, in coordination with her close ally Rajkumari Amrit Kaur, directly intervened to ensure that the Article made state obligation clear: 'While the non-justiciable rights shall not be cognizable by any court, we [Kaur and Mehta] would respectfully urge that they are nonetheless fundamental. We would, therefore, like this to be stressed either in the forward or at the end of clause 35 so that it shall be the duty of the State to take, as soon as possible, the necessary action in fulfillment of the directives.' Letter from Rajkumari Amrit Kaur to B.N. Rau, on behalf of herself and Hansa Mehta, 31 March 1947, in Shiva Rao, vol. 2, pp. 146–47.
71. 'Human Rights in the New Constitution of India.' Speeches by Hansa Mehta, Mehta Papers, Sub-file no. 4, 1949, NMML.
72. Normand and Zaidi, *Human Rights at the UN*, pp. 197–204. Positive rights required that governments (positively) act—the government had to provide things for there to be a right to food or a right to health care. Negative rights required non-intervention by governments, except to protect people whose rights were violated. The right to free speech, for instance, required nothing of the government except that the government protect rather than persecute or prosecute people for what they said.

6. TOWARDS A BETTER FUTURE

1. Pandit, *The Scope of Happiness*, pp. 235–64.
2. Truman Library Photographs, Accession no. 72–613.
3. In an exchange of letters shortly after the visit, Einstein told Nehru that he felt 'grateful for your honest attempts to bring about a peaceful solution in the present dangerous situation.' Einstein to Nehru, 24 July 1950, Einstein Papers, 32–736, Princeton University Special Collections. Nehru responded that he appreciated Einstein's support of 'the ideals for which we have worked'. He noted: 'Unfortunately it is difficult to fit in ideals to reality and all kinds of forces and interests come in the way. But we have to struggle onwards in spite of these obstructions.' Nehru to Einstein, 28 February 1950, Einstein Papers, 32–735.
4. 'A Welcome Visitor', *The New York Times*, 11 October 1949, p. 30.
5. http://clerk.house.gov/art_history/highlights.html?action= view&int ID=485
6. Report of the fifth session of the Commission on Human Rights, 1949, E/CN.4/350, pp. 48–51, UNODS. See also Steiner, Alston and Goodman, *International Human Rights in Context*, p. 270.
7. 'Nehru Bars Neutrality in Injustice; Talk Suggests India as Conciliator', 14 October 1949, *The New York Times*, pp. 1, 8.
8. Ibid.
9. 'Mankind in a Revolutionary Age', *University of Chicago Roundtable*, no. 606, 30 October 1949, especially pp. 7–8.
10. Guha, *India after Gandhi*, p. 143.
11. India: Draft Resolution concerning the inclusion of economic, social and cultural rights in the draft International Covenant on Human Rights, E/CN.4/619/Rev.1, 14 May 1951, UNODS.
12. Annotations on the text of the draft International Covenants on Human Rights. Document A/2929, p. 8, UNODS.
13. E/CN.4/SR.248, 18 May 1951, p. 25, Columbia Law Library.
14. See Skaria, 'The Strange Violence of *Satyagraha*: Gandhi, *Itihaas*, and History', pp. 142–85.
15. Report of the seventh session of the HRC, 16 April to 19 May 1951, reproduced in the Official Records of the Economic and Social Council, thirteenth session, supplement no. 9, p. 29, UNODS.
16. Annotations on the text of the draft International Covenants on Human Rights. Document A/2929, p. 7, UNODS.
17. Mehta specifically uses the word 'harmonize' when discussing a way to bring different methods of implementation together during the

meetings of the seventh session. See 'Summary Records of the Seventh Session', Columbia Law Library.

18. 'Text of Willkie's Address to the Nation Renewing His Plea for a Second Front', *The New York Times*, 27 October 1942, p. 8. See also Chapter 2 of this volume.
19. E/CN.4/SR.248, 18 May 1951, pp. 12–15, Columbia Law Library.
20. E/CN.4/SR.248, 18 May 1951, p. 17, Columbia Law Library.
21. Annotations on the text of the draft International Covenants on Human Rights. Document A/2929, pp. 4–5, UNODS.
22. Details of the Economic and Social Council's resolution can be found in the 'Official Records of the Economic and Social Council, Sixth Year, Thirteenth Session', E/2152, 30 July–21 September 1951, supplement no. 1, pp. 35–36. *The Report of the Indian Delegation to the 13th Session of the United Nations' Economic & Social Council* (New Delhi: Ministry of External Affairs) notes that India jointly sponsored (with Uruguay, Belgium, the US and the UK) the 'invitation' to the General Assembly 'to reconsider its decision in Resolution 421 (V) to include in one single Covenant. [sic] Articles [sic] on economic, social and cultural rights together with civil and political rights.' See p. 29. For the General Assembly discussions, see *Yearbook of the United Nations*, 1951, pp. 477–91. The report notes that India's General Assembly team, along with Lebanon, commented that economic and social rights were dependent on civil and political rights (p. 483). These were not the views expressed in the HRC (where they were both interdependent), so this comment seems likely to be a personal opinion of one of the representatives to the General Assembly than India's official stand. India's team in 1951 (carrying over to early 1952) included B.N. Rau, K.M. Pannikar (see Chapter 5 of this volume), Reverend Jerome D'Souza and two others (p. 31).
23. 'World Consciousness before One World', 1951, in K.M. Munshi, *Our Greatest Need and Other Addresses* (Bombay: Bharatiya Vidya Bhavan, 1958), pp. 214–16. Nehru also sat down for an interview with Norman Cousins that appeared in two parts in the 14th and 21st April issues of *The Saturday Review of Literature* (*SRL*). Cousins, a famed peace activist and leader of the world federalist movement, was the editor-in-chief of *SRL*. In the interview, made at the outset of the seventh session's deliberations, Nehru again reiterated his support of One World, and of the United Nations, but was coy on the idea of difference. *Saturday Review of Literature*, 21 April 1951, pp. 7–8, in 'Nehru 1949–1950', United World Federalists Mss., Lilly Library, Indiana University. Cousins would be the person who brought Nehru the news of Einstein's

death in 1955. Both Cousins and Nehru were attending the Bandung Conference. See 'The Spirit of Bandung' section, this chapter. Nehru immediately penned a short testimonial to Einstein. 32 752, 19 April 1955, Einstein Papers, Princeton University Special Collections.

24. Pandit Papers, I Inst., press clippings, F. no. 5 (Pt. 2), p. 163, clipping from Indianapolis, 13 May 1949.
25. Ibid., p. 159. *Labor*, Washington DC, 14 May 1949.
26. Ibid., clipping from Indianapolis, 13 May 1949.
27. Ibid., p. 164.
28. Ibid., p. 171. *The Washington Post*, 9 May 1949, p. 2.
29. Ibid., pp. 18–19.
30. Ibid., p. 112. *The New York Post*, 1 September 1949.
31. Ibid., p. 93. *The New York Times*, 9 May 1950.
32. Ibid., p. 25, and no number given. Quote from *Daytona Beach Morning Journal*, 3 April 1951, p. 2. Story on Pandit and UN from *Minneapolis Sunday Tribune*, 12 November 1950, p. 4.
33. Pandit Papers, I Inst., press clippings, F. no. 5 (Pt. I), p. 1. *The Washington Post*.
34. Ibid., p. 2.. *The New York Times*, 13 August 1951.
35. Guha, *India after Gandhi*, pp. 137–59, especially pp. 149–50, 153, 158.
36. Eleanor Roosevelt, *The Autobiography of Eleanor Roosevelt*, p. 330. Mrs Roosevelt records that Nehru spoke with thirty million people, and that his miles of travel did not include distance he had covered on foot.
37. Guha, *India after Gandhi*, p. 155.
38. 'Mme. President', 16 September 1953, *The New York Times*, p. 32.
39. Judith M. Brown, *Nehru: A Political Life* (New Haven: Yale University Press, 2003), p. 256. Nehru prepared a 'secret and personal' memo for Churchill, at the Briton's request, outlining his views on a number of international affairs. Brown cites the note, dated 8 June 1953, from Nehru's post-1947 papers, second installment, correspondence with Winston Churchill, no. 70. These papers remain closed to the scholarly public and I was not allowed access to them.
40. Annotations on the text of the draft International Covenants on Human Rights. Document A/2929, pp. 5–6, UNODS.
41. For an overview and analysis of Bandung, see also Vijay Prashad, *The Darker Nations: A People's History of the Third World* (New York: The New Press, 2007), pp. 31–50.
42. 'Asia and Africa Awake', speech at Bandung, 24 April 1955, in Nehru, *India's Foreign Policy*, pp. 269–72.

43. 'The Bandung Conference', Statement in the Lok Sabha, 30 April 1955, in Nehru, *India's Foreign Policy*, pp. 272–80, especially p. 279.
44. See Abraham, 'Bandung and State Formation in Post-colonial Asia', pp. 48–67.
45. 'Asia and Africa Awake', speech at Bandung, 24 April 1955, in Nehru, *India's Foreign Policy*, p. 271. Among the staunchest of Nehru's critics was US Secretary of State John Foster Dulles. He had a good relationship with Madame Pandit, but was generally more hostile to Nehru. Eleanor Roosevelt thought that Dulles' approach to Nehru was 'unfortunate and unwise'. Eleanor Roosevelt, *The Autobiography of Eleanor Roosevelt*, p. 295. Dulles did make a trip to India in 1956. Guha, *India after Gandhi*, pp. 167–70. Dulles–Pandit correspondence, John Foster Dulles Papers, MC016, Princeton University Mudd Library.
46. 'Soviet Crowd Cheers Nehru', Reuter's story in *The Spokesman-Review*, 8 June 1955, p. 4.
47. United Press reporter Charles McCann, 'India's Nehru Ends Visit to Russia with Excellent Display of Diplomacy', *The Times-News*, 22 June 1955, p. 2.
48. Nehru's welcome in Delhi, as appearing in *Pravda* and *Izvestia*, the official newspapers of the Communist Party and the Soviet government, 20 November 1950, p. 2. Translated into English by the Joint Committee on Slavic Studies, *The Current Digest of the Soviet Press* 7 (47), 4 January 1956, pp. 13–17. I am most grateful to my just-retired colleague, Michael Luther, for his authoritative knowledge of Soviet Russia, and for bringing this resource material to my attention.
49. 'Bulganin's Report to the Supreme Soviet Legislature on the Recent Trip to Asia.' Condensed, as appearing in *Pravda* and *Izvestia*, 30 December 1950, pp. 1–2. *The Current Digest of the Soviet Press* 7 (51), 1 February 1956, pp. 13–17.
50. Bulganin's speech to the Indian Parliament, as appearing in *Pravda* and *Izvestia*, 22 November 1950, pp. 1–2. *The Current Digest of the Soviet Press* 7 (47), 4 January 1956, p. 2.
51. 'Bulganin's Report to the Supreme Soviet Legislature on the Recent Trip to Asia.' Translated into English by the Joint Committee on Slavic Studies, *The Current Digest of the Soviet Press* 7 (51), 1 February 1956, p. 14.
52. Guha, *India after Gandhi*, p. 171.
53. This was made clear when the UN adopted the Panchsheel in 1957. See the 'Towards a Better Future' section of this chapter.
54. 'The Concept of Panchsheel', in Nehru, *India's Foreign Policy*, pp. 99–102, especially p. 99, n. 1.

55. Ibid., p. 100.
56. 'Nehru Is Privately Ashamed of Soviet Leaders' Actions', *The Modesto Bee*, 22 December 1955, p. 1. Nehru's thoughts were widely reported in the Western press, indicating that he wanted to publicly distance himself from the Soviet comments.
57. The above material is summarized from Steve Morewood, 'Prelude to the Suez Crisis', in Simon C. Smith, ed., *Reassessing Suez 1956: New Perspectives on the Crisis and Its Aftermath* (Hampshire, England: Ashgate, 2008), pp. 14–34.
58. 'Nationalization of the Suez Canal', in Nehru, *India's Foreign Policy*, pp. 527–32.
59. Brown, *Nehru*, pp. 263–65.
60. Circumstantial evidence from 1955 leads me to believe it is quite possible that Nehru urged Khrushchev to make this famous move, but until serious research can be done in the Soviet archives from this period, this remains mere conjecture. In any event, Krushchev's speech led first to an uprising in Poland and then to one in Hungary. The Polish did not ask for multi-party democracy, and their issues were brought to a resolution. The Hungarians did and that led to the harsh response, signalling clear limits to Khrushchev's approach. I thank my colleague, Benjamin Hett, for clarifying this point.
61. 'Top secret' note from Pillai to Nehru, 2 November 1956, cited in Brown, *Nehru*, p. 381, n. 64.
62. See references to Menon throughout Pandit, *The Scope of Happiness*. In an 'angry outburst' she also once told a reporter: 'Don't pay any attention to anything that man tells you.' 'Menon Ousts Pandit as Nehru's Advisor', Chicago Daily News Services, 17 August. No year given, but context indicates the story is from 1954. Pandit Papers, II Inst., press clippings, F. no. 11. File page number possibly is 11, but unclear.
63. 'Menon Ousts Pandit as Nehru's Advisor.'
64. Brown, *Nehru*, p. 265. The material in this section is largely based on information found in ibid., pp. 256–66; and Guha, *India after Gandhi*, pp. 172–75. Brown's work is based on access to Nehru's post-1947 papers, which, as noted earlier, remain closed to the general scholarly public at the Nehru Library in New Delhi. I did not have access to them.
65. While Nehru had delivered numerous addresses on peace and on One World before, including one in Hamburg as recently as July 1956, all of those had been to much more narrow audiences. The speech he delivers in December 1956 at the UN is his first on the

subject to the entire global audience. 'Nehru on "One World",' *The Glasgow Herald*, 17 July 1956, p. 4. In his summer 1956 trip to Germany, he met with German Chancellor Konrad Adenauer, via facilitation by Cyrus Sulzberger, the editor of *The New York Times*. My colleague, the historian Benjamin Hett, translating from the German scholar Hans-Peter Schwarz's book on the chancellor, indicates that Adenauer was a hard-edged Cold Warrior, and a realist, disinclined to like Nehru. But Nehru made 'a strong impression' and the two leaders 'dealt with each other respectfully'. Hans-Peter Schwarz, *Adenauer*, vol. 2, *Der Staatsmann: 1952–1967* (Stuttgart: Deutsche Verlags-Anstalt, 1991), p. 318. Hett takes this as clear indication of Nehru's considerable talents. Interestingly, but tangentially, the German newspaper *Der Spiegel* (again as translated by Hett) reported on 4 November 1959 that Nehru was growing increasingly concerned about his growing cult of personality in India, and saw this as the 'greatest danger' to Indian democracy.

66. Nehru spoke to an 'informal gathering', rather than an 'official meeting', but all UN delegates were present, along with a number of prominent US officials and others. See 'Nehru, Here, Asks End of "Cold War" and Armed Pacts', 21 December 1956, *The New York Times*, pp. 1, 4.
67. 'Towards a World Community', Nehru, *India's Foreign Policy*, pp. 173–79.
68. 'Question of Peaceful Co-Existence and Relations', *Yearbook of the United Nations*, 1957, pp. 105–09. And 'U.N. Resolution on Co-Existence'. Speech to the Lok Sabha, 17 December 1957, in Nehru, *India's Foreign Policy*, pp. 102–04.
69. 'U.N. Resolution on Co-Existence.'
70. 'Nehru Urges End of Atomic Terror', 11 November 1961, *The New York Times*, p. 3.

EPILOGUE

1. Nehru, *The Hindu*, 26 October 1962, quoted in Mithi Mukherjee, '"A World of Illusion": The Legacy of Empire in India's Foreign Relations, 1947–1962', *The International History Review* 32 (2), June 2010, p. 253.
2. Ibid., pp. 253–71.
3. The Cuban Missile Crisis began when the Soviets secretly placed nuclear missiles in Cuba, within easy striking distance of the United States, partially in response to US missiles in Turkey. Nehru's reputation suffered another major blow when he ordered the Indian army into

the Portuguese colony of Goa, on India's west coast. While there was indigenous opposition to Portuguese control, and political opinion from right to left was united in support of military action, Nehru's use of force in that instance (though he had long advocated non-violence on this issue as on all others) screamed hypocrisy. His primary sin appears to have been his faith in Krishna Menon, who blundered at the UN in 1956. The Goan affair was, in part, meant to shore up Menon's parliamentary re-election bid. It did, and Menon won, but the result was that he was also the bungling minister in charge of defence during the war with China. See Guha, *India after Gandhi*, pp. 331–33. For more on the Cuban Missile Crisis, see Aleksandr Fursenko and Timothy Naftali, *One Hell of a Gamble: Khrushchev, Castro, and Kennedy, 1958–1964: The Secret History of the Cuban Missile Crisis* (New York: Norton, 1997); Ernest R. May and Philip D. Zelikow, eds, *The Kennedy Tapes: Inside the White House during the Cuban Missile Crisis* (New York: Norton, concise edition, 2002).

4. Jagat Narain points out that the sixteenth amendment passed because of 'political pressures' rather than 'judicial interpretation'. He also notes that the amendment 'does constitute an additional, independent ground for imposing restrictions . . .' on rights and freedoms, certainly the opposite of everything Nehru had been advocating. See Jagat Narain, 'Constitutional Changes in India', *The International and Comparative Law Quarterly* 17 (4), 1968, pp. 884–85. Although similar language related to sovereignty and integrity was used in the Panchsheel agreements, those were always meant as mutual or multi-lateral pacts, and thus signalled mutual respect and cooperation. The sixteenth amendment was a unilateral defence of sovereignty and territorial integrity, and thus markedly different—a national(-ist) act—as opposed to an internationalist one.
5. Untitled fourteen-page speech on Non-alignment, 1962, Pandit Papers, II Inst., Speeches/Writings by Her, F. no. 16. It is unclear if this was ever published.
6. S. Radhakrishnan, K. Chattopadhyay and K. Kalelkar, *Mahatma Gandhi and One World* (New Delhi: Government of India, 1966, reprinted 1994), pp. 7–9. P.C. Joshi Archives, Jawaharlal Nehru University.
7. Ibid., pp. 13, 19.
8. Various newspapers, 1963–65, Pandit Papers, II Inst., press clippings, F. no. 4.
9. 'Nothing So Important as Genuine International Cooperation.' Speech by Madame Pandit to the World Council of YMCA's at Gotemba,

Shizuoka-ken, Japan, n.d., Pandit Papers, II Inst., press clippings, F. no. 4, p. 85.

10. Madame Pandit railed in 1977 that this 'erosion of our cherished values must be stopped and we must go back to the ideals to which we are pledged'. See Katherine Frank, *Indira: The Life of Indira Nehru Gandhi* (New York: Houghton Mifflin, 2002), p. 412. More generally, see Pandit, *The Scope of Happiness*, pp. 1–23.
11. In perhaps the most sincere sign of Radhakrishnan's providence, the high commissioner since 2008, Navanethem Pillay, is a South African of South Indian descent.
12. For important criticisms of the modern human rights framework, see Kristen Ross, 'Ethics and the Rearmament of Imperialism: the French Case', in Jeffrey N. Wasserstrom, Greg Grandin, Lynn Hunt and Marilyn B. Young, eds, *Human Rights and Revolutions* (New York: Rowman and Littlefield, second edition, 2007), pp. 155–67; and Upendra Baxi, *The Future of Human Rights* (New Delhi: Oxford University Press, third edition, 2009, first published 2008). These are but samples of a vast literature.
13. Sudan suffered from ethnic conflict and civil war particularly fierce prior to the creation of the new state of South Sudan in 2011; atrocities continue in both states. Katrina was a hurricane that struck the southern US city of New Orleans. Poor planning and aid relief devastated many city communities and hit minority populations especially hard.
14. Cf. Marnia Lazreg, *Torture and the Twilight of Empire: From Algiers to Baghdad* (Princeton: Princeton University Press, 2008).
15. See Garrett Wallace Brown and David Held, *The Cosmopolitanism Reader* (Cambridge, UK: Polity Press, 2010). For an important critique, see David Harvey, *Cosmopolitanism and the Geographies of Freedom* (New York: Columbia University Press, 2009). See also David Held, *Cosmopolitanism: Ideals, Realities & Deficits* (Cambridge, UK: Polity Press, 2010).
16. See, for instance, Thomas G. Weiss, *What's Wrong with the United Nations and How to Fix It* (Cambridge, UK: Polity Press, 2008); and Joseph E. Schwartzberg, *Revitalizing the United Nations* (New York: Institute for Global Policy, 2004). Online at: http://globalsolutions.org/files/public/documents/Schwartzberg_Weighted_Voting.pdf. Last accessed 16 December 2010. See also Schwartzberg's *Designs for a Workable World*, forthcoming. I am grateful to Prof. Schwartzberg for sharing some of the unpublished manuscript with me.
17. Nehru, *India's Foreign Policy*, pp. 182–83.

INDEX

Bibliography

Primary Sources

Ali, Asaf. 'India's Role in One World', *Annals of the American Academy of Political and Social Science*, vol. 259, July 1948.

Asian Relations: Being Report of the Proceedings and Documentation of the First Asian Relations Conference. New Delhi: Asian Relations Organizations, 1948.

Briggs, Herbert W. 'Implementation of the Proposed International Covenant on Human Rights', *The American Journal of International Law* 42 (2), 1948.

Campaign for World Government, Records of the New York Office, Manuscripts and Archives Division, New York Public Library, Astor, Lenox and Tilden Foundations.

Collier's Weekly. February–December 1945.

Cordier, Andrew W. and Foote, Wilder, eds. *Public Papers of the Secretaries-General of the United Nations: Trygve Lie, 1946–1953*. New York: Columbia University Press, vol. 1, 1969.

——. *Public Papers of the Secretaries-General of the United Nations: Dag Hammarskjöld, 1953–1956*. New York: Columbia University Press, vol. 2, 1972.

Council on Foreign Relations Records, Princeton University Mudd Library.

Dalton, Dennis, ed. *Mahatma Gandhi: Selected Political Writings*. Indianapolis: Hackett Publishing Company, 1996.

David E. Lilienthal Papers, Princeton University Mudd Library.

Foreign Office of the United Kingdom. A *Commentary on the Charter of the United Nations*, Cmd. 6666, Misc. no. 9, London, 1945.

Gandhi, Mohandas K. *An Autobiography: The Story of My Experiments with Truth.* Boston: Beacon Press, 1993, first published 1957.

——. *The Collected Works of Mahatma Gandhi (CWMG).* Online at: http://www.gandhiserve.org/cwmg.

Hamilton Fish Armstrong Papers, Princeton University Mudd Library.

Jinnah, Mohammad Ali. *Quaid-i-Azam Mohammad Ali Jinnah Papers.* First series, Islamabad, Pakistan, 1996.

John Foster Dulles Papers, Princeton University Mudd Library.

India and the United Nations: Report of a Study Group Set up by the Indian Council of World Affairs. New York: Manhattan Publishing Company, 1957.

Institute of Pacific Relations. *Security in the Pacific: A Preliminary Report of the Ninth Conference of the Institute of Pacific Relations, 6–17 January 1945.* New York, 1945.

International League for Human Rights, Manuscripts and Archives Division, New York Public Library, Astor, Lenox and Tilden Foundations.

Khipple, R.L. *Vijaya Lakshmi Pandit: The Woman Who Swayed America.* Lahore: Lion Press, 1946.

Madhavan, S.K., ed. *India at the United Nations.* New Delhi: APH Publishing Corp., vols 1–3, 1999.

Mansergh, Nicholas, Lumby, E.W. and Moon, Penderel, eds. *The Transfer of Power, 1942–7.* London: Her Majesty's Stationary Office, 1970–83.

Mehta, Hansa, Kaur, Rajkumari Amrit and Menon, Lakshmi. *The Indian Woman's Charter of Rights and Duties*, July 1946.

Mehta, Chandralekha, Sahgal, Nayantara and Dar, Rita. *Sunlight Surround You.* New Delhi: Orient Longman, 1970.

Menon, V.P. *Integration of the Indian States.* Madras: Orient Longman, 1985, first published 1956.

Munshi, K.M. *Indian Constitutional Documents: Pilgrimage to Freedom, 1902–1950.* Bombay: Bharatiya Vidya Bhavan, vols 1–2, 1967.

——. *Our Greatest Need and Other Addresses.* Bombay: Bharatiya Vidya Bhavan, 1958.

——. *The End of an Era: Hyderabad Memoirs.* Mumbai: Bharatiya Vidya Bhavan, 1998, first published 1957.

Nehru, Jawaharlal. *Autobiography.* London: John Lane, 1936.

——. *Essential Writings.* Edited by S. Gopal and Uma Iyengar. Delhi: Oxford University Press, vols 1–3, 2003.

——. *India's Foreign Policy.* Delhi: Government of India, 1961.

——. *Speeches*. Delhi: Government of India, vol. 3, 1958.

——. *The Discovery of India*. New York: John Day, 1946.

——. *The Selected Works of Jawaharlal Nehru* (*SWJN*). Edited by S. Gopal. New Delhi: Jawaharlal Nehru Memorial Fund, first series.

——. *The Selected Works of Jawaharlal Nehru* (*SWJN*). Edited by S. Gopal. New Delhi: Jawaharlal Nehru Memorial Fund, second series, distributed by Oxford University Press.

——. *The Unity of India*. New York: John Day, 1942.

'Nehru 1949–1950', in Box 36 of United World Federalists Mss. Courtesy of the Lilly Library, Indiana University, Bloomington, Indiana.

Official United Nations Documents, Dag Hammarskjöld Library, United Nations Headquarters, New York.

Pandit, Vijaya Lakshmi. *The Evolution of India*. London: Oxford University Press, 1958.

——. *The Scope of Happiness: A Personal Memoir*. New York: Crown Publishers, 1979.

Pannikar, K.M. *An Autobiography*. Translated by K. Krishnamurthy. Madras: Oxford University Press, 1977, first published 1954.

Papers of Albert Einstein, Princeton University Special Collections.

Papers of Eleanor Roosevelt, 1933–45. Franklin D. Roosevelt Library, Hyde Park, New York.

Papers of the External Affairs Ministry, National Archives of India, New Delhi.

Papers of Pearl S. Buck, Warren Sherk Collection, Randolph College Archives.

Papers of Isador Lubin, Franklin D. Roosevelt Library, Hyde Park, New York.

Papers of Clare Booth Luce, Library of Congress, Washington DC.

Papers of Henry Luce, Library of Congress, Washington DC.

Papers related to the visit of Vijaya Lakshmi Pandit to the United States, National Archives, United Kingdom.

Private Papers of Hansa Mehta Nehru Memorial Museum and Library, New Delhi.

Papers of the National Association for the Advancement of Colored People, via Hunter College Interlibrary Loan.

Papers of the United Nations, UN Archives, New York.

Poplai, S.L. *Select Documents: India, 1947–1950*. London: Oxford University Press, vols 1–2, 1959.

Private Papers of Vijaya Lakshmi Pandit, Nehru Memorial Museum and Library.

Radhakrishnan, S., Chattopadhyay, K. and Kalelkar, K. *Mahatma Gandhi and One World*. New Delhi: Government of India, 1966, reprinted 1994.

Rao, B. Shiva. *The Framing of India's Constitution: Select Documents*. New Delhi: Universal Law Publishing, vols 1–5, 2006, first published 1967.

Report of the Indian Delegation to the Second Part of the First Session of General Assembly of the United Nations. New Delhi: Government of India, 1946, Nehru Memorial Museum and Library.

Roosevelt, Eleanor. *The Autobiography of Eleanor Roosevelt*. New York: De Capo, 1992.

Sahgal, Nayantara. *Before Freedom: Nehru's Letters to His Sister*. New Delhi: HarperCollins, 2000.

Security in the Pacific: A Preliminary Report of the Ninth Conference of the Institute of Pacific Relations. New York: Institute of Pacific Relations, 1945.

Sidney Hertzberg Papers, Manuscripts and Archives Division, New York Public Library, Astor, Lenox and Tilden Foundations.

The Current Digest of the Soviet Press. Translated into English by the Joint Committee on Slavic Studies (Includes *Pravda* and *Izvestia*).

The Report of the Indian Delegation to the 13th Session of the United Nations' Economic & Social Council. New Delhi: Ministry of External Affairs.

The University of Chicago Roundtable, pamphlets, in cooperation with the National Broadcasting Company.

Town Meeting: Bulletin of America's Town Meeting of the Air (collected as *Town Hall*), vol. 10, no. 44, 1 March 1945.

United States Department of State Records, National Archives of the United States, College Park, Maryland.

Willkie, Wendell L. *One World*. New York: Simon and Shuster, 1943.

SECONDARY SOURCES

Abraham, Itty. 'Migration and Citizenship in Asian International Relations and State Formation.' In Tan, See Seng and Acharya, Amitav, eds. *Bandung Revisited: The Legacy of the 1955 Asian-African Conference for International Order*. Singapore: National University of Singapore Press, 2008.

Anderson, Carol. 'Allies of a Kind: India and the NAACP's Alliance against South Africa's Colonialism and *Apartheid*, 1946–1951.' Unpublished conference paper. Cited by permission of the author.

——. *Bourgeois Radicals: The NAACP and the Struggle for Colonial Liberation, 1941–1960*. Manuscript cited by permission of the author.

——. *Eyes off the Prize: The United Nations and the African American Struggle for Human Rights, 1944–1955*. Cambridge: Cambridge University Press, 2009, first published 2003.

——. 'International Conscience, the Cold War, and Apartheid: The NAACP's Alliance with the Reverend Michael Scott for South West Africa's Liberation, 1946–1951', *Journal of World History*. 19 (3), September 2008.

Andrews, Robert Hardy. *A Lamp for India: The Story of Madame Pandit*. Englewood Cliffs, New Jersey: Prentice-Hall, 1967.

Ansari, Sarah. *Life after Partition: Migration, Community and Strife in Sindh, 1947–1962*. Karachi: Oxford University Press, 2005.

Austin, Granville. *The Indian Constitution: Cornerstone of a Nation*. New Delhi, Oxford University Press, 2000, first published 1966.

Basu, Tapan, Datta, Pradip, Sarkar, Sumit, Sarkar, Tanika and Sen, Sambuddha. *Khaki Shorts, Saffron Flags: A Critique of the Hindu Right*. Hyderabad: Orient Longman, 1993.

Baxi, Upendra. *The Future of Human Rights*. Delhi: Oxford University Press, third edition, 2009, first published 2008.

Berkes, Ross and Bedi, Mohinder. *The Diplomacy of India: Indian Foreign Policy and the United Nations*. Stanford: Stanford University Press, 1958.

Bhagavan, Manu. 'A New Hope: India, the United Nations, and the Making of the Universal Declaration of Human Rights', *Modern Asian Studies*, online 13 June 2008, print edition forthcoming.

——, ed. *Heterotopias: Nationalism and the Possibility of History in South Asia*. New Delhi: Oxford University Press, 2010.

——. 'Princely States and the Hindu Imaginary: Exploring the Cartography of Hindu Nationalism in Colonial India', *The Journal of Asian Studies* 67 (3), August 2008.

——. 'Princely States and the Making of Modern India', *The Indian Economic and Social History Review* 46 (3), 2009.

——. *Sovereign Spheres: Princes, Education and Empire in Colonial India*. New Delhi: Oxford University Press, 2003.

——. 'The Hindutva Underground: Hindu Nationalism and the Indian National Congress in Late Colonial and Early Postcolonial India', *The Economic and Political Weekly*, special article, 13 September 2008.

Borgwardt, Elizabeth. *A New Deal for the World: America's Vision for Human Rights*. Cambridge, Massachusetts: Harvard University Press, 2005.

Brittain, Vera. *Envoy Extraordinary: A Study of Vijaya Lakshmi Pandit and Her Contribution to Modern India*. London: George Allen, 1965.

Brown, Garrett Wallace and Held, David. *The Cosmopolitanism Reader*. Cambridge, UK: Polity Press, 2010.

Brown, Judith. *Nehru: A Political Life*. New Haven: Yale University Press, 2003.

Burke, Roland. '"The Compelling Dialogue of Freedom": Human Rights at the Bandung Conference', *Human Rights Quarterly* 28 (4), November 2006.

Casolari, Marzia. 'Hindutva's Foreign Tie-up in the 1930s: Archival Evidence', *Economic and Political Weekly*, 22–28 January 2000.

Chakrabarty, Dipesh, Majumdar, Rochona and Sartori, Andrew, eds. *From the Colonial to the Postcolonial*. New Delhi: Oxford University Press, 2007.

Chatterjee, Partha. *Nationalist Thought and the Colonial World: A Derivative Discourse?* Minneapolis: University of Minnesota Press, 2004, first published 1986.

Chaterrji, Joya. *The Spoils of Partition: Bengal and India, 1947–1967*. Cambridge: Cambridge University Press, 2011.

Clymer, Kenton. *Quest for Freedom: The United States and India's Independence*. New York: Columbia University Press, 1995.

Connelly, Matthew. *A Diplomatic Revolution: Algeria's Fight for Independence and the Origins of the Post-Cold War Era*. New York: Oxford University Press, 2002.

Copland, Ian. *The Princes of India in the Endgame of Empire 1917–1947*. New Delhi: Cambridge University Press, 1999.

——. *State, Community and Neighbourhood in Princely North India, c. 1900–1950*. New York: Palgrave Macmillan, 2005.

Corbridge, Stuart and Harriss, John. *Reinventing India: Liberalization, Hindu Nationalism and Popular Democracy*. New Delhi: Oxford University Press, second edition, 2000.

Divine, Robert. *Second Chance: The Triumph of Internationalism in America during World War II*. New York: Atheneum, 1967.

Dunning, John. *On the Air: The Encyclopedia of Old-time Radio*. New York: Oxford University Press, 1998.

Eisenhower, John D. *Allies: Pearl Harbor to D-day*. New York: Doubleday, 1982.

Frank, Katherine. *Indira: The Life of Indira Nehru Gandhi*. New York: Houghton Mifflin, 2002.

Gaddis, John Lewis. *The Cold War: A New History*. New York: Penguin, 2005.

Gangal, S.C. *The Gandhian Way to World Peace*. Bombay: Vora, 1960.

Garson, Robert and Kidd, Stuart. *The Roosevelt Years: New Perspectives on American History, 1933–1945*. Edinburgh: Edinburgh University Press, 1999.

Gilbert, Martin. *Road to Victory: Winston S. Churchill, 1941–1945*. Boston: Houghton Mifflin, vol. 7, 1986.

Glendon, Mary Ann. *A World Made New: Eleanor Roosevelt and the Universal Declaration of Human Rights*. New York, Random House, 2002, first published 2001.

Gopal, Sarvepalli. *Jawaharlal Nehru: A Biography*. Cambridge: Harvard University Press, vols 1–3, 1976–84.

Goswami, Manu. 'Autonomy and Comparability: Notes on the Anticolonial and the Postcolonial', *boundary 2* 32 (2), Summer 2005.

Guha, Ramachandra. *India after Gandhi: The History of the World's Largest Democracy*. New York: HarperCollins, 2007.

Guthrie, Anne. *Madame Ambassador: The Life of Vijaya Lakshmi Pandit*. New York: Harcourt, Brace & World, 1962.

Hardgrave, Robert and Kochanek, Stanley. *India: Government and Politics in a Developing Nation*. New York: Harcourt Brace & World, fifth edition, 1993.

Hardiman, David. *Gandhi in His Time and Ours: The Global Legacy of His Ideas*. New York: Columbia University Press, 2003.

Harvey, David. *Cosmopolitanism and the Geographies of Freedom*. New York: Columbia University Press, 2009.

Held, David. *Cosmopolitanism: Ideals, Realities & Deficits*. Cambridge, UK: Polity Press, 2010.

Hess, Gary R. *America Encounters India, 1941–1947*. Baltimore: The Johns Hopkins University Press, 1971.

Hunt, Lynn. *Inventing Human Rights: A History*. New York: W.W. Norton, 2007.

Ibhawoh, Bonny. *Imperialism and Human Rights: Colonial Discourses of Rights and Liberties in African History*. New York: State University of New York Press, 2007.

Imperato, Pascal James and Eleanor M. *They Married Adventure: The Wandering Lives of Martin and Osa Johnson*. Rutgers: Rutgers University Press, 1999.

Jacoby, Susan. *Alger Hiss and the Battle for History*. New Haven: Yale University Press, 2009.

Jaffrelot, Christophe. *The Hindu Nationalist Movement in India*. New York: Columbia University Press, 1996, first published 1993.

Jalal, Ayesha. *Democracy and Authoritarianism in South Asia: A Comparative and Historical Perspective*. Cambridge: Cambridge University Press, 1995.

——. and Bose, Sugata. *Modern South Asia: History, Culture, Political Economy*. New York, Routledge, second edition, 2004.

——. *The Sole Spokesman: Jinnah, the Muslim League and the Demand for Pakistan*. Cambridge: Cambridge University Press 1985.

——. *The State of Martial Rule: The Origins of Pakistan's Political Economy of Defence*. Cambridge: Cambridge University Press, 1990.

James, Robert Rhodes. *Robert Boothby: A Portrait of Churchill's Ally*. New York: Viking, 1991.

Jeffery, Keith. *The Secret History of MI6*. New York: Penguin, 2010.

Jeffrey, Robin, ed. *People, Princes, and Paramount Power: Society and Politics in the Indian Princely States*. New Delhi: Oxford University Press, 1978.

Johnson, Richard L., ed. *Gandhi's Experiments with Truth: Essential Writings by and about Mahatma Gandhi*. New York: Lexington Books, 2006.

Judt, Tony. *Postwar: A History of Europe since 1945*. London: Vintage Press, 2010, first published 2005.

Kennedy, David M. *Freedom from Fear: The American People in Depression and War, 1929–1945*. New York: Oxford University Press, 2005.

Kennedy, Paul. *The Parliament of Man: The Past, Present, and Future of the United Nations*. New York: Random House, 2006.

Khalidi, Rashid. *Sowing Crisis: The Cold War and American Hegemony in the Middle East*. Boston: Beacon Press, 2009.

Khilnani, Sunil. 'Nehru's Faith.' In Needham, Anuradha Dingwaney and Rajan, Rajeswari Sunder, eds. *The Crisis of Secularism in India*. Durham, North Carolina: Duke University Press, 2007.

Klug, Heinz. 'Transnational Human Rights: Exploring the Persistence and Globalization of Human Rights', *Annual Review of Law and Social Science*, vol.1, December 2005.

Kooiman, Dick. *Communalism and Indian Princely States: Travancore, Baroda, and Hyderabad in the 1930s*. New Delhi: Manohar, 2002.

Kumar, C. Raj and Chockalingam, K., eds. *Human Rights, Justice, and Constitutional Empowerment*. New Delhi: Oxford University Press, 2007.

Lazreg, Marnia. *Torture and the Twilight of Empire: From Algiers to Baghdad*. Princeton: Princeton University Press, 2008.

Leonard, Karen. *Making Ethnic Choices: California's Punjabi Mexican Americans*. Philadelphia: Temple University Press, 1994.

——. *The South Asian Americans*. Westport, Connecticut: Greenwood Press, 1997.

Lévinas, Emmanuel. *Totality and Infinity: An Essay on Exteriority*. Translated by Alphonso Lingis. Pittsburgh: Duquesne University Press, 2007.

Lloyd, Lorna. '"A Most Auspicious Beginning": The 1946 United Nations General Assembly and the Question of the Treatment of Indians in South Africa', *Review of International Studies* 16 (2), April 1990.

Manela, Erez. 'The "Wilsonian Moment" in India and the Crisis of Empire in 1919.' In Louis, Wm. Roger, ed. *Yet More Adventures with Britannia: Personalities, Politics and Culture in Britain*. New York: I.B. Tauris, 2005.

——. *The Wilsonian Moment: Self-determination and the International Origins of Anticolonial Nationalism*. New York: Oxford University Press, 2007.

May, Ernest R. and Zelikow, Philip D., eds. *The Kennedy Tapes: Inside the White House during the Cuban Missile Crisis*. New York: Norton, concise edition, 2002.

Mayaram, Shail. *Resisting Regimes: Myth, Memory and the Shaping of a Muslim Identity*. New Delhi: Oxford University Press, 1997.

Mazower, Mark. *No Enchanted Palace: Empire, War and the Making of the United Nations*. Princeton: Princeton University Press, 2010.

——. 'The Strange Triumph of Human Rights, 1933–1950', *The Historical Journal* 47 (2), 2004.

McLeod, John. *Sovereignty, Power, Control: Politics in the States of Western India, 1916–1947*. Boston: Brill, 1999.

Moore, John Allphin and Pubantz, Jerry. *Encyclopedia of the United Nations*. New York: Facts on File, second edition, 2002.

Morsink, Johannes. *The Universal Declaration of Human Rights: Origins, Drafting & Intent*. Philadelphia: University of Pennsylvania Press, 1999.

Moyn, Samuel. *Origins of the Other: Emmanuel Levinas between Revelation and Ethics*. Ithaca, New York: Cornell University Press, 2005.

——. *The Last Utopia: Human Rights in History*. Cambridge, Massachusetts: Harvard University Press, 2010.

Mukherjee, Madhusree. *Churchill's Secret War: The British Empire and the Ravaging of India during World War II*. New York: Basic Books, 2010.

Mukherjee, Mithi, '"A World of Illusion": The Legacy of Empire in India's Foreign Relations, 1947–1962', *The International History Review* 32 (2), June 2010.

Naftali, Timothy and Fursenko, Aleksandr. *One Hell of a Gamble: Khrushchev, Castro, and Kennedy, 1958–1964: The Secret History of the Cuban Missile Crisis*. New York: Norton, 1997.

Nandy, Ashis. *The Illegitimacy of Nationalism: Rabindranath Tagore and the Politics of Self*. New Delhi: Oxford University Press, 1996, first published 1994.

Narain, Jagat. 'Constitutional Changes in India', *The International and Comparative Law Quarterly* 17 (4), 1968.

Newton, Jim. *Justice for All: Earl Warren and the Nation He Made*. New York: Penguin, 2006.

Normand, Roger and Zaidi, Sarah. *Human Rights at the UN: The Political History of Universal Justice*. Bloomington: Indiana University Press, 2007.

Palit, D.K. *Major General A.A. Rudra: His Service in Three Armies and Two World Wars*. New Delhi: Reliance, 2006.

Pernau, Margrit. *The Passing of Patrimonialism: Politics and Political Culture in Hyderabad, 1911–1948*. New Delhi: Manohar, 2000.

Prashad, Vijay, *The Darker Nations: A People's History of the Third World*. New York: The New Press, 2007.

Purohit, B.R. 'Indian Fundamental Rights and the Universal Declaration of Human Rights', *Central India Law Quarterly*, vol. 14, 2001. http://www.cili.in/article/view/1377/981, last accessed 8 December 2008.

Rai, Mridu. *Hindu Rulers, Muslim Subjects: Islam, Rights, and the History of Kashmir*. Delhi: Permanent Black, 2004.

Ramusack, Barbara N. *The Indian Princes and Their States*. Cambridge: Cambridge University Press, 2004.

——. *The Princes of India in the Twilight of Empire: Dissolution of a Patron–Client System, 1914–1939*. Columbus: Ohio State University Press,1978.

Rana, Swadesh. 'The Changing Indian Diplomacy at the United Nations', *International Organization* 24 (1), Winter 1970.

Robinson, Kenneth. 'World Opinion and Colonial Status', *International Organization* 8 (4), 1954.

Rosenberg, Jonathan. *How Far the Promised Land? World Affairs and the American Civil Rights Movement from the First World War to Vietnam*. Princeton: Princeton University Press, 2006.

Said, Edward W. *Orientalism*. New York: Vintage Books, 1994, first published 1978.

Saikia, Yasmin. *Women, War and the Making of Bangladesh: Remembering 1971*. Durham, North Carolina: Duke University Press, 2011.

SarDesai, D.R. *India: The Definitive History*. Boulder, Colorado: Westview Press, 2008.

Schwartzberg, Joseph. *Designs for a Workable World*, forthcoming.

Schwarz, Hans-Peter. *Adenauer*, vol. 2, *Der Staatsmann: 1952–1967*. Stuttgart: Deutsche Verlags-Anstalt, 1991.

Sherman, Taylor. 'The Integration of the Princely State of Hyderabad and the Making of the Postcolonial State in India, 1948–1956', *Indian Economic and Social History Review*, vol. 44, 2007.

Sherwood, Marika. 'India at the Founding of the United Nations', *International Studies* 33 (4), 1996.

Sen, Amartya. *Poverty and Famines: An Essay on Entitlement and Deprivation*. New Delhi: Oxford University Press, 1999, first published 1981.

Smith, Neil. *The Endgame of Globalization*. New York: Routledge, 2005.

Smith, Simon C., ed. *Reassessing Suez 1956: New Perspectives on the Crisis and Its Aftermath*. Hampshire, England: Ashgate, 2008.

Steiner, Henry J., Alston, Philip and Goodman, Ryan. *International Human*

Rights in Context: Law, Politics, Morals. New York: Oxford University Press, third edition, 2008.

Talbott, Strobe. *The Great Experiment: The Story of Ancient Empires, Modern States, and the Quest for a Global Nation*. New York: Simon and Schuster, 2008.

Takaki, Ronald. *Strangers from a Different Shore: A History of Asian Americans*. New York: Little, Brown, and Co., updated and revised, 1998, first published 1989.

Tharoor, Shashi. *Nehru: The Invention of India*. New York: Arcade Publishing, 2003.

Tignor, Robert, Prakash, Gyan, et. al. *Worlds Together, Worlds Apart: A History of the World from the Beginnings of Humankind to the Present*. New York: W.W. Norton, 2002.

Twitchett, Kenneth. 'The Colonial Powers and the United Nations', *Journal of Contemporary History* 4 (1), 1969.

Venkataramani, M.S. and Shrivastava, B.K. *Quit India: The American Response to the 1942 Struggle*. New Delhi: Vikas Publishing, 1979.

Von Eschen, Penny. *Race against Empire: Black Americans and Anticolonialism, 1937–1957*. Ithaca, New York: Cornell University Press, 1997.

Von Tunzleman, Alex. *Indian Summer: The Secret History of the End of an Empire*. New York: Henry Holt, 2007.

Wasserstrom, Jeffrey, Hunt, Lynn, et. al., eds. *Human Rights and Revolutions*. New York: Rowman and Littlefield, second edition, 2007.

Weiss, Thomas G. *What's Wrong with the United Nations and How to Fix It*. Cambridge, UK: Polity Press, 2008.

Westad, Odd Arne. *The Global Cold War: Third World Interventions and the Making of Our Times*. Cambridge: Cambridge University Press, 2005.

Wood, John. 'British Versus Princely Legacies and the Political Integration of Gujarat', *The Journal of Asian Studies* 44 (1), 1984.

Woodward, C. Vann. *The Strange Career of Jim Crow*. New York: Oxford University Press, third edition, 1974.

Zachariah, Benjamin. *Nehru*. London: Routledge, 2005, first published 2004.

Zutshi, Chitralekha. *Languages of Belonging: Islam, Regional Identity, and the Making of Kashmir*. New York: Oxford University Press, 2004.

NEWSPAPERS

Baltimore Afro-American

Chicago Daily Tribune

Der Spiegel (translated by Benjamin Hett)

The Indian Express

The Glasgow Herald

The Modesto Bee

The New York Times

The Spokesman-Review

The Times-News

WEBSITES

http://avalon.law.yale.edu/wwii/atlantic.asp

http://www.bl.uk/reshelp/findhelpregion/asia/india/indianindependence/transfer/transfer1iindex.htm

http://clerk.house.gov/art_history/highlights.html?action=view&intID=485

http://www.doaks.org/about/the_dumbarton_oaks_conversations.html

http://www.gandhiserve.org/information/listen_to_gandhi/lec_2_iarc/lec_2_iarc.html

http://globalsolutions.org/files/public/documents/Schwartzberg_Weighted_Voting.pdf

http://www.ibiblio.org/pha/policy/1942/420427a.html

http://indiacode.nic.in/coiweb/welcome.html

http://www.liberation.org.za/collections/sacp/dadoo/dadoo03.php

http://www.mkgandhi.org/swarajya/coverpage.htm

http://www.otrcat.com/

http://parliamentofindia.nic.in/ls/debates/debates.htm

http://www.un.org/aboutun/charter/

http://www.un.org/aboutun/history.htm

http://www.un.org/en/documents/charter/chapter11.shtml

http://unyearbook.un.org/

http://usinfo.org/docs/democracy/53.htm

http://www.washingtonpost.com/wpdyn/content/video/2008/06/27/VI2008062703016.html

ARCHIVES CONSULTED

Archives of the United Nations

British Library/India Office Records

Central Intelligence Agency, USA (no material, but reference to other material acquired)

Columbia University Law Library

Dag Hammarskjöld Library, United Nations

Federal Bureau of Investigations, USA

Franklin D. Roosevelt Library, Hyde Park, New York

Hunter College Interlibrary Loan

Indian Society for International Law, New Delhi (no material, but redirected)

Library of Congress, Washington DC

Lilly Library, Indiana University, Bloomington

Manuscripts and Archives Division, New York Public Library, Astor, Lenox and Tilden Foundations

National Archives of India, New Delhi

National Archives of the United Kingdom

National Archives of the United States, College Park

Nehru Memorial Museum and Library, New Delhi

Official Document System, United Nations (online)

P.C. Joshi Archives, Jawaharlal Nehru University

Princeton University Mudd Library

Princeton University Special Collections (via Hebrew University, Jerusalem)

Randolph College, Warren Sherk Collection

Truman Library

United Nations DPI/NMD/MRU Photo Library

University of Chicago (no material, but redirected)

University of Hawaii

Acknowledgements

This is a book that spans several different areas of focus, from the histories of World War II and the Cold War, to the development and application of human rights law. Geographically, it travels from the East Coast of the United States to the West, from Delhi to Moscow, and from London to Bandung.

It has been an exciting challenge, if a humbling one, to research such interesting times and places. I would not have gotten very far without the incredible support and assistance I have received from many different quarters. I leant heavily on friends and colleagues, imposing on their time and hospitality.

For conversations or written exchanges from which I gained many insights, I am grateful to: Itty Abraham, Carol Anderson, Granville Austin, Karna Basu, Rick Belsky, Keyne Cheshire, Ellen Chesler, Margaret Crahan, Veena Das, Mallika Dutt, Marc Edelman, Jonathan Fanton, Judith Friedlander, Mohan Lal Gautam, Robert Hardgrave, Tom Head, Syed Akbar Hyder, Rob Jenkins, Michael Luther, Mark Mazower, C. Raja Mohan, Samuel Moyn, Rupal Oza, Gyanendra Pandey, Marta Petrusewicz, Sangeeta Pratap, Anupama Rao, Mary Roldán,

Liana Romulo, Helena Rosenblatt, Nayantara Sahgal, Christopher Schmidt-Nowara, Joseph Schwartzberg, Nancy Siraisi, the late Ambassador Phillips Talbot, Romila Thapar, J. Michael Turner, Thomas Weiss and Barbara Welter.

I am especially grateful to two fellow members of the Hunter History faculty, Benjamin Hett and Jonathan Rosenberg. Each read through the entire manuscript carefully and offered detailed criticisms. This book has been buttressed by their mastery of mid-twentieth-century European and American history. More to the point, I am glad to count the two—funny, helpful and brilliant—among my close friends.

The Peacemakers was written with the support of a fellowship from the American Council of Learned Societies, two PSC-CUNY Research Grants, three Hunter College Presidential Travel Awards, a George N. Shuster Faculty fellowship, an official Hunter College sabbatical leave, and a Mellon Mid-career Fellowship at the CUNY Graduate Center. For their generosity and encouragement, I am especially grateful to President Jennifer Raab and Provost Vita Rabinowitz.

Many of the ideas that are expressed in this book were first batted around classroom conference tables at CUNY, and so I owe a tremendous debt of gratitude to my students, who never fail to inspire me. Alexander Bacha, Brittany Gleixner-Hayat and Mona Mady especially stand out. Brittany and Mona have both gone on to do graduate work, and Mona also provided assistance with some of the Princeton papers I used. Alex, a Hunter MA student, was my research assistant for a year.

This work simply would not have been possible without the assistance of the superb librarians and archivists who keep the many record rooms I visited running smoothly and efficiently. Their good humour also made my research that much more enjoyable. I would like to single out Linda Dickinson and

Norman Clarius at Hunter; Julie Miller, John Haynes and Karen Fishman at the Library of Congress; and Gabriel Swift at Princeton University for their time.

I presented elements of this book at the nineteenth European Conference on Modern South Asian Studies in Leiden, the Netherlands; the 'Beyond Independence' Conference at Royal Holloway, the University of London; the Eleanor Roosevelt Faculty Seminar on Public Policy at Hunter; the Ralph Bunche Institute for International Studies at the CUNY Graduate Center; the Gandhian Forum for Peace and Justice at William Patterson University of New Jersey; the seminar of the Society of Indian Academics in America; the Human Rights Program Seminar at the Roosevelt House Institute for Public Policy at Hunter College; and the National Strategy Project of the Institute for Defence Studies and Analyses, New Delhi. I learned a great deal from the fruitful exchanges with participants and audience members that resulted from these meetings, and I thank the organizers, particularly Bernardo Michael, Sarah Ansari, Yasmin Khan, M.G. Prasad, John Wallach, Krishnappa Venkatshamy and Balmurli Natarajan for inviting my involvement.

Material spread over several chapters first appeared as 'A New Hope: India, the United Nations and the Making of the Universal Declaration of Human Rights', *Modern Asian Studies* 44 (2), March 2010, pp. 311–47, © Cambridge University Press; 'Princely States and the Making of Modern India', *The Indian Economic and Social History Review* 46 (3), September 2009, pp. 427–56, © The Indian Economic and Social History Association New Delhi, all rights reserved; and 'The Hindutva Underground: Hindu Nationalism and the Indian National Congress in Late Colonial and Early Postcolonial India', *The Economic and Political Weekly*, Special Article, 13 September 2008, pp. 39–48. I thank Cambridge University Press, *EPW* and the copyright holders and the publishers Sage Publications India Pvt. Ltd (New Delhi) for permission to reproduce that material in altered form here.

Krishan Chopra, Publisher and Chief Editor, Non-fiction, at HarperCollins has been incredibly kind and generous. I am thankful for all his help. Debasri Rakshit has been a tireless and meticulous editor.

Finally, as always, I am so thankful for the love and affection, and sometimes wicked humour, of my family. My 'godfather', Edmund 'Uncle Bud' Beacham, did not live to see this book, but I did have the pleasure of sharing some of the early material with him. He landed at Normandy and, as a medical officer who tended to the wounded, fought the Nazis. I learned from him what it means to act heroically, and humbly. My interest in this period of history generally stems from the many stories I heard sitting around his armchair.

My mother, Leela Bhagavan, also did not live to see this book. But what she accomplished in her life, the people she touched through her humanity and compassion, remind me every day of the incomparable power of love.

I have found little that exceeds the pleasure of debating and sometimes arguing with my family over ideas. For this and for so many other things that I simply cannot express, I thank Minni, Ajei, Prajit, Rohit, Sharad and Shobha. I can't yet argue with my one-year-old niece Saanvi, but I am looking forward to the quick arrival of that day. I stand in awe of my father, Belur, for all his energy, his curiosity, his generosity and his ethics. In India, I thank Chinmayya Ajji, Hari, Roopa and Chubbi and my parents-in-law, Kalpana and Dasu, for good food, hilarious jokes and a sense of home.

To my vast extended family I also remain in debt. The world of Gandhi and Nehru first came alive for me nearly thirty years ago when my uncle, Bellur S. Prabhakar, baited me to write an essay on the two Indian titans in exchange for a video game. That game is long forgotten, but the essay grew into this book.

My world revolves around my wife Sree and my daughter Priyanka. I love the laughter, the silliness, the serious discussion, and the plain, old fun that we have. It is to them, with the deepest and most sincere expression of affection, that this book is dedicated.